The Prairie Builder

Walter C. Murray
Sketch by Ernest Lindner, 1927

The Prairie Builder
Walter Murray of Saskatchewan

David R. and Robert A. Murray

■

NeWest Press
Edmonton

Canadian Cataloguing in Publication Data

Murray, David Robert.
The Prairie Builder

Includes index.
ISBN 0-920316-75-1 (bound). — ISBN 0-920316-73-5 (paper)

1. Murray, Walter, 1866-1945. 2. College presidents - Saskatchewan - Biography. 3. University of Saskatchewan - History. I. Murray, Robert A., 1910- II. Title.
LE3.S7217 1908 378.7124'2'0924 C84-091459-8

Credits

Cover and book design: S. Colberg
Photographs: University of Saskatchewan Archives
Typesetting: J. Charter
Printing and binding: Friesen Printers Limited

Financial Assistance

Alberta Culture
The Canada Council
University of Saskatchewan

Cover photograph

Walter C. Murray sitting at the desk which he bought on becoming President and used throughout his years at the University of Saskatchewan.

NeWest Publishers Limited
Suite 204, 8631 - 109 Street
Edmonton, Alberta
Canada   T6G 1E8

To Margaret Beattie Murray

■

■ Contents

Preface

We wish to express our gratitude to the University of Saskatchewan for commissioning the publication of this biography of Walter Charles Murray, the first President of the University. Dr. Jean Murray, a longtime faculty member in the History Department of the University of Saskatchewan, had hoped to write her father's biography and spent much time researching it. However, she was unable to carry out the task. When we approached her with our plan, she expressed her approval, cooperated with us, and gave us written permission to use her father's papers. We interviewed her a number of times, gleaning important insights on the Murray family. Sadly, she died before this book was completed.

We are not related to Walter Murray, but one of us attended the University of Saskatchewan when he was its President and knew him then as well as any student could. The research and writing have been a father-and-son undertaking, and we are indebted to Walter Murray for, among other things, the joint satisfaction involved in writing this biography.

Many people have generously assisted us. Dr. J. Francis Leddy, President Emeritus of Windsor University and a former Vice-President Academic of Saskatchewan, read the manuscript and made many helpful comments and suggestions. His help and support were very valuable indeed. Mrs. Marion A. Stayner provided superb hospitality in Saskatoon to both of us on numerous occasions and acted as a research assistant when she was needed. Mrs. Helen Fischer-Morrison examined the Tory papers at the University of Alberta on our behalf. We are especially indebted to Mr. Stan Hanson, the University of Saskatchewan Archivist, who took a special interest in this project from the beginning and helped us in innumerable ways. More than thirty people who knew Dr. Murray granted us interviews.

We gratefully acknowledge the assistance of the following archives and their staffs: The University of Saskatchewan Archives, Saskatchewan Archives, St. Andrew's College Archives, Public

Archives of Canada, University of Alberta Archives, University of Dalhousie Archives, Atlantic School of Theology Archives, Nova Scotia Provincial Archives, University of New Brunswick Archives, Province of New Brunswick Archives, United Church Archives, and the Saskatchewan Conference of the United Church Archives. We acknowledge permission to quote material from the following: The Carnegie Corporation, the United Church of Canada Archives, and the official records of the University of Toronto.

The University of Guelph Research Advisory Board helped offset some of the research costs.

We thank Mrs. Ruth Mickus who expertly typed the various drafts of the manuscript.

In one way or another, each member of our family assisted us in the preparation and writing of the book. We thank them all warmly, but to one especially, whose love and inspiration as wife and mother has helped us see it through to completion, we are particularly grateful; to her we dedicate this book.

We take full responsibility for its content and for any errors or omissions.

David R. Murray
Robert A. Murray

Foreword

Few individuals have the opportunity to create a university. Walter Murray was one of those few. He was the first President of the University of Saskatchewan. His letter of application in 1908 sketched the plan for the unborn institution. When he retired twenty-nine years later in 1937, much of that outline had taken shape on the once bare prairie above and beside the Saskatchewan River.

This was the central task of his life. He was a man of great imagination and drive. His capacity to perform was matched by equally impressive accomplishments. Yet neither Murray nor the young university escaped controversy. The crisis surrounding the dismissal of four senior members of the university in 1919 placed his career and his job in jeopardy. It caused him to have a nervous breakdown. The loyalty and work of the majority of his faculty and the support of both the Board of Governors and the provincial government saved him. He recovered his health and returned to continue his life's work as President at the beginning of the 1920's.

His second great driving interest arose from his deep religious conviction. It found an outlet in his twenty-year crusade in support of the union that created the United Church of Canada in 1925. For Walter Murray this was a momentous personal triumph, one he savoured the rest of his life.

The third central theme of his life was serving the community, a service that embraced people of all classes, the province, the nation, and the Empire. He served on innumerable boards, committees, councils, and Royal Commissions. Many disciplines, including Education, Agriculture, Art, Music, Science, History and Letters, benefitted directly from Murray's contributions. So did a very large number of individuals, people from all walks of life.

This book tells the story of an extraordinary man, his achievements and his failures.

Chapter 1

The Maritimer

Charles Murray, then in his sixties, his wife, eight children, and five grandchildren arrived in St. John, New Brunswick, on a leaky ship after spending nine weeks crossing the Atlantic. The year was 1819. Walter Murray, his great-grandson, was born forty-seven years later on a farm a few miles from the one on which his immigrant ancestor had settled three generations earlier.

The Murray family came to New Brunswick from Liddlesdale in Roxboroughshire. It was Border Country and it was Covenanters' Country. The spirit of John Knox was still abroad in the land and permeated the dales. His stern faith continued here as did the arrangement by which tithes supported both the church and the teacher in every congregation. The latter was the foundation of universal education that remained the prerogative of the Scottish Church for two hundred years, practically into the lifetime of the immigrant to New Brunswick.

These stern traditions survived the leaky ship and took strong root in the new land. Political freedom, education for all, and the strict moral code of the covenant were the ruling forces for these Scots. Such was the case with Walter Murray's grandfather, after whom he was named. He was a successful farmer and a formidable figure. Walter wrote of his grandfather, "Though naturally a kindly man, the conscientious observances of the practices of the strictest sect of Presbyterians gave him a reputation which touched with something of awe the respect the younger folk felt for him."[1] With his father and brothers he had found his first home at Studville. There he married the girl next door, Elizabeth Pearson, whose family came from Castle Garrick near Carlisle. The border heritage continued although the Pearsons were English and Anglican. These border traditions were to exert a strong influence on the grandson through the grandmother.

They were married in 1827, four years after Elizabeth came to Canada. By 1832 there were three children and doubtless too many mouths for Studville to feed. Walter's grandfather moved his family upstream and settled on the farm in the English Settlement where Walter was born in 1866. Years later, Walter described this pioneer land:

> The district to which these settlers came is hilly, traversed by five or six brooks, running down deep valleys, some to join the Belleisle on the east; the others the long creek on the west. The great rivers and lakes were the arteries along which the immigrants passed into the country. As the broad valleys were peopled by the Loyalists and their children, the later arrivals were forced to ascend the tributaries to their sources in the hills. From the Kennebecasis and the Millstream one group of immigrants seems to have entered the eastern end of the settlement; while from the Washademoak and up the long creek another, and probably earlier group, seems to have penetrated the hills. The pioneers moved from hilltop to hilltop and naturally settled on the high lands which were dry and more easily cleared. The hardwood, the maples, birches, and beeches, disappeared from the ridges long before the cedars and the spruce were cut in the swamps and valleys. The trails of the pioneers . . . became in time a highway picturesque to the eye, difficult and dangerous to the traveller.[2]

His grandfather indeed had settled on high land. The farm, located in Studholme parish ten miles northwest of Sussex, New Brunswick, then, as now, was a fine piece of land. Except for fifteen to twenty acres of swamp, now drained, the rest is high tableland, fertile and easily cultivated, not dissimilar to the Vale of Teviot where the Murrays had originated, although the farm in Studholme possessed richer soil and land more pleasing to the eye. The lovely large farm is still worked by a distant relative. The hardwood is largely gone as is much of the cedar and spruce, and a fine crop flourishes where the swamp once produced only hay. Here Walter's grandfather prospered. He was a founding member of the church located about a mile away. He became a Rye Roads Commissioner. His son Charles became first a schoolteacher, then apprenticed to a doctor in St. John, and finally went to New York where he graduated from the College of Physicians and Surgeons, which was later to become the Columbia Medical School. When he graduated in 1861, his mother persuaded him to forego his inclination to remain in the United States. He returned to the farm in the English settlement and practised there as a pioneer country doctor for more than a quarter of a century.

Like father, like son; the doctor was also a formidable figure. His reputation as a bill collector outlived him and survives in the records of the King's County Registry Office by the liens in his name. To his family he was, in the words of one of his daughters, "a handsome big man, nearly six feet tall, full of fun and very jolly." Apart from medicine, he had a passion for horsebreeding. He married Elizabeth Mackenzie of St. Stephen, a woman fifteen years younger than he was and someone to whom he was utterly devoted. She was petite, vivacious, full of energy, and possessed an infectious delight in life. She ruled the Murray family. Her daughter remembered that "she sang like a lark, danced, skated, cut figures on the ice, swam, but above all she was born for horses."

Charles Murray had worked hard himself to obtain his medical education, and his wife was equally committed to learning. One of her children recalled that "Mother used to sweep with a Latin Grammar tied to the broom handle."[3] Charles and Elizabeth together passed on their devotion to education both for itself and as a means of self-improvement to their children. Five of the seven who survived graduated from university, surely a remarkable record in the last half of the nineteenth century in rural New Brunswick.

Walter Charles Murray was the eldest and a favourite of his mother. He was brought up on the family farm remote from town or city. He worked on the farm; he drove with his father on sick visits; he went to church and to school. When he had finished at the nearby primary school, he walked four miles morning and evening to the continuation school at Collina. Work and study were his life. Then and later he demonstrated a remarkable capacity for both. He inherited and developed a deep and abiding religious faith; in it and in him faith without works was dead.

The stern traditions of his ancestors exemplified by his father and grandfather were supped by Walter with his porridge, but both his English, Anglican grandmother and his Presbyterian mother helped to soften this forbidding inheritance. Each woman, but especially his mother, had a lasting imprint on young Walter. He was no dour Scot, but he did retain a driving ambition to build a moral world of educated, free men responsible for their government and destiny. It was an ambition which remained central in and unifying to his life. His mother persuaded Walter's father to return to Presbyterianism, but she did not succeed in converting him from his Conservative political leanings. Walter happily followed his mother both in religion and in politics, growing up a liberal, a reformer and a Presbyterian. Above all and always he would be a driven man. The engine of this drive was an enormous determination to excel himself and to teach others to excel. It was coupled with a powerful intellect.

After Collina School with its daily, weary, eight-mile trudge, he was sent to Fredericton, first to a city school and then to the Collegiate School, where George Parkin was the principal, to be trained for admission to university. Parkin planned the Collegiate School as "a central school for the whole Province."[4] He had absorbed the philosophy of Edward Thring and became his lifelong follower and later his official biographer. Thring was then in his prime as the renowned headmaster of the English public school, Uppingham. During the year's stay at Oxford in 1874, Parkin had visited Uppingham and met Thring. Parkin attempted to create in the Collegiate School a model of Uppingham, but the obstacles were too numerous. However, he did infuse it with the spirit of an elite English public school.

Thring's philosophy was to educate the sons of the wealthy for leadership in society. This was to be done in a residential "public school." Here every boy would receive equal attention and training and individual attention in the residential dormitory where the master could take a special interest in the life of each pupil. While classics were the academic foundation of the curriculum, the overriding purpose of the school was to build character.

When Walter Murray arrived at the Collegiate School in January, 1882, it was indeed the elite school in New Brunswick. Here Parkin, great teacher that he was, moulded his students in preparation for success in university and leadership in society. He did this through a rigorous training in classics with an accompanying program in character-building, just as Thring prescribed. Parkin taught the classics and took the lead in the character-building program. He took a personal interest in each student, spending hours outside the classroom with them in all manner of extracurricular activities: sports, tutoring, hikes, picnics, and holiday tours in the summer. Small wonder that he cast a powerful spell over his students, especially the ablest. Bliss Carman wrote: "I cannot conceive of a teacher with greater power to arouse and inspire his pupils than Mr. Parkin had—a power he possessed in such abundance and spent so lavishly."[5] Carman and Charles G.D. Roberts, both Fredericton poets and students of Parkin, were touched by it all their lives. Walter Murray was another who was deeply changed by Parkin. He inherited Parkin's devotion to Thring and his educational ideas; he later prescribed Thring's *Theory and Practice of Education*, published in 1883, as a textbook for his own students, and he taught those principles and ideas for almost a quarter of a century in Dalhousie and Saskatchewan.

The impression Parkin made remained etched in Murray's memory years later. Murray arrived with scant knowledge of Greek and Latin. Parkin's teaching gifts and the eager pupil produced an early harvest. In the Christmas examination of 1882, Murray stood third in Latin. The following spring in the matriculation examination he topped the class winning both the Douglas silver medal and the Governor General's medal. He was also awarded the King's County scholarship providing the equivalent of free tuition at the University of New Brunswick. His short stay at the Collegiate School with George Parkin was the springboard to future academic distinction. Perhaps even more remarkable, in this short period George Parkin implanted the ideas and ideals of teaching that were to guide him throughout his career.

At the University of New Brunswick academic distinction continued. He took the highest mark in every class in every year. When he graduated in 1886 he won the Alumni Gold Medal, graduating with first class honours in Classics and Mathematics. He also won the Mathematics scholarship. Academic work took up nearly all of his time, but he participated in the Literary and Debating Club, becoming its President in his senior year.

While an undergraduate, Walter had been caught up in what the Senate Minutes described as "a grave case of discipline and general insubordination."[6] He never forgot the affair, and his own attitude of leniency to student offences at Saskatchewan was a direct result of his experience at New Brunswick. It began as a harmless, student prank. One of Walter's fellow students in the junior year threw a slipper in a mathematics class, and the instructor, who happened to be the aging President of the institution, took it as a personal insult. The class rallied behind the student to protect him from punishment. A special disciplinary meeting of the Faculty decided to rusticate the entire class for the remainder of the term and not to readmit any of them until the slipper-thrower owned up. At this juncture Walter applied for admission to Dalhousie on behalf of the class, but he was refused on the grounds that he was a rusticated member of another university. The issue was finally resolved when all the class members submitted formal apologies and then were permitted to continue their studies. Ironically for Walter Murray, one of the members of the UNB Senate at the time was Edward L. Wetmore, later to be the first chancellor of the University of Saskatchewan. The affair at New Brunswick went west in the memories of both men as one of the many bonds of friendship between them.

After graduating, Murray spent the next year training to be a teacher. He obtained a license to teach in the province's grammar school. That license he never used. During the year, he had also written an examination, open to students in the Empire, for the Gilchrist Scholarship. Murray stood first among Canadians competing and third overall and won one of the coveted scholarships. He had attained the peak of academic distinction then available to a Canadian student.

Walter Murray retained many happy memories of his university days at the University of New Brunswick. He recalled some of them in an article he wrote for that university's student newspaper in 1942, after his retirement as President of the University of Saskatchewan:

> The great events of the College year to Freshmen were the "initiation," most dreaded of all College rites; the Hallowe'en celebrations when all the spirits of evil were let loose to the discomfort of the faculty; the rugby game with the city; and the Encaenia Night, when recent graduates proclaimed their freedom from discipline by firing the Old Cannon which had remained buried and hidden during the past year. Its roar from the hill, behind the College, terrified old ladies and wakened the children in the city.[7]

Earlier, in a Convocation address in 1905 to his alma mater, he passed on some of his academic reminiscences to a later generation. He told them that as a student he had taken Greek, French, Philosophy, Physics, Analytics, and Geology "in equal doses with nearly equal relish." But he admitted that the university, during the 1880s, had been very weak in science, especially on the practical side. "A laboratory was to us a dark and mysterious place into which it was better not to peer." Lacking a proper scientific background and brought up within a strict religious creed, he and his fellow students were taught to see Darwin's idea of evolution as religious heresy. Murray recounted: "Well do I remember the feeling of alarm with which we first heard that evil word 'Evolution' and the delight with which we heard Joseph Cook denounce the Evolutionist and all his ways."[8]

With the award of the Gilchrist Scholarship, the door was open to a new career teaching in a university rather than a grammar school. This scholarship had been awarded since 1868 to the Canadian with the highest standing in the matriculation examination of the University of London.[9] No scholarship had been awarded in Canada in the two years prior to Murray's triumph, and his was the last given to a Canadian.

In terms of academic prestige the Gilchrist Scholarships were the forerunners of the Rhodes Scholarships, with which Murray would later be closely associated. However, the number awarded and the method of selection differed markedly. Only one Gilchrist was available to Canadians each year, and it was awarded by competitive examination. It was a rich prize worth one hundred pounds annually for three years. The holder could study at either University College, London, or at the University of Edinburgh.

The guarantee of an academic career relieved him of the farm labour he certainly did not enjoy. His father's extended medical practice laid much of the burden of farm labour and tedious chores on the shoulders of Walter and his brothers. The news of the Gilchrist award reached him in the hay field. Pitching hay was a job he particularly detested. He immediately threw down his pitchfork and proclaimed, "That's the last load of hay I'll ever pitch."[10] It was.

As a Gilchrist Scholar, Murray was a celebrity. On the eve of his departure for Europe, he was feted at a lavish banquet in the Queen Hotel, Fredericton. The Speaker of the New Brunswick House of Assembly presided. After everyone was sated with food, George Parkin rose to toast his brilliant pupil. Parkin praised his intellectual abilities and added that "Through all his competitions and successes at college, Mr. Murray had borne himself with becoming modesty, but with a dogged earnestness which could not but win success."[11] For Parkin, Walter Murray was a prize example of the success of Edward Thring's educational methods.

Now, with the praise of his accomplishments ringing in his ears, Murray was off to the Presbyterian land of his forefathers and Edinburgh University, a scholarly mecca for Scots from the Maritimes. Here Murray made friends who were to be his intimates for life. They included Robert Falconer, his brother James, Clarence MacKinnon, and Arthur Morton. Except for Murray they were theological students. Each was destined to be prominent in Canada, but all were able students with much in common, and they grew into a close-knit group. Together with some medical students, they occupied their weekends visiting the teaching hospitals or the slums, and on Sundays they made the round of Edinburgh's churches hearing the preachers of the day. It was a golden age of intellectual awakening whose glow shone in their memories for the rest of their lives. Sir Robert Falconer wrote fifty years later that he was there "at the height of the Victorian Age. The spirit of the period was confident, its mind clear, its character stable. We did not realize we were standing on the verge of a new world . . . "[12]

There is no record of deep friendships formed by Murray at New Brunswick as there is at Edinburgh. Was the warm empathy so characteristic of the man only now coming to full flower away from the stern farm life which he did not relish? Was it the inner security and independence the Gilchrist Scholarship brought? Certainly one hundred pounds per annum in the later 1880s was relative affluence and the scholarship gave definite status. Be that as it may, the fire that fueled the extraordinary drive within him burned as hot as ever. Not only did he take medals in his specialty, philosophy, but he also garnered medals and prizes in mathematics and natural science. In 1891 he graduated with first class honours. His academic record, otherwise brilliant, was marred by one failure. He failed a French exam, which prevented him from receiving a B.A. from London as well as his Edinburgh degree.

Murray studied philosophy under one of the leading metaphysicians in Britain, Alexander Campbell Fraser, then nearing the end of his long career of thirty-five years as Edinburgh's Professor of Logic and Metaphysics. From him Murray absorbed the philosophy of New Idealism, concentrating on Kant, Hegel, and such British Idealists as T.H. Green. In company with others of his generation, Walter Murray found this philosophy useful to re-interpret his Presbyterian beliefs, challenged as they were by scientific advances and the theory of evolution. For him there was never any incompatibility between philosophy and religion; the former served the latter, and his devout faith remained untroubled by doubt. He enjoyed the intellectual challenge of philosophy and rose to it, but he was constantly searching for ways to apply his philosophical knowledge. The emerging social science of psychology, still in its early infancy, and the application of ethics to education were two areas that held special appeal because of their practical utility. Murray, as a trained teacher, always remained close to the needs of the classroom.

From Edinburgh Walter Murray went to Berlin for a brief period of study, but brief it was. He was offered, and accepted, the chair of Mental and Moral Philosophy and Political Economy at his alma mater. At age twenty-five he returned to Canada brim full of the confident optimism of the age to make his mark in the academic world. In September 1891 he took up his post at the University of New Brunswick. His tenure here was to be short but important in his life. Here he met his future wife, who was one of his students. He married her four years later. Here, also, he started extension lectures; he would be involved in university extension work for almost fifty years.

The chair of philosophy he held was funded by Alumni donations, and Walter Murray was uniquely qualified to convince that body that their money was well spent. In his inaugural lecture, he set out to justify the place of philosophy in a liberal education. The lecture was entitled "The Function of Philosophy in a Liberal Education."[13] He argued that education should aim at the perfection of man through the "full, harmonious, perfect development" of his capacities. In a liberal arts curriculum with this aim, philosophy holds a fundamental place. It fosters "reflection, criticism, independent thinking (and) judgment." Each of these characteristics, in turn, helps to produce better human beings. Man is humanized through reflection; he understands belief through the tempered discipline of critical judgment; criticism develops independent thought; independent thought transforms individuals and through them the societies and nations in which they live. "All true national progress must ultimately come from the individual." Edward Thring would have applauded the general thrust of the argument. To the assertion that progress came from the individual, John Knox would have uttered a hearty "aye."

Murray went on to compare the teaching of philosophy with the sciences. The latter "disciplines man in accuracy"; the former "encourages its students to look beyond the immediate facts, to consider a thing in all its beginnings, to look to the principles which give meaning to the present facts, to judge of the value of things." He summarized his case: "Theology and science are entwined in the folds of metaphysics. Logic casts a light on the pathway of every reasoner who bears it with him. Ethics presents us with the plan of the good life. Psychology places on the table of the educator reports on the characteristics and development of the instrument which he perfects. Political Economy is the statesman's guidebook." It was an eloquent and persuasive lecture, and it established him firmly in the Maritime academic community. For a man of twenty-five this was a well-rounded credo revealing him as a builder and a doer, someone who had come to terms with life. Walter Murray was ready to go to work.

He took an active part in all aspects of the university. Despite poor health that confined him to bed for a period, he undertook a new university venture by giving extension lectures to classes in St. John. From the end of January to the close of the academic year, he travelled regularly to that city to lecture in political economy. For the next year he planned a further series in psychology.

These plans were changed by the sudden offer of the chair of philosophy at Dalhousie, the leading university of the Maritimes, in the spring of 1892. This was an opportunity not to be missed, especially when it was accompanied by a salary of $2,000 a year, twice what he was paid at New Brunswick. Several of Murray's colleagues at UNB tried unsuccessfully to get the university to raise his salary in hopes of retaining him, but Murray's mind was made up. He accepted the Dalhousie offer and spent the next sixteen years as the George Munro Professor of Philosophy at Dalhousie. He was not the only one to be pleased. *The Halifax Chronicle* welcomed Murray's appointment. The Dalhousie Board of Governors "have chosen a young man, who has not only proven himself to be a thorough scholar, but an enthusiastic and successful teacher; and they have not found it necessary to go beyond the limits of Canada for the man of their choice. The day has gone by when Canadians were considered necessarily incompetent to fill the highest teaching positions in their own country."[14] Murray's selection was a victory for the fledgling cause of Canadian academic nationalism.

To hold the chair of philosophy at Dalhousie at the age of twenty-six was a signal achievement, but it was also a place where international recognition could be won as his two predecessors in this chair, Seth and Schurman, had proved. Although the university was still small in terms of faculty and students, it had entered an era of expansion in the previous decade. At a time when the provincial government was about to withdraw its annual grant in the early 1880s, which could have been fatal to the university, it was rescued by the benefactions of three men led by George Munro.[15] These gifts amounted to $350,000, an unparalleled sum in British North America. They enabled the university to guarantee teaching in eight departments through endowed chairs. The Munro chair of Metaphysics, or Philosophy as it became known, dated from 1884, and Walter Murray was the third person to hold it.

When he came to Dalhousie in 1892, he was one of ten faculty members. There were approximately two hundred students. Dalhousie had doubled in size by the time he left in 1908, but it still retained the intimacy of a small college where the faculty knew every student by name. Certainly Murray did. As the only professor of philosophy for most of these years, he taught all the undergraduate courses as well as a course in education and usually supervised two or three students taking graduate work. He never taught less than five basic courses and, in later years, six was the usual number. Compared to present-day university teachers, Walter Murray carried a heavy teaching load, and he did it without a sabbatical break for sixteen years.

The first course was junior philosophy, consisting of lectures on logic one year and in the following year of lectures on psychology, including its application to educational methods. Senior philosophy was either a history of modern philosophy (Descartes to Kant) or a history of ancient philosophy combined with a critical study of a basic text such as Locke's *Essay Concerning Human Understanding* or Plato's *Republic*. Two other courses covered Ethics and the intensive study of a modern philosopher, normally Kant or Hegel. Occasionally he substituted a history of English Ethics as his advanced philosophy course. When James Seth, his immediate predecessor, published his *Study of Ethical Principles* in 1894, Murray adopted it as a text for his ethics course. He advertised it then as moral philosophy covering four sections: the moral ideal, the metaphysics of morality, the moral life, and moral institutions. Except for the addition of a course in psychology in 1904, these courses remained the basic philosophy curriculum during his sixteen-year tenure of the chair.

Walter Murray's particular favorite was his education course. The year he arrived he had organized a department of education to give advanced training for prospective teachers. His own contribution to the education curriculum lay in the history and theory of education, a course he offered in one form or another every year. It was an elective for arts students in their senior year and a basic requirement for those who wanted to become teachers. He described it as dealing with the principal questions of educational science concerning the ends of education, its methods, materials, curriculum, the teacher, and the school. By 1900 the course had evolved into the theory of education, beginning with a short history of educational theories from Ascham to Thring and moving on to the issues described above. Two years later, Murray began to incorporate the psychological basis of education into his course, tracing the mental development of the child from infancy to maturity. This split between educational theory and psychology continued as long as he taught education at Dalhousie. He later used his psychological knowledge in a teacher's manual he wrote for the Presbyterian church, *From One to Twenty-One: Studies in Mind Growth*, a widely used Sunday School text from 1904 to World War I.

By profession Murray was a philosopher; by inclination he was a teacher. He was happiest intellectually when he could merge the two. This is evident in the Convocation address he delivered in September 1893, on "Educational Ideals."[16] Going back to the Greek philosophers, Murray traced the development of two contrasting ideals: instructionism, the belief "that the aim of education should be to instruct, to impart useful information," and disciplinism, the belief "that the educator try to develop capacity, power through exercise." Instructionism was "realistic, utilitarian" whereas disciplinism was "formal, scholastic." Instructionism had its parallel in utilitarianism and disciplinism in asceticism. He argued that, as in the study of ethics, the blending of these opposites created "a higher unity," so in educational ideals this Hegelian dialectic resulted in "a more comprehensive ideal, which we may call Culture, and which we may attribute to Plato."

After discussing the merits and defects of all three ideals, Murray advanced Edward Thring's philosophy as expressed in his *Theory and Practice of Teaching* as "the ideal of Culture." The aim of the ideal of culture was to develop intelligence, which Murray defined as including characteristics such as thoughtfulness and many-sided interests, "to arouse an inward spiritual activity, to develop capacities for thought, for feelings and for decision, and so form character." Murray took up where Parkin left off, preaching Thring's philosophy of education to a wider Maritime audience. Through Murray a whole generation of Dalhousie students was exposed to the educational ideals of Edward Thring.

Walter Murray's activities at Dalhousie during his sixteen-year tenure were remarkable for their extent and variety but with one notable exception: he produced no work of scholarship in his own discipline. His predecessors, Seth and Schurman, had built themselves international reputations while at Halifax. Murray was a different man; scholarship was not his primary interest. People, administration, and education absorbed him. But his interest in, and contribution to, Maritime primary and secondary education went well beyond his university teaching. He regularly delivered papers to provincial education associations in each of these provinces. In 1896, for example, he presented a paper on "Public Schools and Ethical Culture" to the Educational Institute of New Brunswick, stressing the importance of regular and systematic moral training.[17] His message was simple: "Place the pupil in a healthy moral atmosphere and he will grow up a good man and a good citizen."

He was a featured writer in *The Education Review,* published in St. John, New Brunswick, that boasted a circulation encompassing every teacher in the Maritimes. He contributed many columns and book reviews, all of which were welcomed by the editors. In a series on prominent Maritime educators in 1897, Murray was given a centrepiece spread with laudatory editorial comment.

Murray's contributions were frequently short, pungent articles criticising narrow-minded school texts or offering diagnosis and remedy for poor spelling habits. His homily on spelling ended with a characteristic injunction: "But above all study the peculiarities of each pupil. Diagnosis must precede successful treatment." His father's medical training was not without effect in the next generation. Murray's educational journalism continued for twelve years. At the end of the period he was introducing his readers to recent psychological findings on improvements in methods to teach mathematics.

In addition to his heavy teaching load and his work and writing in the field of education, university administration at Dalhousie claimed considerable time and effort. As the George Munro professor of philosophy, he sat on the Senate from the time of his appointment. With his chair he inherited the position of University Librarian, which entailed responsibility for its operation, the preparation of annual reports, and the acknowledgement of gifts. The last was particularly important. The library was totally dependent on voluntary gifts from alumni, professors, and students. Murray added his own philosophical journals to its shelves.

By 1900 the library had only approximately 8000 volumes, and these were largely in the field of arts and science. As new professional faculties developed, these inadequacies grew still more serious; without any regular appropriation for purchases no remedy was apparent. In 1899, after repeatedly calling attention to this serious lack, Murray pointed out that three departments each had no more than "a score or two of books." He relinquished the post in 1902 although he continued to serve on the Senate Library Committee until he left Dalhousie in 1908. In his last year as librarian he was delighted to receive a small endowment fund for the purchase of books, and he urged strongly that this should be increased to $5000 within the next few years. Meantime, in some departments professors had to lend their own books to students to enable them to complete assignments. Murray went to Saskatchewan persuaded that a university library could not exist on charity, that it must have an assured purchasing allotment and he so arranged.

His administrative duties went far beyond the library. He was the Secretary of the Senate in his last three years at Dalhousie with its attendant duties of record keeping and correspondence. He served on committees to arrange convocation and to prepare the calendar, and he was regularly involved with discipline matters. In 1901, after reports that the medical examinations had been stolen, Murray was one of a three-man committee to find the culprits and tighten up examination procedures. When medical students that same year stole the French cannon belonging to the university, he was one of the faculty asked to provide proposals to protect university property. The following year he formed part of a Senate Committee to meet with the Board of Governors to work out funding for two chairs in Mining and Metallurgy.

He was the representative of the University to deal with the Rhodes Scholarships. By 1902 the Gilchrist Scholarships had long since lapsed—Murray was the last Canadian to hold one. He was acutely aware of the lack of assistance to students for postgraduate training abroad, and he was determined that the Maritimes should not be excluded from the opportunities the Rhodes Scholarships provided. Cecil Rhodes' will recognized only Quebec and Ontario students as eligible for scholarships. As soon as the will became public, Murray set to work. He drafted a memorial petitioning the trustees to treat the Maritimes equally with Quebec and Ontario and with other political units of the Empire and the United States. The trustees accepted the justice of these representations and decided to send the Secretary of the Rhodes Trust to Canada to meet with Canadian educators. The Secretary was none other than Walter Murray's old schoolteacher, George Parkin, and Parkin's first meeting was in the Maritimes. Here the key questions of how the scholarships were to be apportioned and the method of selection were discussed.

Representatives of the Maritime universities met with Parkin at Sackville, New Brunswick, in December 1902.[18] Murray represented Dalhousie, served as the secretary of the meeting, and took a leading role in working out the problems. The recommendations were adopted unanimously. With these in hand, Parkin had little trouble persuading the rest of Canada to concur.

Walter Murray's double success in the Rhodes affair was notable first in helping to persuade the Rhodes Trustees to award a scholarship to each of the Maritime provinces, then in obtaining unanimous agreement among the Maritime universities' representatives to support the idea. The latter was perhaps the more difficult. Murray had to counter the argument of those who wanted the scholarships for Canada pooled in order to bind the regions of Canada more closely together. Murray fought hard and successfully for regional autonomy and for the right of colleges to nominate candidates.

When Dalhousie received the right to nominate the first Nova Scotian scholar in 1904, Walter Murray was at the centre of the process. Three faculty members met with the students to develop the procedure, then the Senate debated for three days before agreeing on the candidate. He did not carry this procedure with him to

Saskatchewan, but he was just as forceful an advocate in the west for the right of the prairie universities each to nominate their Rhodes Scholars.

If the philosophical mantle of his predecessors in the George Munro chair of philosophy was not meant for him, Walter Murray's impact on Dalhousie was no less significant. He was beloved as a professor, as a warm friend and colleague to the rest of the staff, and as someone who was always willing to shoulder responsibility. When he left Dalhousie, its Senate paid tribute to his "distinction to find work which seemed to be no one's particular concern and to do it himself."[19]

Writing about the history of Dalhousie for the student *Gazette* in 1903, Murray tackled the question of whether Dalhousie was a university or a college. "If a university is a place for the prosecution of research, then Dalhousie is primarily a teaching institution, a College, although not a few of its professors and students have made valuable contributions to science, literature and philosophy."[20] For Murray, Dalhousie was a college, and he was first and foremost a college man.

Although not a Haligonian by birth, Murray soon emerged as one of its more prominent citizens. His position in the university and his dedication to the Presbyterian church gave him a place of influence in the community. Moreover, he was an active, amateur historian of both the city and the university. He wrote articles on the history of Dalhousie for the student newspaper, and he presented a paper on the history of his own church to the Nova Scotia Historical Society in 1903.[21] He began his paper: "Haligonians pride themselves on the antiquity of their city," and, as virtually an adopted son, he shared that pride.

His research into the history of Halifax institutions spread to embrace more contemporary issues of local government. Over the years he became an acknowledged expert on the subject. He lectured in a series on "The Science of Government" sponsored by the Y.M.C.A. during 1904-5, and the following year he participated in a program of the Civic League. By 1905, with local elections approaching, the press began mentioning his name as a possible candidate. By then he was well known in the city, and his assets enabled him to meet the aldermanic qualifications of $1000 in real estate, $1500 in real and personal property, or $3000 "clear of the world."

Why, in the midst of all his other activities, did he contemplate seeking elective office? One reason was his strong opposition to what he saw as a growing trend towards centralization in Nova Scotia government. He described his own philosophy in his study of Maritime local government:

> Whatever be the cause, whether a demand for a greater efficiency or a desire for greater patronage, or a distrust of elected bodies as agencies for executive work, the fact remains that an important part of the machinery of government in local affairs appears to be passing away from the residents of the locality; at the same time one is surprised at the apathy or tacit approval which greets the change. We may purchase efficiency or patronage at too great a price. Direct popular government is indeed an educational agency that should not be valued lightly.[22]

When Murray decided to run just a month before the election, he received the endorsement of "Scrutator," the *Daily Echo's* columnist on municipal affairs. Murray's candidature was an example of a man "of ability and standing in the community" offering himself to the electors:

> Professor Murray, as is well known, takes a deep interest in civic government. In fact, he has made it a particular study—is not fettered with 'hobbies'—is young and energetic—has more time than the ordinary business man to give to civic affairs and should, if elected, be a most useful Alderman.[23]

In short, Walter Murray was an ideal candidate.

His opponent was a druggist who had been canvassing for some time, so Murray's late start was a handicap. Murray published his "card" in the local papers, promising to "do his best to secure an efficient, honest and non-partisan administration of the affairs of the city." He then campaigned door-to-door, finding this a tiring, footslogging business. Every night he returned home footsore from canvassing. It paid off. On polling day, Murray squeaked past his opponent with a bare 13 votes. In all, 917 ballots of a possible 1200 had been cast, a relatively high total for a civic election. The *Echo*, doubtless with some self-satisfaction, congratulated Murray in glowing terms: "He fought a grand fight, coming into the contest late in the day and working strenuously to win. His victory is most popular and at the close of the day's contest he was warmly congratulated."[24]

The papers attributed the narrowness of Murray's victory to his late start. Murray never denied this, but he had another explanation,

one he always recounted with an impish glint in his eye. It was his
favorite story. He claimed he owed his victory to the madames of the
red-light district in ward two. He never elaborated.

His electoral triumph brought him congratulations from
colleagues and friends, but the one he enjoyed most came from three
former students. Addressing him with all his titles, "Doctor,
Professor, Elder and Alderman," the students gently poked fun at
their old philosophy teacher:

> Upon your accession to new and enlarged honours, we, your
> former subjects . . . [resolve that] whereas further Plato rightly
> saith that the philosopher is king and ought to rule . . . and
> whereas further the dissolution of popular superstitions is a
> thing well befitting the contemplation of a philosopher . . .
> congratulations to Halifax and to you. But when do you
> sleep?[25]

When indeed!

As an alderman, he shouldered an administrative burden that
alone constituted a full-time job. He served as chairman of the
Citizen's Free Library Committee and of the Camp Hill Cemetery
Committee. He was a Director of Point Pleasant Park, a
Commissioner of the County Court House, and member of the City
Council's Tender Committee. He also served as one of the Halifax
Commissioners of Public Schools and as a member of the Greater
Halifax committee. These were continuing appointments. There
were also other special committees of which two were particularly
important.

He had notable success on a committee which dealt with pensions
for municipal employees. The current method of inducing the
retirement of elderly employees was for Council to vote a retiring
allowance. Invariably the Council came under criticism each time
this was done. Murray candidly admitted, after the problem was
solved, "in self-defence the City and its employees have been forced to
establish a fund from which the official can draw an allowance as a
right and not as a privilege."[26] His committee drafted the plan, got
the approval of Council, then drafted the legislation which the
Council recommended to the legislature. He then wrote an article for
The Canadian Municipal Journal to publicize it. The legislation was
passed and went into effect while he was still an alderman. Later he
looked back with considerable satisfaction on this achievement. As
he put it in his article, "a civic pension fund blesses the city which
gives and the employee who receives." Friends and opponents alike

praised the pension scheme as Murray's greatest contribution to Halifax. At a testimonial dinner held in 1909 in Halifax to honour the new President of the University of Saskatchewan, the President of the Halifax Board of Trade highlighted this: "The day would come, too, when broken-down teachers, worn-out firemen and city officials, as they went down to get their pension would thank God that Murray had been on the Council."[27]

Certain municipal issues were time consuming and frustrating. Writing later he observed wryly that, "revision of electoral lists, liquor license control and assessment are responsible for most of the local municipal conflicts. As the burdens of taxation increase, the inequalities of the system become more galling and the demand for reform more insistent."[28] With the liquor licenses he dealt pragmatically with each individual case trying to minimize conflict. The story was very different with municipal assessment.

Halifax raised most of its revenue from personal property taxes, but there was continuing controversy over conflicting definitions of personal property. Ten years before Murray was elected, a local tax expert, F.H. Bell, had pointed out how unfair the Halifax system was.[29] In the ensuing years the disputes continued. In 1906, searching for new sources of revenue, the City Council reimposed a poll tax. Murray concluded that a poll tax, in addition to the obvious inequities of the personal property tax, inhibited the growth of commerce and manufacturing in Halifax.

In April 1907 he got Council to approve a committee to study the system of municipal assessment and recommend improvements. Under Murray's leadership, the committee spent a year studying assessment practices all over North America. Finally, they decided to base their recommendations on the system adopted by Ontario in 1904. In March, 1908, the committee's report recommended the abolition of the poll tax and the introduction of an income tax.

This proposal provoked a storm of controversy with Murray the main target of angry taxpayers. His efforts to defend the tax reform before the Board of Trade and in the newspapers only succeeded in increasing the opposition. He and other reformers were accused of trying to turn the City Council into a legislative body instead of being content to administer the city on laws "as they find them." One opponent branded Murray as a member of a clique seeking to spring radical change on an unsuspecting and unprepared municipality. After a four-hour debate the Council voted down the proposals. Two months later Murray's term as Alderman ended. Never again did he seek elective office.

Murray was identified as a progressive, and he allied himself with the progressives on the Halifax City Council. As a well-known Liberal supporter, most of his allies were Liberals and his opponents were mainly Conservatives since partisan considerations were closely interwoven with Halifax municipal politics. Murray's progressivism had yielded some results apart from the municipal pension plans. Along with his Council allies, he had fought hard and successfully for a series of improvements including permanent paving for key business streets, concrete sidewalks, sewerage extension, new fire stations and fire-fighting equipment, and a water-meter system. He also obtained salary increases for teachers, especially female teachers, in his capacity as School Commissioner. He earned himself very favourable reviews on his performance as Alderman. The journalist, "Scrutator," summed up Murray as "a clear thinker, a close student of civics: a man who approached every subject coming before him without bias or prejudice but with a perfectly open mind—an ideal Alderman in short."[30]

Through his success in civic politics, Walter Murray helped to break down the barriers of isolation between Dalhousie and the Halifax community in which it was located. This and his undoubted accomplishments were just cause for pride, but it was mixed with a stronger sense of frustration at what he had been unable to do. This frustration at the unwillingness of Haligonians whether in the city or the university to move forward influenced his decision to move west when the opportunity came. There, in a fluid and new society, a man of ideas might be more successful than in an old colonial society where traditions and people were resistant to change. After Murray had been settled in Saskatoon for two years, he wrote to an old friend how depressing it was to hear that little had altered in Halifax:

> The good old city has enough advantages and has had enough opportunities to become one of the leading cities in the country. All that is needed is more vision, more daring and more enterprise on the part of a larger number of its citizens. The dead weight of the croakers was enough to hold back and discourage those who used to do something. When men had to spend about half of their time and energy in trying to persuade some narrow-minded obstinate and short-sighted citizens that every reform suggested is not necessarily an impending calamity, it is hardly worthwhile making the effort.[31]

In 1907 Murray had been at the centre of another public dispute, this time with a happy ending. For four years the Intercolonial

Railway and the Freight Handlers Union in Halifax had wrangled over job classification and local wages. A strike was called in the summer of 1907. Late in July the Minister of Labour, Rodolphe Lemieux, telegraphed Murray to ask him to act as Chairman of a conciliation committee.[32] Walter accepted without hesitation. When conciliation failed to resolve the dispute, he agreed to head the arbitration board which met continuously for a week at the beginning of August. The Board submitted a unanimous report which was accepted by both sides. Both Lemieux and his deputy, Mackenzie King, were delighted with Murray's success and insisted over Murray's initial protest that he accept the full fee of $220 for his work.

The Murray family's vacation had been postponed while conciliation and arbitration ran their courses. As soon as the report was submitted, the family prepared to leave. But the successful mediator turned out to be one of the strike's victims, as he ruefully recalled.[33] Murray was forced to carry his family's luggage and load it on the train. The handlers were not yet back at work.

They had been "the happy years," or so Murray remembered the sixteen years spent in Halifax.[34] He had gone there as a bachelor to live in college rooms. To begin with, it was a lonely life, but in 1895 he married Christina Cameron, his former student and, like him, a gold medallist. The bride and groom moved into their first home, 141 Spring Garden Road, where they lived until they moved to Saskatchewan. There their three daughters spent their early childhood. It was within easy walking distance of the university and St. Matthew's, one of the oldest Protestant churches in Canada, where the Murrays worshipped and where Walter soon became a church elder. His interest and activity in the church led him to play an increasingly important part in the national affairs of the church; he was to be a leader in the church-union movement culminating in the formation of the United Church of Canada in 1925.

The home on Spring Garden Road was not far from the Halifax Curling Club, his one sport and one at which he excelled. He curled regularly in the inter-city matches for his club. He was its President in 1902 when the first Scottish team to tour Canada was entertained. The Scots presented him with a gold-headed cane in honour of the occasion and for arranging their reception on the first stop on their tour. Murray welcomed them with the curler's traditional complaint about the quality of the ice; it didn't bother the Scots, who won the six-game match.[35]

The catalogue of Murray's activities, the university with his teaching and administrative duties, the church, the School

Commission, the City Council, his writings on educational and municipal affairs, as well as his activities in clubs and on committees, reveals a man who had to be occupied every minute of his waking hours. What drove this man that he must be so involved, take up every task, and accomplish more than seems reasonably possible for one person? His "drive" was extraordinary, a compulsion "to do" much more than ordinary folk would call normal. His academic record had been outstanding, but the record of his years in Halifax was even more so. He saw tasks everywhere, and he had to do them. This drive was combined with an intense interest in people. His friend from Edinburgh days, James Falconer, described Murray in a farewell tribute for *The Dalhousie Gazette:*

> But as attractive as he is as a lecturer he is yet more noteworthy because of his broad humanity. Few in college had a larger circle of friends than he; and these were drawn from every quarter. He was *persona grata* in every society. He would breakfast with philosophers, dine with doctors and sup with theologians, and whenever he came his happy laugh and ingenious discussions were the life of the company. . . . He is essentially a peacemaker; and whether in college, or city council, or church courts, it is ever the same that he refuses no labor, counts nothing too much trouble, if only he can bring people to see eye to eye. Energetic to the last degree, ready for hard work, sane in judgment, he is a man who is always sure to come to the front in the counsels of men.[36]

Murray had lived all his life in the Maritimes except for his period of study in Edinburgh. Now like many other Maritimers before and after him, he was moving west. By the middle of August 1908, Walter Murray was on the train for Saskatchewan and his new career. No longer would he have to worry about the educational problems of the Maritimes; those of the prairies awaited him. There was nothing in Saskatchewan yet but the legislative framework of a university with its Board of Governors waiting to greet their new President. He would have to start from scratch.

■

above:
Walter Murray's birthplace,
Studholme, New Brunswick.

left:
The earliest photograph of
Walter Murray.

top:
A.W. Duff, F. Walker and
Walter Murray, Edinburgh,
1889.

above:
Walter Murray, the student
c. 1885.

Chapter 2

Plain and Province

The land to which Walter Murray came and in which he would live and work for the rest of his life was a vast, empty plain just thirty years before. A few explorers had traversed its space and followed its rivers. The Gentlemen Adventurers Trading into Hudson's Bay had divided the land into districts and sub-districts, putting factors in charge who traded with the Indians, shipped their furs to Britain, sometimes married their squaws, and who provided both the organization and the stability necessary to carry on commerce. Finally the Hudson's Bay Company surrendered its title to the territory for £300,000, millions of acres of land, and untold (and then largely unknown) mineral and oil rights.

Boats continued to navigate the rivers bringing supplies. The railways had not yet crossed and criss-crossed the plains, but slowly a few settlements grew along the rivers. They spread onto the prairie at Wood Mountain, Duck Lake, and at Forts Edmonton and Macleod. Supplies now slowly snaked their way west in Red River carts, their wooden axles groaning and screeching, each pulled by a single animal. From Winnipeg they followed the Boundary Trail to Wood Mountain, Fort Macleod, Calgary, Edmonton, and thence to Fort Saskatchewan and the Peace and Smoky confluence. Others went to Fort Qu'Appelle, Battleford, Duck Lake, and Prince Albert. In 1876 between four and five thousand carts, each carrying a thousand pounds of supplies, left from Winnipeg on a noisy, tiring journey of four to eight weeks.

The 1880s saw only a thin stream of settlers trickle into this land. Between the decennial censuses of 1881 and 1891, the population of the whole territory increased by only 10,000, an average of 1,000 per year, in an area of more than 500,000 square miles. A continent-wide depression contributed to this slow growth. Frost and drought exacerbated the hard times and reduced the return from the small crops. The North-West Rebellion of 1885 symbolized the end of an era for the Canadian plains. The Rebellion was quickly suppressed, the casualties were few, and the determination of the Canadian government to enforce the law was made abundantly clear. The Rebellion put the North-West on the front page of every newspaper in Canada and made the affairs of the frontier known and discussed across Canada and beyond its boundaries. The publicity of the North-West and its revolution in transportation (created by the completion of the transcontinental railway in 1886) paved the way for a considerable increase in settlement in the next decade.

Two other events of great future benefit to the settlers occurred in the latter half of the 1880s. Red Fife wheat with its shorter growth period, high yield and excellent milling quality came to the prairies. Red Fife enhanced the farmer's prospects through a better return both in bushels and dollars and it reduced, somewhat, the great frost danger to the wheat crop. The Dominion government's establishment of the experimental farm program heralded a new era for western agriculture. Angus MacKay established an experimental farm at Indian Head to try to improve western farming practices. The "Dry Land Farming" program pioneered at Indian Head and at other experimental farms still continues. The smut problem, that affected a third of the wheat crop in the late 1880s, was also solved. It was at Indian Head, strong evidence indicates, that the first stalks of Marquis wheat, a new and sturdier variety better suited to the climatic conditions, first took root. Even though, after three quarters of a century, it is no longer grown as a wheat crop, it is still the standard by which the milling quality, colour, hardness and protein content of wheat are compared and assessed.

In 1877, the land which was to become the province of Saskatchewan had no schools, no taxation and very few people, but it had an active government. Ordinances were provided for the administration of justice, the transfer of real estate by married women, the prevention of forest fires, the issuance of licenses, the regulation of gambling, and the organization of a Board of Health. (There was only one doctor between Regina and Prince Albert.) The government also passed an ordinance for the protection of buffalo.

It was too late for the buffalo. Their weather-whitened bones were already scattered over wide areas of the prairie. For the next forty years settlers would pitchfork those white bones onto hayracks and garner a few dollars a ton when they were shipped out by the carload to be ground up for fertilizer. Grain, livestock and buffalo bones would be the real domestic product of the prairie settlers for many decades to come.

Meantime, the small and very slowly growing population began its quarter-century struggle toward self-government and, finally,

Christina and Walter Murray

provincial stature. The Legislative Council governed for ten years from 1877 to 1887. Then, the first Legislative Assembly of the North-West Territories with twenty-two elected members took over the duties of government; sixteen of the twenty-two representatives were born in Ontario. All were men accustomed to self-government, and none was about to accept quietly either the colonial status imposed by the North-West Territories Act or the continuing mandate of the Dominion Department of the Interior.

First, after a stiff struggle, they wrested control from the Lieutenant Governor, then set their sights on provincial status. Up until 1903, memorials on their grievances flowed in a steady stream to Ottawa. Land grants figured prominently. The allocation of land in each township of thirty-six sections allowed only sixteen to be open for homesteaders. Two were reserved for the Hudson's Bay Company;

the even-numbered sections were held for sale by the Dominion government or given in aid of railway companies; two more were set aside for school lands. The huge grants of land to "land companies" for settlement were bitterly resented. The litany of complaints about the Canadian Pacific Railway began with their enormous land grant, which was tax exempt, and continued with the company's erratic service, or worse, the failure to provide it. The C.P.R.'s high freight rates were unpopular as was the alleged propensity of C.P.R. locomotives to cause prairie fires from their smoke stacks or through the train crew's dumping hot coals and ashes along the right of way for the wind to scatter.

The settlers had a lot to complain about. In 1899 Premier Haultain summarized the major problems in a letter to the Minister of the Interior.[1] Some of the funds included in the federal appropriation had not been turned over to the territorial government. The government had no means of raising revenue except from the sale of licenses or similar fees. There was no means to implement a system of municipal organization. Expenditures for education had to be borne entirely by local residents of a district. Property holders were called on to make improvements on land held by railroads or other companies for speculative purposes and the companies themselves did nothing to help. The people complaining had grown up with a responsible government, and they were determined to have one, believing that with it they could solve their other problems.

While their elected representatives fought for provincial stature, the settlers struggled to survive. In the 1880s and 1890s, frost and drought blighted crops. Gophers were a continual menace, multiplying as they did without hindrance on those sections reserved from settlement. Doctors and hospitals, when they existed at all, were many miles distant while disease was an ever-present threat. In 1890 there were two doctors, who were also coroners, in the whole of the North-West. That year there were more than 900 babies born, 449 in the area that is now Saskatchewan, and for many years to come deaths from smallpox, diphtheria, and childbed fever were commonplace. Prairie fires were a constant menace; in 1886 the districts surrounding Grenfell, Broadview, Whitewood, Wapella, Moosomin and Carlyle were devastated by a single fire.

Almost as soon as the seasonal danger of prairie fires passed, the deadly cold menaced the settler. Sod huts were reasonably efficient at holding the severe prairie winters at bay, but the wooden shacks that replaced them were not. The newspapers reported deaths from freezing each winter as well as deaths in blizzards with the bodies discovered only when the snow melted. The Saskatoon *Star-Phoenix* listed the following deaths between January 21 and March 23, 1907:[2]

John Bergin in his shack near Dundurn;

Bodies of two Scotch homesteaders found near Davidson, partly devoured by wolves;

Joseph Coarsan—missing from his shack—body found 60 miles south-east of Saskatoon;

A homesteader by the name of Reed has been found dead in his shack six miles east of town (Lashburn).

Winters exacted a heavy toll among the prairie homesteaders. Isolation reduced opportunities for social intercourse almost to nil in the harsh weather of winter. Schools often operated only in summer. Long journeys to bring wheat to the nearest grain elevator or grist mill were commonplace and arduous—a sixty-mile journey was not unusual. Fresh fruit and vegetables were unknown for at least eight months of the year; fortunately though, prairie chicken, ducks, geese and antelope were in abundance. The settlers often lived on the very edge of survival.

As well as the usual crop menaces of drought, frost, prairie fires, smut, and bunt, the disease of wheat rust was reported for the first time in 1896. It returned in 1900 when it was classed as moderate. In 1903 its effect was "slight to considerable,"[3] but it would always return and increase.

Slowly the sod huts were replaced by whitewashed houses with thatched roofs, which came with the central European settlers. Then came lumber construction. Horses replaced oxen and drills replaced the broadcasting of seed as modernization brought greater efficiency to prairie agriculture. With increased settlement and improved methods, the wheat crop itself was increased. It rose from 1.5 million bushels in 1883 to between 4 and 5 million in 1895. Ten years later it reached 16 million, then in 1906, the year of the first great bumper crop, 26 million bushels of wheat were harvested. With bumper crops came prosperity and rapid expansion.

The early settlers' dedication to education borders on the amazing considering that they were living on the very edge of survival. They devoted a large percentage of their scanty resources to education. Moise Ouellette and Pierre Landry sought help to establish a school at St. Laurent in 1877, but they were refused by the North-West Council which had no funds for schools. Two years later in 1879, the Council's estimates included the figure of $2,000 in aid of schools. In 1885, Lieutenant Governor Dewdney's address to Council reported "sixty-five applications for the formation of school districts" in addition to 38 districts with 918 pupils already proclaimed and a further 12 schools with 301 pupils receiving government aid.[4] The government allotted the largest portion of its budget for schools year after year. In 1889, 46.8% of government expenditures went to schools and by 1892 the figure was 55%. Not only was education the single largest expenditure, but it was almost double that for roads and bridges, the next largest item.

The first ordinance of the North-West Territories on education was passed by the Council in 1884 and, as amended in 1885, established separate Protestant and Catholic school systems; in a word, the Quebec system of education. The first Legislature of the Territory set about changing the system radically. The Quebec system was dismantled and in its place came a non-denominational school system with English as the only language of instruction. This move had widespread and popular support, spearheaded by Premier F.W.G. Haultain and J.A. Calder, Commissioner and Deputy Commissioner of Education respectively. When a last-gasp motion supporting the Quebec system was put before the Assembly in 1896, not only was it voted down but the mover and seconder could not muster even one other member to vote with them.

Even before the first territorial ordinance on education was passed, the Anglican Diocese of Saskatchewan had obtained a Dominion charter for a University of Saskatchewan.[5] The Bishop of Saskatchewan was the chancellor; he would name the vice-chancellor who would be the chief executive officer. Under this Act the Senate of the University was given authority to establish a college at Prince Albert. Although the Act provided that the University would be non-sectarian, the influence of the Anglican Church was paramount. The times were not propitious for the first University of Saskatchewan. Crop failures, depression, and rebellion all struck the area within two years, and the decision of the CPR to build a railroad through the southern part of the North-West Territories caused a decline in land values at Prince Albert. The charter remained dormant until the new province of Saskatchewan created a state university.

Haultain and Calder also took up the University question in the 1880s. The first legislature of the Territories approached the Dominion government in 1889, requesting a land grant for a university. Such a grant of 150,000 acres had been authorized in Manitoba, but the resolution from the Legislative Assembly pointed out that each of the three districts—Alberta, Assiniboia, and Saskatchewan—was larger than Manitoba and thus "entitled to a grant for university purposes in proportion. . . ."[6] Ottawa refused to endow a university in the Territories with a land grant, saying that the question was premature. The university issue faded, then came into public prominence again in 1903.

By this time the Methodists were planning a denominational college in Edmonton, and The Western Canada College had been incorporated at Calgary as a non-denominational college. It was controlled by a private company, authorized to raise $50,000 through the sale of shares. At this point the territorial government acted by introducing a Bill to establish a state university with the exclusive right to grant degrees (except in theology) throughout the Territory. Haultain's philosophy envisioned a state university, but not under rigid state control. As he put it, "the first principle taken into consideration is to make the university free from all influence of government, sect, or politics; in fact the institution is to be governed by its graduates."[7] Haultain's University Ordinance of 1903 specifically excluded religious tests as a condition of entry to university and made admission an equal right of women as well as men.

Shortly after the formation of Alberta and Saskatchewan as provinces in 1905, the new Saskatchewan Liberal government headed by Premier Walter Scott introduced a Bill in the Saskatchewan Legislature to create the University of Saskatchewan. The Bill, introduced in March 1907, owed much to Haultain's Ordinance, but it also drew upon the principles embodied in the reform of the University of Toronto in 1906.

The University of Toronto Act of 1906 created a Board of Governors that assumed responsibility for the business affairs of the university, leaving academic matters in the hands of a Senate. Academic appointments were to be made by the Board on the recommendation of the President. The Saskatchewan Act of 1907 contained some provisions which went beyond its Toronto counterpart, most notably in the limitation of possible political interference. The Saskatchewan government limited its appointees on the University Board of Governors to three, leaving the majority of the members of the Board, five, to be elected by the Senate of the University.

Yet, because the location of the university was not decided by the Act, the university became entangled with provincial politics until the issue was settled. This entanglement occurred in a rather unusual manner. Premier Scott, who as a member of the House of Commons had a good deal to do with the Act creating the new Province, assisted in having a clause inserted locating the provincial capital at Regina, unless the Legislature should decide otherwise by vote. In the provincial election following the establishment of the province, the larger number of Liberal members was elected from the north of the province. Within this group there was a movement to change the location of the capital from Regina to Saskatoon. A motion to do this was introduced into the Legislature. It placed the Premier in an untenable position, because, if the motion were to come to a vote and the Liberals from the north voted for it, his government would be saved only through the votes of opposition members from the south of the province. Scott could not allow this to happen, and he did not.

The night before the vote took place, he held a caucus of his party and persuaded the members from the north to vote for Regina. When the vote was held the following day, observers were surprised at the large margin of victory for Regina. Why did these members, who felt so strongly that the provincial capital should be located in Saskatoon, suddenly change their minds? The answer is hinted at in two telegrams from members of Scott's party to the Premier when the University Bill was before the Legislature the following year. The first, dated March 5, 1907 from the Saskatoon member, W.C. Sutherland, reads:

> Saskatoon very anxious to have university location settled this session. In view of promise to me do you object my bringing matter up caucus?[8]

The second, dated March 16, was signed by eight members of Scott's caucus.

> We desire that location university be decided this session. Answer requested.[9]

No answer to either telegram has been found in the Premier's papers, but it is not difficult to guess what the "promise to me" in the first telegram was. Scott clearly had committed himself to locating the university at Saskatoon.

The Premier was not only a man of his word but an adroit politician. He proclaimed publicly that the location of the university would be settled by its Board of Governors. It was, but Scott and his Minister of Education, J.A. Calder, carefully selected the three government appointees. The University Act provided that five of the nine governors would be elected by the Senate. They were elected in January 1908. When the government appointments were made, ostensibly the north/south representation on the board was even. Conceivably, the University President, once appointed, would have the deciding vote, but this was not to be the case. Two of the Board members from the southern part of the province, Levi Thompson and John Dixon, were close to the Minister of Education and to the Premier, and as a consequence both voted for Saskatoon. But the Board did make the actual decision, and the Premier kept his promise. The University was too important for the fledgling province to remain immune from political rivalries, especially over its location, a decision which would have a profound effect on the fortunate community that received it.

Now a newcomer entered the picture. It was mid-August of 1908 in Regina. The train clanked to a stop, and Walter Murray stepped out onto the wooden plank railway platform. He came as an educator, and the gifts he brought were ideas; one, in particular, was the concept of a university to be built on the Saskatchewan prairie.

■

Chapter 3

Selecting a President

The creation of the University of Saskatchewan by legislative enactment in the spring of 1907 paved the way for the summoning of Convocation, consisting of all graduates of British and Canadian universities who had been resident in the province for three months. Convocation first assembled in Regina on October 16, 1907, and the graduates gathered there proceeded to ratify the nomination of Saskatchewan's Chief Justice, Edward Wetmore, as Chancellor of their new university. They then elected the twelve men who would form the first Senate of the University. At its second meeting in January 1908, Senate elected five men as its nominees to the Board of Governors. This meeting, held on January 7, coincided with the formal inauguration of the University, celebrated by a public assembly in Regina's Metropolitan Church. The university was in being although the Board of Governors was not yet complete. A site still had to be selected, and most important of all, the first President had to be chosen.

Chancellor Wetmore recognized the necessity of selecting the right man for President in his opening address at the inauguration: "To get a man of that order, you must pay him . . . pay him the salary that that man is entitled to have, and without which we cannot get the man."[1] At first glance, this suggests a belief that Saskatchewan was out to buy the best man available, but what Wetmore meant was that the university could not afford to be niggardly in recruiting for the most vital position in the new university. But in the event, salary itself was not the determining element in recruiting the man the Board wanted.

What sort of person did they want? The university's members and supporters sought a leader, someone who could build their provincial university, and this required special attributes. The Regina *Morning Leader* described these in an article even before the first Convocation had been convened:

At this stage it is impossible to refrain from referring to the vital importance of obtaining a president of the right stamp. Let us hope there is such a man available. He certainly will be hard to find. He should be imbued with academic traditions, and yet broad minded, a scholar, and yet a man of affairs, possessing high educational ideals, and full of the progressive spirit of the west. On this man, whenever he may be found, depends largely the growth of the University of Saskatchewan.[2]

With unanimous agreement on the need to choose the right man, the question was how to find him? This was a task for the Board of Governors, but the composition of the Board itself was not complete until the Saskatchewan government named its three representatives late in March 1908. The three government appointees—A.P. McNab from Saskatoon, James MacKay from Prince Albert, and Levi Thompson from Wolseley—had one thing in common with the five elected representatives of the university's Senate: none had any previous experience of running a university or of finding a president.

The Board members, nevertheless, were a remarkable group of men with strong loyalties to the province. James MacKay's forbears had been distinguished Hudson's Bay Company officers for several generations. James Clinkskill, a Scot, had set up a store at Battleford in the late 1870s and helped to defend the settlement during the Riel Rebellion. He also served in the legislature of the North-West Territories. John Dixon started his store in a tent at Maple Creek before the railway crossed the plains. Levi Thompson made three trips from Winnipeg to Wolseley between April and freeze-up in 1882 and still managed to build his sod hut before winter set in. Each trip meant a horseback ride of two hundred and fifty miles to and from the end of steel at Oak Lake, Manitoba (then called Flat Creek). If none of these men was familiar with running a university, all were pioneers used to dealing with the unknown and confident of their ability to do so.

Saskatchewan was not unique in looking for a university president. Other Canadian universities had preceded her in the previous two years. The new President of the University of Alberta, H.M. Tory, had been personally recruited from McGill by Premier Rutherford of Alberta. More interesting was the experience of the University of Toronto. The Saskatchewan government consciously followed the new University of Toronto Act of 1906 in framing its legislation enacting the University of Saskatchewan. When the University of Toronto Act of 1906 was implemented, President Loudon resigned, and the Toronto Board of Governors faced the task of finding his successor. It created a special committee which searched "far and wide," as the university's historian admitted. It took nine months before appointing Robert Falconer, the Principal of Pine Hill Divinity College in Halifax.[3]

Just over a year later, the Board of Governors of the new University of Saskatchewan chose one of Falconer's closest friends, Walter C. Murray, to be Saskatchewan's first President. Murray's name had surfaced during the Toronto search. J.A. Macdonald, editor of the Toronto *Globe* and a member of the Board of Governors at Toronto, submitted a written assessment early in 1907 of possible candidates in other Canadian universities. He compared Murray and Falconer as potential candidates:

> As regards the men in the Maritime Provinces there are only two names that are deserving of consideration. One of them is Prof. Walter C. Murray of Dalhousie University, the other, Principal Falconer of Pine Hill College, Halifax. Prof. Murray is a distinctly strong man, well-furnished educationally, and also is a leader of men. He would have made a good man for the Department of Education, and his presence in the University would have strengthened the qualities of leadership in the staff, but in my judgment he is scarcely large enough for the presidency. He is a very much stronger man than the great majority of those whose names were submitted from the United States. Principal Falconer is the strongest man, or is the man with the best qualities for this position, to be found in the Maritime Provinces. . . . His sympathies are broad, his ideals are high, and were he appointed I am quite sure no offence would be given by him to any section of the entire circle of the friends of the University. In the list of Canadian names I would think Dr. Falconer's name would stand among the very first.[4]

This letter is the best surviving evidence of why Falconer's name, and not Murray's, went on the short list of the Toronto candidates, and he eventually emerged as the Board's choice as President. Macdonald's opinions, influential as they were in Toronto, were not passed on to Saskatchewan. When the Board of Governors at Saskatchewan began the search for the President in the spring of 1908, they did not seek recommendations from any members of the Toronto Board of Governors. How, then, did the Saskatchewan Board set about its task without any precedents, and how did Walter Murray's name emerge as a candidate?

The process actually began before the Board had formally met. D.P. McColl, the secretary of the Board and a Toronto graduate himself, obtained the approval of the Board members late in April

1908 to write to university presidents in North America to solicit nominations which would be considered at the Board's first meeting. One of the Board members, Clinkskill, from Saskatoon, stressed how important it was to acquire information on all possible candidates. "This appointment is one of the most important duties of the governors and should not be decided in haste. We must get the best man available regardless of money considerations."[5] In retrospect, Clinkskill's caution seems out of tune with the mood of the rest of the Board. They acted quickly and decisively. Their choice was made within two months, and the appointment was confirmed before the end of August, by which time their new President was actually in Regina at work creating the university

McColl's letter to university presidents across Canada, the United States, and Britain elicited recommendations from men such as Woodrow Wilson, Nicholas Murray Butler of Columbia, Elliott of Harvard, Peterson of McGill, and the new President of Toronto, Robert Falconer. Not surprisingly, the man at the top of Falconer's list was Walter Murray of Dalhousie University. Falconer wrote, "The only opinion that will be really valuable to you is one based upon personal acquaintance," and on this basis Walter Murray was the person "possessing most qualifications for the position." After detailing Murray's academic background, Falconer added: "His splendid common sense, tact and clear sightedness makes his judgment of uncommon value. He is not perhaps an eloquent speaker, but he is effective and has a fine conception of educational ideals, and is a leader among men."[6]

Falconer recommended two other Canadians: A.T. DeLury, a Professor of Mathematics at the University of Toronto, and J.A. MacLean, a graduate of Toronto, who was then serving as the President of the University of Idaho. All three of the names Falconer suggested were placed on Saskatchewan's short list when the Board of Governors convened for its first full meeting on May 22, 1908. The man who headed the list was Adam Shortt of Queen's. When approached formally he withdrew his name, although not before news of the overture was leaked to the press in Kingston.

With Shortt's withdrawal, Murray's name advanced to the top of the list. The Board authorized its Secretary, McColl, to write to each of the men on the short list to find out "whether in case the Presidency of the University were offered you, you would consider the offer."[7] The letter was ambiguous, and two of the candidates, DeLury and MacLean, each assumed he was being offered the job. This caused some embarrassment before McColl clarified the University's position. McColl's letter also mentioned a salary of

$5,000, although the possibility of raising it to attract "a suitable person" was left open.

When McColl's letter arrived in Halifax, Walter Murray sat down at his desk and drafted a reply which he mailed two days later. He said he would seriously consider the offer of the Presidency, "with a strong possibility of accepting it."[8] His letter really was a remarkable document for in it he sketched out a bold concept for the structure of the new University, a concept that he would translate into reality. He was the only one of the candidates on the Board's list to attempt this, and Murray's vision of what the University of Saskatchewan might be obviously caught the imagination of the Board.

When he wrote, Murray had not yet examined personally, as he would do later, the state universities of the American mid-west. He had crossed the prairies once, but the fleeting view from the window of a C.P.R. train had not given him much opportunity to assess their potential or analyse their resources. He admitted having only the scantiest information "apart from that contained in the Board's letter." His ideas were the product of his Maritime experience, and his years of study in the philosophy of education. The concept of the state university as set out in the Toronto model attracted him, but to that model he added some innovations of his own.

Murray envisaged "a large University with Faculties of Arts, Science, Engineering, Agriculture, Education, Law, Medicine and probably Dentistry and Commerce." His major innovation was the inclusion of agriculture in the University, which was at that time a novel idea for Canada. He highlighted the importance of agriculture in a striking naval metaphor: "The College or School of Agriculture must be regarded as the sheet anchor of the University." Because of the importance of agriculture to the people of Saskatchewan, the University, with agriculture as its centrepiece, could identify with the people's needs much more than was possible in any of the Eastern universities.

Yet he was emphatic that the humanities must not be subordinated. He wanted to know whether there were "any signs of a contempt for the humanities or a fanatical devotion to utility that would try to convert the University into a huge Agricultural and Engineering College and nothing more." If there were, then Saskatchewan was not the place for him. He summed up in a sentence what the proper balance should be: "I believe that the College of Agriculture, while distinct from the other Faculties and probably more isolated and independent, should yet be within the University, receiving from the liberal studies a humanizing influence and giving to the whole life of the University a sense of the close relationship between the daily life of the people and the pursuits of the scholar and the scientist."

In spite of his enthusiasm at the prospect of going to Saskatchewan to build a new university, his loyalty to Dalhousie tugged at his conscience and crept in at the end of his letter of application: "I do not like to think of leaving this University. Poverty has been our lot and our ambitions for a strong University have been great; but I have received nothing but kindness and have here friends who have been tried and never found wanting; and in spite of all our struggles and disappointments we have been very happy. Perhaps I should not have mentioned this." The frustrations of Dalhousie made the offer at Saskatchewan more tempting for Murray than it might have been otherwise, but leaving a place where he had given so much energy for sixteen years would be a wrenching break. His experience in the Maritimes convinced him of the absolute necessity, as he put it, "of beginning well." "Saskatchewan should have the best and the reputation of its University from the outset should be good."

Walter Murray's letter undoubtedly confirmed the tentative decision that the Board members had already made on the strength of Falconer's recommendation. But, because their decision was so important for the future of the university, they were not willing to hire anyone without seeing him first. Political pressure had added another person to the short list, so the Board struck a three-man committee to travel east and interview the leading candidates. George Locke, a Professor of Education at McDonald College, in Montreal, had sought the aid of several politicians to advance his cause. Calder, the Saskatchewan Minister of Education, wrote to one of the Board members that Locke was "a very likely candidate." Two days later, Scott, the Saskatchewan Premier, informed one of his political cronies in Ottawa that "the eye of those here, whose duty it is to find a President for the University, is turned in Professor Locke's direction in a way which I fancy puts him strictly in the running for selection."[9] Locke's efforts ultimately were not successful, but he was not the only candidate to use political influence.

Before Walter Murray met the selection committee for his interview in Montreal, he had enlisted the services of his political friends from Halifax as references on his behalf. One of them, A.K. Maclean, then the M.P. for Halifax, wrote to Murray the day before his interview:

> I saw the Committee today, who are to interview you tomorrow. I did everything I could, and our friend, the Senator, is trying to do the best he can. I cannot ascertain how severe the

competition is. I think there are one or two others who are being vigorously promoted but the delegation have cut their selection to four in number.[10]

Murray certainly was not backward in promoting his own candidacy.

Walter Murray had made up his mind to move west. If he was offered the post of President of the new University of Saskatchewan, he would accept without hesitation. Why, at age 42, was he prepared to forsake the Maritimes, where he had spent all his life, and Dalhousie, to which he had given sixteen years? The lure of the west beckoned him as it did other Maritimers. Murray had crossed the Prairies in 1903. The thought of creating a new provincial university there was an exciting prospect, especially for a man who had grown tired of trying to change old institutions weighted down with the barnacles of tradition.

He shared this frustration with one of his closest friends on the faculty at Dalhousie, A. Stanley MacKenzie, who had just come as the Professor of Physics in 1905 and with whom Murray struck up an immediate friendship. MacKenzie became the President of Dalhousie in 1911 and remained until 1931. The two men were regular correspondents and close friends. In 1910 when Stanley MacKenzie, too, was about to leave Dalhousie but only for a year, he described his feelings about Dalhousie in words which echoed Murray's feelings two years before:

> I have tried to stir them up, tried to see it make progress, tried to pull here and push there—and yet I can see no result; I cannot flatter myself that my being here has made the position of the College now different from what it was 5 years ago. It seems, if anything, deader than ever—or what is worse, apathetic.[11]

Apathy, the perennial shortage of money, and a President who carried "twenty years of accounts in a pocket memo book" and who dealt with university matters in an equally eccentric manner discouraged ambitious and able men. Murray was glad to leave this behind, while his friend, Stanley MacKenzie, returned after a year's absence to help Dalhousie move into the twentieth century.

When the chance came, Murray seized it. His selection came as a devastating blow to the aging President of Dalhousie, John Forrest. He was on a holiday in Europe, and the first news he had of Murray's imminent departure was a letter Murray sent with the news that he had been placed on the short list and invited to an interview. Forrest replied, "The truth is I am so upset that I do not know what to say. . . .

I cherished the hope that in the very near future you would be my successor and I did not hesitate to express my views to more than one of the Governors with their cordial approval. Of course the salary offered is larger but I feel confident that the position in the Maritimes would suit you and your family better."[12] Forrest's plans for Dalhousie were shattered by Murray's decision and a further exchange of letters succeeded neither in changing Murray's mind nor in reconciling Forrest to the decision. The hold of the Maritimes was not enough to compensate for the assured financial support a state university would receive and, above all, for the unique opportunity to design his own university.

When news of his selection reached Halifax, Murray's friends shared his delight. MacKenzie wrote, "You darned old runaway—but I am glad for your sake, and for the reputation of the moral city of Halifax. . . . I am so certain that you will make an unmistakable success of it that I congratulate you without hesitation."[13] Murray's other close friend among his colleagues, the distinguished Professor of English, Archibald MacMechan, was just as warm in his praise: "You are eminently fitted for it in your administrative gifts, business habits, ability to get on with men and your mastery of educational methods and problems. I think the new university is fortunate in getting you for its head. But what are *we* going to do? Poor old Dalhousie is becoming a sort of turnstile." Both MacKenzie and MacMechan were envious of Murray's good fortune, as they gently chided him, but most of all they were sad to lose him as a colleague. As MacMechan lamented, "There is nobody to take your place."[14]

When the three-man committee returned from the east after interviewing their candidates, Walter Murray's name headed their list. All that remained was the formal process of appointment. D.P. McColl informed Murray that he would be formally recommended for the position, at an annual salary of $5,000, when the Board next met on August 20th. Murray was to be present in Regina on that date.

He arrived very early in the morning, and alighting onto the wooden platform, he was met by the Chairman of the Board of Governors, A.F. Angus, the manager of the Bank of Montreal in Regina. Years later Murray recalled that scene:[15] Victoria Square was "little more than a bald prairie field, in the process of being ploughed up, not a tree or even a shrub in it, a scene of utter desolation." Into this "dreary" picture came "a tall man with a black bag in his hand" hurrying to board the train. It was Walter Scott, the Premier of the province, and Murray met him for the first time. Scott greeted him with a few words which Murray never forgot: "This is a great country and it needs men with large ideas." Murray was one of those men.

Murray also remembered vividly the actual circumstances of his appointment:

> The Governors met in the new City Hall in Regina and for what seemed like a decade I sat on a seat in an outer room reeking with fresh paint. I never liked fresh paint and to this day it has been associated with all the horrors of the doomed. The interview which followed was less painful than I had feared.[16]

He was confirmed by the Board as President that afternoon. There was no time for reflection or for settling affairs in Halifax. Murray did, however, brush aside a suggestion from the President of Dalhousie that he withdraw his name and return to Halifax. Everyone in Saskatchewan, it seemed, was in a hurry; the Governors wanted him to start work immediately. Murray commenced his duties the very next morning, using the office in Regina's City Hall intended for the city solicitor. "It, too, was reeking with fresh paint. I was given a small desk, a chair, a copy of the University Act and told practically 'to hop to it' and create a University."[17] The task was a daunting one, but the Board of Governors was confident that he would succeed. Scarcely three weeks after Murray's arrival, one of them wrote to Premier Scott: "Professor Murry [sic] is taking well under all conditions. The chances are we have the right man for the position. . . ."[18] They did.

■

Chapter 4

Locating the University

In August 1908, Walter Murray sat in the railway car on his way to Regina and his new job. He watched the changing scenes of the Canadian summer pass by and mused about the challenge awaiting him. To build a great provincial university from the ground up was awesome to contemplate. Where should he begin? He sketched a partial list of the immediate issues in a letter he wrote on the train to one of his old Dalhousie colleagues, Archibald MacMechan:

> How to reconcile the Liberal Arts and Agriculture? What should be the determining factors in the selection of a site for a new university? What provision should be made for College residences—the Dormitory or the English College? How to provide for the education of women? You might also give me your ideas of College Architecture and of the campus. There is hardly a University problem that must not to some extent be considered by us. In laying our foundation we must remember that we are building for centuries. The University will ultimately be large and I hope sound educationally. A state university cannot confine itself to the realization of one idea but must serve the many-sided life of the community. It must keep in close touch with present needs and yet must be true to the best university traditions.[1]

Murray's determination to fuse the "best university traditions" to Saskatchewan's needs for a state university is the key to the plans he brought west with him. To do that he had to find answers to the questions he had raised. None was more important in his mind nor more pressing than the location of the university. What Murray did not know, but soon began to suspect, was that the real decision may already have been made.

In his letter of application for President, written early in June, Murray included queries about the site:

Has the location of the University been decided? Do you think there is any likelihood of its being dismembered and the fragments scattered over the province to satisfy the wishes of ambitious towns? If the question of location has not been settled, by whom will it be decided?[2]

He clearly set down his own criteria. The "supreme consideration," as he put it, "will be what locality will enable the University to serve the whole province best. . . ." It would have to be a large site to accommodate the state university he had in mind, and it must contain "ample room for expansion in the years to come," which he foresaw would be as rapid as in the American state universities of the middle west. If his criteria were at least partly formed when he arrived in Regina at the end of the summer, he was still open minded as to where the actual location should be.

Ambitious Saskatchewan towns had been competing fiercely for the university prize long before Murray was appointed President. Saskatoon, Moose Jaw, Battleford, Prince Albert, and Regina all waged vigorous campaigns, first to persuade the government of the province, and then to convince the university's Board of Governors that each was the best location for the new university. Faced with great and irreconcilable political pressure from these towns, Premier Scott in the spring of 1908 placed the responsibility for choosing the site on the shoulders of the Board of Governors, adding that it would then be up to the government to accept or reject the advice of the Board. So great was the attraction of the university for these rival towns that the issue surfaced again during the provincial election of July 1908. Candidates running for both the Liberal and Conservative parties made bold statements about bringing the university to their own cities. The election results returning Scott and the Liberals to power reduced the real contenders, if political influence was to be the deciding criterion.

Both Moose Jaw and Prince Albert elected Conservative members, while Saskatoon and Regina returned Liberals. The Liberal member from Saskatoon, A.P. McNab, was also a member of the University's Board of Governors. During his campaign McNab pledged himself to bring the university to Saskatoon and promised to resign his seat if he was not successful. The Scott government had been committed since 1905 to a policy of decentralization which seemed to favour Saskatoon since Regina had already been chosen as the province's capital. But the overriding issue when Walter Murray arrived in Regina was still, who would make the real choice? Had political considerations already tipped the balance to Saskatoon? Would the

Board of Governors be permitted a free choice, and, most important to Murray, would the President's views receive a fair hearing?[3]

Murray was acutely conscious of the political maelstrom into which he had been thrown. The very day the Board confirmed his appointment, the site issue arose, and as he wrote his wife, "at once the passions flared up. It seems that the elections have intensified the ambitions of the towns."[4] Before he could do any thinking or planning about the university itself, he found himself in company with other members of the Board, visiting the rival towns to hear their presentations and to talk to them about the prospective university. He could not afford to alienate anyone. Only one place would be chosen, but if the university was going to succeed it had to rely on the support of people all across the province. On his first tour of the province, Walter Murray was both an ambassador and an inspector, with no time to prepare for either role.

The presentations to the Board of Governors on behalf of the leading contenders in September gave full play to creative imagination. Each town extolled its own virtues, and Murray was obviously amused by the attempts to draw comparisons with the great universities of Britain. He wrote later:

> Oxford and the Isis were to be found at Moose Jaw and the Creek. Edinburgh might be repeated in Battleford, the ancient capital and the scene of a siege. Beautiful and historic Prince Albert poured contempt on 'Pile O' Bones'. . . . Saskatoon had not forgotten the struggle over the capital and was anxious.[5]

While touring the province, Murray had a chance to get to know the Board and had many opportunities to convince them of his views on how a state university should operate. The one issue that they delicately skated around was the site, as he told his wife in another letter:

> We were driven around at Prince Albert, Saskatoon and Battleford and were feasted in each place and treated to speeches and upon me fell the burden of speech-making—just imagine it. No preparation and plenty of tossing up and down to mix-up one's ideas. Well I surprised myself and everybody. Apparently I got the ear of the crowd and have got the Governors into my way of thinking about such things as general policy, agriculture, salaries, buildings, etc., everything except location, which we have carefully avoided except in so far as they have agreed to keep the University together and to place it where it can do its work best and not where the towns clamour for it.[6]

After barely two weeks in the job, Murray had reason to be optimistic.

At the second meeting of the Board that Murray attended (held in Prince Albert on September 2), the Board agreed to send its new President, with two other Board members, on a tour of American state universities to learn from their experience. Before they left early in October, Walter Murray's growing fear of political interference over the location of the university prompted him to write the Premier.[7] He agonized over the letter and finally sent it just before he left for the States. In his letter, Murray drew the Premier's attention to the conflict of interest of A.P. McNab who had promised the university to Saskatoon in his successful electoral campaign that summer and who still remained a member of the Board of Governors. McNab, according to Murray, "would consider not the good of the University but what would please some of his friends. If I were to adopt this same attitude with regard to a single appointment, a single purchase or a single proposal, I would surely deserve at least immediate dismissal, if not heavy penalties. If we settle University affairs in this manner what can we expect of the young men and women who come to that institution for instruction in the best things of life? I would rather see a priest rob the charity boxes than see a university pollute the springs of education."

His letter was long and detailed. In it he argued very eloquently the case for political non-interference in the location of the university. Murray suggested there could be only two reasons for government interference: political expediency or the incompetency of the Board of Governors. The importance of the issue in Murray's mind transcended the problem of the site itself; to him it had become symbolic of the relationship between government and university. "I believe that this question is vital. Its settlement will determine whether University affairs are to be administered solely in the interest of the University or in that of self seekers."

Murray did not ask for an interview with the Premier to discuss the matter nor did he wait for a reply. His letter embodying his strong feelings was a challenge to the Liberal government not to become involved in University affairs. Having cast down the gauntlet, Murray departed for the United States. He was a worried man, and there had been no opportunity to discuss his difficulties with his wife, who had remained in Halifax. The first she heard of it was a letter he wrote to her from St. Louis, Missouri, late in October:

> After careful[ly] thinking the thing over I believe I should protest most strongly against the Government interfering in the settlement of the question of location, should they so decide. If

so I must be ready to back up my protest by resignation if necessary. I shall write you if things begin to look dangerous.[8]

This letter to his wife announcing he might have to resign after barely two months in the job came as a complete shock to her. She received it the day before Thanksgiving, 1908, and Teenie, as Walter called her, nearly cancelled the Thanksgiving dinner she had planned for family and friends. She wrote back immediately, pointing out to her husband that if he resigned "we shall be back to our old financial difficulties and worse, for you will be a man without a job."[9] She urged him to consult his great friend Robert Falconer, President of the University of Toronto, before deciding. "If he says you are justified I shall be resigned." Then in a pointed remark she told him, "You would have made a good martyr. I am afraid I was not cut out for one."

They were not able to discuss the crisis with one another except by mail, but as husband and wife they held opposing views. Walter believed he had to stand on principle even if resignation was his only course of action. Christina was much more the pragmatist; although she was prepared to support her husband if he decided to resign, she tried to persuade him against a precipitate decision.

The trip through the American mid-west was strenuous, but it helped to take Murray's mind off the worrisome site problem. As he told his wife, "We go to sleep in one place, wake up in another and interview a College President. Then eat and go to sleep again." The tour was a succession of contrasts. "Chicago is the noisiest, smokiest hole in America. Our visit was like a descent into Hades. The only bright spot was the trip to the university." St. Louis, on the other hand, provided inspiration for the greystone buildings Murray's university was to make famous. He wrote after visiting Washington University, "The buildings are beautiful, my idea of university buildings."[10]

As he toured the American universities, his own views on the location of the University of Saskatchewan were clarified. He also believed, naively as it turned out, that he had converted the two Board members who were travelling with him: McColl, the Board's Secretary, and John Dixon. Shortly before he returned to Regina, he summed up the site difficulties for his wife:

It is good politics to locate the University at Saskatoon, but I think bad University policy. Hitherto the Premier has declared that he will not interfere about the location but Saskatoon is bringing pressure to bear. If they change their attitude it will be due purely to party expediency. I feel that if they once break away we will never be secure and that it is better to settle this question now and forever.[11]

Yet even after he returned to Regina he could not rid himself of the nagging suspicion that party politics and not the good of the University would determine its location. Early in November he wrote to his wife that the chances were about even that the government would not intervene. He told her, however, that if the government intervened he would have to resign. Even though he privately feared he might be making a mountain out of a molehill, he felt he had to justify his possible resignation, both to himself and to his wife:

> If they interfere they establish a dangerous precedent. My resignation in protest may at least direct public attention to the magnitude of the evil and will probably prevent a recurrence. In this way I can do the University, I believe, great and lasting service, probably the greatest service. On the other hand if I stay, I confess my weakness to fight for the right and lay myself open to all sorts of influences or pressures in the interests of anything but the University.[12]

His wife's obvious concern did not sway him. He had consulted Falconer and wrote to her again a week later that "I cannot see my way clear in any other direction. The thing has not come to a head and may never get worse. I hope so, but one must be prepared for the worst."[13] His wife remained supportive and tried to cheer him up. She assured him they would be able to survive until the next autumn on the money from the sale of their Halifax house. Her chief regret, she wrote, would be Walter's disappointment "not to have the opportunity of building up a new University." Fatalistically, she would accept what her husband decided. "But if you must resign, why then you must." She confessed, however, her puzzlement that a man like Falconer, who must also be subject to government interference, would keep working and yet advise Walter to resign in protest. In contrast to her husband, Christina accepted the reality of government interference: "I feel sure that the Government will interfere, for what man in politics would withstand so influential a place as Saskatoon. Scott may be a 'decent' enough man; so is Premier Murray [of Nova Scotia]. But I notice when it comes to doing a thing out and out against colleagues these men seldom have the courage of their convictions."[14] Christina's political acumen on this subject was sharper than Walter's. Perhaps her distance from both her husband and Saskatchewan gave her greater objectivity. She could live with the result even if it was a political decision which went counter to her husband's advice. The major question for both of them, however, was whether Walter could swallow such a defeat and still carry on.

In spite of his bold declarations to his wife, Walter Murray did not seek martyrdom through resignation. Nor when the issue was finally decided did he resign. What he worked feverishly to do in the autumn of 1908 was to convince the Saskatchewan government to let the University Board of Governors decide, without any outside political pressure, where the university would be built.

An added complication was that Walter no longer was uncommitted himself. He had decided on his American trip where the University ought to be situated. His conviction was so strong that he was unshakeable: the University had to be located at Regina. His task, as he saw it, was twofold: persuading the rest of the Board to agree with him, and keeping the government out of the decision. Ultimately he failed to win over the Board, and the suspicion lingered for the rest of his life that party politics really had determined the site for Saskatchewan's provincial university. His suspicions were undoubtedly correct, although the government went to great lengths to make sure there was no overt interference with the decision of the Board of Governors.

In the notes he made on his trip he set down five points which should govern the University's location. It must have an ample site with good soil; it had to be easy of access, in direct communication with all parts of the province and, ideally, at the centre of the concentration of population; it should be in or near a large city; it should be at the seat of government because this would ensure support, enable the University to give greater service to the state, and make available to the University such facilities as provincial libraries, museums and laboratories; and it should be placed at the point of greatest strategic value. Using his five criteria, Murray compared Regina and Saskatoon. The only heading under which Saskatoon came out ahead was scenic beauty. "In all others Regina surpasses."[15]

Even Murray's geopolitical analysis of the province's future favoured Regina. He divided the province into three belts, using the railway lines. One belt lay south of the C.P.R., another north, and a third in between. The southern belt had in the past proved highly suitable for farming; it also contained large amounts of low grade coal which might be the foundation for future industrialization. The middle belt had fertile soil in the east and the possibility of agricultural development in the west. The northern belt had potential for mixed farming, lumbering and mining. The railway lines in between the belts had determined the economic, as well as the political, importance of Regina. Murray also observed that for the next twenty-five years, the great majority of Saskatchewan's high school students would be drawn from southern Saskatchewan. Everything pointed to Regina; therefore that was where the University had to be.

He could not separate the location of the University from his philosophy of what a state University should do:

> *A false conception of the University* had led some to think lightly of the importance of locating a University wisely. A generation ago a University or College, as it was called, was looked upon as a Boarding School, or a Retreat for troublesome boys, to be placed in some shady spot, beside a pleasant stream remote from the marketplace and the current of national life. Today the University is regarded as the great instrument of the State for the discovery of the truths of science to the problems that arise in our agriculture, industries, commerce, government, and social life. To be of the greatest service, the University must be placed where it is easy of access and in close touch with the life of the province.[16]

Murray's views on why Regina was the only possible choice did not change between October 1908, when he formed them, and April 1909 when the decision was made to select Saskatoon. Moreover, they were directly opposed to the decentralization philosophy of Scott's government which pointed to Saskatoon as the likely site, since Regina had been named the provincial capital. The outcome and the fact that Murray did not resign suggests a victory for the politically adroit Premier over the inexperienced University President.

Murray vigorously lobbied both the Board members and government Ministers in November and December of 1908 against government interference in the selection of a site. No one in the government could possibly have been unaware of the President's strong views. In public, the Saskatchewan government adopted a neutral stance on the issue and in private the Premier reassured Murray that no political interference would take place. Murray sent his own analysis of where the University should be to Premier Scott early in December, so the government knew that Murray strongly favoured Regina. When A.P. McNab, the Liberal member for Saskatoon, was brought into Scott's cabinet in December, he had to stand for re-election. A week before the election he resigned from the University's Board of Governors, another welcome sign to Murray that direct political interference would not occur.

In a letter he wrote to McNab in December, Premier Scott made it clear that the University would not be awarded to any town which had made the mistake of electing Conservatives in the provincial election of the previous July.[17] That would eliminate Moose Jaw and Prince Albert. The only two competitors left were Saskatoon and Regina; the race was indeed between these two. The Premier was known to favour Saskatoon and the University President was behind Regina. Scott, however, had no desire to force Murray's resignation over the choice. The provincial government was very happy with Murray's work. From Scott's perspective, the dilemma was how to ensure that Saskatoon was selected without precipitating an open confrontation with Murray. The answer seemed to lie in indirect persuasion. Scott had promised Murray there would be no direct political interference and he kept his promise.

The site question dragged on through the winter and spring of 1909. The Board of Governors would not make a decision without full attendance of every member. When one Board member had to leave for New York because of the death of his father, the decision was postponed until April. Murray found the delay very trying, but he was determined not to lose heart. He wrote to Henry Tory, the President of the University of Alberta, that the site issue had to be fought out to the finish.[18]

Murray was terribly homesick for his wife and family as he waited throughout the winter and early spring for the Board to meet and choose the site. The loneliness got on his nerves. His only outlet came in letters to his wife; in them he confessed his uncertainties about what the Board would do. As the date for the decisive meeting approached, his letters reveal a determined man, whistling to keep his courage up. On March 21 he wrote his "Teenie":

> The betting about the location is keen and wild. There are rumours of all kinds flying about; but I say nothing and at the meeting will put up the fight of a lifetime, and if I win I will go home in comfort; if not, then I must make the best of it, unless there is crooked work. If there is, look out for trouble. But there will be no trouble. There is only one chance in a thousand.[19]

The Board of Governors made the final decision on April 7, 1909, in Regina's City Hall. Regina had made its presentation to the Board that very day, so on the surface things could not have been more favourable for the capital's interest. When the item "University location" was reached in the Board's business, everyone in the room was conscious of the tension rising. Every member of the Board gave his view before voting started. Murray reiterated the same arguments in favour of Regina which he had presented to the Premier the previous December. The voting then proceeded, with the town receiving the fewest votes being discarded at each ballot until one place received a majority of votes. The contest quickly narrowed to Regina and Saskatoon, with Murray voting for Regina on every ballot. On the final ballot, Regina received three votes to Saskatoon's six. In the end, as Murray immediately recognized, politics won out over what he regarded as the interests of the University.[20]

Privately, Murray was acutely disappointed over the outcome and again contemplated his resignation. Chancellor Wetmore, his old acquaintance from New Brunswick days, helped to talk him out of it. Publicly, the President put on a gracious face. When asked by the editor of the Saskatoon *Daily Phoenix* for a word of congratulations to the newly selected University city, Murray replied, "May the devotion of Saskatoon to the best interests of the University spur the University to the highest service of the province."[21] He did not, however, immediately go up to Saskatoon to join in the revelry.

Upon hearing news of the decision, President Tory of Alberta wrote a letter of consolation to Murray.[22] He pointed out that one good feature would be the close proximity between the two state universities of Alberta and Saskatchewan, which the Alberta President hoped would engender "a tradition of good fellowship in competition between the students of the two Universities." Tory also drew an obvious moral from the defeat he knew Murray had suffered: "I imagine both you and I have already found out that it is not altogether smooth sailing in getting things started in the West."

Murray was certainly not alone in his disappointment over the Board's choice. Premier Scott was in Florida when the decision was announced, but the hot sun of St. Augustine was cool compared to the hot anger of some of his Liberal supporters in Regina. His personal secretary described the reaction of the Regina Liberals for the Premier:

> The majority of them were so genuinely flabbergasted with the decision that very little was said for a day or two, but the longer they thought it over the angrier most of them became, and by Saturday there were quite a number of prominent Grits vowing summary vengeance upon all and sundry connected with the Government. A hurry-up meeting of about twenty or so of the workers was held and I believe the gathering was one of the warmest which has taken place in Regina for many moons....[23]

But the lawyers and the educators were the angriest of all. One was reported to have "paced his office all day very much after the manner of a caged tiger, while the air was positively blue in his vicinity." Their immediate reaction was to contemplate seeking financial assistance from the Government to establish a Law School and a Medical School in Regina. Out of the anger of the professional men in Regina was born the seeds of rivalry—a situation Murray would have to contend with throughout his term of office.

The only other criticisms of the decision heard by the Premier's Secretary had come from Tories which he dismissed, and from real estate men in Regina, who stood out in their hyprocrisy. "One of the most remarkable features of the whole question is that the real estate men who are grousing are not doing so because their pockets will be affected but solely on account of the great disadvantages the University will be placed under through being located at Saskatoon."[24] But outside Regina, especially in the north of the province, the decision was warmly welcomed. Many people in smaller towns away from the capital were not unhappy to see Regina snubbed.

Murray rationalized his decision not to resign over the location of the university in a letter to his beloved Teenie. He was still wrestling with his conscience even if the outcome was no longer in doubt:

> Here I think I have made good so far as winning the confidence of the people who are concerned, particularly in this town and generally where I have been. There has been no burst of enthusiasm but quiet regard and confidence. In the Senate everything I have proposed has carried. In the Board of Governors the same is true except the site question; even the Government has listened and accepted. But on the site their ears were closed and political considerations alone won out. The interests of the University were simply ignored. I could have taken many rebuffs on other things with equanimity, but the introduction of politics is a vital blow. It will take many a day to adjust oneself if it can be done.[25]

His assessment of his accomplishments was modest, but the defeat he had suffered was so galling to him it blurred any celebration of the great progress he had made towards establishing the University. He could not accept that political considerations had swept aside his carefully argued case, and that on such a key issue the President's advice had quite simply been ignored.

With time, Murray fully reconciled himself to the decision in favour of Saskatoon. He came to feel that the distance of Regina and the provincial legislature from Saskatoon offered the university extra protection from direct political interference: a haunting, though largely imaginary, spectre throughout Murray's presidency. On the positive side, he believed with good reason that the Legislature was likely to be more generous in its support of the university as the major public institution in the northern half of the province, than it might have been if the university had been placed in the south. Thus the political philosophy of decentralization to which Premier Scott had committed himself was eventually accepted by Murray. What he would not accept and fought against all his life was any idea of creating a rival university at Regina. For Murray, there could be only one state university in Saskatchewan.

The site question vexed him until the land was actually purchased. He hurried onto the train for Saskatoon from Regina early in June 1909 with the signed options to buy the university land, only to discover forty miles up the line that he had misplaced his suitcase with the papers. He borrowed a team of horses and spent five agitated hours on a return trip to Regina. Fortunately, the suitcase was found and he was able to reach Saskatoon before the options expired.

Once Saskatoon was chosen, he set his reservations aside and worked to build the new university there with all the vigour of which he was capable. Five months after the Board decided in favour of Saskatoon, the first classes began at Saskatchewan's provincial university. Murray had no time for brooding; there was too much to do. In short order the Board approved his recommendations for the first faculty members, and appointed the firm of Brown and Vallance of Montreal as architects to design the plans for the university.

His enthusiasm for the land itself was an obvious tonic and was very evident in his letters to his family. He wrote in June:

> We have had three good rains in one week, a most unusual occurrence. The wheat is looking fine and the air after the rain, when the sun is shining, is perfection itself. There is nothing better.[26]

Walter Murray had become a Westerner.

■

Chapter 5

Building the University

Next to the location of the university, the role of agriculture loomed as the most urgent question confronting the new President of the University of Saskatchewan. Would the university include a Faculty of Agriculture or would a College of Agriculture be established as a separate institution, as was the pattern in eastern Canada? Murray had no doubts about his own position. In his letter of application for the Presidency, he had referred to agriculture as the sheet anchor of the university he planned to construct. Fortunately for Murray, in view of his defeat on the location of the university, Premier Scott and he agreed on the predominance of agriculture in Saskatchewan's university. Just after Murray arrived in Saskatchewan, Scott wrote to a Maritime correspondent:

> Agriculture must be our main industry and if our University cannot and does not turn out men and women with taste and training for agricultural pursuits, it will fail of its mission. . . . My view is that the Saskatchewan University ought to inculcate the principle that the Science of Agriculture is of all the material sciences the best and noblest, and that in its organization such principle should be dominant.[1]

W.R. Motherwell, Scott's Minister of Agriculture, apparently had plans of his own for a separate College of Agriculture. The 1908 government estimates had some provision for a College of Agriculture, and a Supplementary Revenue Act passed in 1907 allocated equal shares from a direct levy on occupied lands in the province to the new university and to an agricultural college.[2] Moreover, it was widely believed that Motherwell had brought W.J. Rutherford, the Deputy Minister of Agriculture, from Manitoba to head this separate agricultural college.

Walter Murray was determined to house the agricultural college within the University, but first he had to persuade the Board of

Governors to agree with him. Less than two weeks after his appointment, on his motion the Board authorized a small committee, including Murray, to tour the universities and colleges of the western and central states as well as Ontario and Manitoba. They were to investigate agricultural education along with other immediate concerns such as building design and teacher training. Murray was optimistic about agriculture, and the Board had every reason to support his views. The President wanted the university to sink deep roots into Saskatchewan's soil.

In his view, university control of agricultural education and teacher training were two key ways of achieving a close relationship with the life of the province. He explained his ideas in a letter to his wife in September 1908:

> There are two pretty things looming up. One concerns the place of the Agricultural College in the University. Of that you have already heard or read enough. The other is a plan to gobble up all the provincial examinations for certificates and teachers' licenses and to take over the normal school and establish a Faculty of Education in the University. If we can do this the University will obtain control of the work of the schools, the training of the teachers and become an integral part of the whole educational system. No province has been able to go so far up to the present but every university wishes it. It is a big thing. If we can put these two things through, the University will get a hold upon the public that will be unique. . . . [3]

Murray did not "gobble the whole thing up" as he wanted. Murray's plan of gobbling up the education ministry, for it nearly amounted to that, was unlikely to win the approval of Calder, the Minister of Education and, next to the Premier, the most powerful man in the government. The idea was audacious, but politically out of the question. Whether or not Murray's eagerness to take over teacher training delayed the creation of an education faculty within the university is an open question. The Faculty of Education had to wait for twenty years—a deep disappointment to the man who had helped to introduce an Education Faculty at Dalhousie. However, Murray was more successful with agriculture.

He obtained the evidence he needed on the whirlwind tour of American and Canadian campuses in the autumn of 1908. Not only did Murray, and the Board members accompanying him, interview College Presidents but they also talked to faculty members with special knowledge of the organization and integration of agricultural colleges. Murray was surprised at the unanimity of opinion on agriculture. He wrote to Tory, the President of the University of Alberta, that "even in institutions which are now separate, such as the Agricultural Colleges at Lansing, Guelph and Indiana, we found the leading men in agriculture of one mind with regard to the wisdom of starting the higher educational work in one institution in a new Province."[4]

The report that Murray wrote and the Board of Governors endorsed after the American trip "strongly recommended" to the Saskatchewan government "that the College of Agriculture in this Province be united with the University and that all departments of University work be concentrated in the same locality."[5] Murray was able to advance some powerful arguments in support of this recommendation: "the overwhelming opinion" in favour of union which he had found on his visits, the "demoralizing rivalry" and waste caused by the existence of separate institutions, the encouragement given to agricultural research and extension work by locating agricultural studies within the university, and the "social advantages" not only to agricultural students but also to those from other faculties. Murray added in his own report appended to the recommendation:

> Of the social advantages of union, there cannot be two opinions. The Agricultural students mix with the other students on the football field, in the literary and musical societies and the social gatherings and not only receive much from them but also contribute much to the general life of the University. All are greatly benefitted by the intercourse and better prepared for service in the State, where the farmer, the doctor, the lawyer, the teacher and the engineer must work together for the public good.[6]

Murray was optimistic about persuading the government to unite the agricultural college and the university. He wrote to his wife after his return from the trip:

> I believe the Minister of Agriculture is opposed to my view and we may have some difficulty in persuading him, but I think the Premier and the Minister of Education are inclined in our direction. I have had two interviews with the Deputy Commissioner of Agriculture, Professor Rutherford. He is a good fellow and I think we can pull together.[7]

Motherwell, the Minister of Agriculture, may have opposed Murray's plan initially, but he soon succumbed. He was preoccupied with fighting a by-election during the fall of 1908, but the niceties of political protocol were observed. When Motherwell had won his seat, he sent Rutherford to retrace Murray's steps and interview many of the university and college officials Murray had already consulted. Quite possibly, Murray had converted Rutherford before the latter's trip, but he returned in full support of Murray's plan and convinced Motherwell to back it. Motherwell did so and transferred many of the educational aspects of his ministry to the new university. Rutherford also moved to the university to become the first Dean of Agriculture.

Once the decision had been made to include a Faculty of Agriculture in the university and to place agriculture at the forefront of the university's activity, the Provincial Department of Agriculture transferred to the university its very popular extension branch. Murray and members of his faculty devoted a great deal of their time to build an extension program. Six years after his appointment and five years after the university opened, one quarter of the total provincial population was directly influenced by courses, lectures, demonstrations, and exhibits provided by the extension department. Murray wrote in 1914 that "through its extension department in agriculture, the university reaches every part of the province and not only makes the people realize that the university is touching their daily life, but prevents the agricultural interests from becoming separated from the other interests of the province."[8]

Saskatchewan was the first Canadian state university to incorporate agriculture as one of its faculties. It was a historic decision for Saskatchewan and for the development of state universities within Canada. Murray's pioneering vision of the link between the university and the province's main industry was borne out by the development of agriculture within the university and by the contribution which Saskatchewan graduates and professors were to make to Canadian agriculture.

Once this decision was made, Murray could proceed with the rest of his plans. On November 21, 1908, a meeting of the University Council approved Murray's motion to establish two Faculties at the earliest possible date, Arts and Science and Agriculture. Classes would begin in the autumn of 1909.

Murray had to grapple with the location of a university and the connection of agriculture to the university again in 1910. He was asked by the British Columbia government to serve on a commission to select the site for the University of British Columbia. Murray accepted the invitation and served as the commission's secretary.[9] The routine was all too familiar. He spent from late May through

June 1910 touring key towns of British Columbia listening to the advantages each proclaimed. The rival claims in British Columbia advanced by Victoria, Vancouver, Nanaimo, New Westminster, Kamloops, Chilliwack, etc. bore many resemblances to those Murray had heard in Saskatchewan two years earlier. The commission worked quickly and before the end of June it recommended that the university be located in Vancouver. The actual report consisted of a seven-line recommendation in Murray's handwriting.[10] Having not had his recommendation on a site for a university accepted in Saskatchewan, it was some consolation at least to have the commission's recommendation for British Columbia accepted immediately.

Murray was equally insistent in British Columbia that the College of Agriculture had to be united with the university. This was a major point in the commission's thinking, as Murray reiterated several years later to President Wesbrook of the University of British Columbia:

> The living and working together of the students of Agriculture and the Arts cannot but result in the establishment of very strong ties between the men who are afterwards to attain positions of importance and power in the different professions and callings of the province. So important do I believe this close tie to be, that I would personally sacrifice nearly everything for its attainment.[11]

Murray's view weighed heavily with the Board of Governors of UBC when they made a presentation to the government to obtain more land for the university in order to keep agriculture together with the rest of the university.[12] Thus he played a key role in uniting agriculture with other faculties in two western Canadian universities.

The University of Saskatchewan Board of Governors' Committee, which visited the American universities in the autumn of 1908, also brought back recommendations for the style and design of the new university campus and its buildings. Here, too, Walter Murray's view predominated. He wrote to his wife after visiting Washington University in St. Louis: "The buildings are beautiful, my ideal of university buildings. I shall send you a book of views."[13] No doubt he returned with books for the Board members as well. The Board agreed with Murray's recommendation that the University of Saskatchewan should be constructed in Collegiate Gothic style as best embodied in Washington University, St. Louis. The Committee also interviewed a number of leading university architects in the United States but only considered seriously Cape and Stewardson of

St. Louis and Brown and Vallance of Montreal. In June 1909, Brown was interviewed and hired. His firm took on the challenge of adapting Collegiate Gothic to the Saskatchewan prairie.

The Saskatchewan Board of Governors approved the architectural style. They were to approve each step in building—layout and site plan, materials of construction, and the sequence in which buildings were erected—but in every case they acted on Murray's recommendations. In a very real sense, Walter Murray designed the physical layout of the university in the same careful and painstaking way he had developed the academic design.

The Montreal architects had to work within two constraints: the style of Collegiate Gothic which had been chosen before they were hired, and the need to incorporate agriculture on the campus. Since the first buildings to be constructed were to be for agriculture, the architects had to neglect the great natural feature of beauty on the Saskatoon sight, the riverbank, and commence building at the point farthest from the river and nearest to the farm. Agricultural needs in the first instance took priority over scenic beauty. It was a practical choice and one Murray defended in his 1910 Annual Report: "It was felt that the latter course was more in keeping with present needs and present resources." From the very beginning the university's physical layout was oriented away from the river, not dictated by it, because of the primacy given to agriculture.

The first three buildings contracted for were the stock pavilion, the power house, and the laboratory for agriculture engineering. Then came the College Building (planned for eventual agricultural use) and the first residence. The following year, 1911, it was decided to build a horse and cattle barn, a sheep barn, an implement shed, and residences for the Dean of Agriculture and the Professor of Field Husbandry. The campus was looking all too much like an Agricultural College.

Murray used a substantial section of his 1911 Annual Report to promote the College of Arts and Science, which had almost three-quarters of the registered students. "The best universities in Canada are those whose Arts Faculties are strong and were strong from the first." Was there some unease developing? Murray may have been feeling uncomfortable for, in the same report, he wrote, "The University of Saskatchewan would be unfaithful to the trust imposed upon it if it neglected its Arts and Science. . . ." When we raised this issue with his daughter, Dr. Jean Murray, who had done much research for a planned biography of her father, her reaction was sharply defensive. To her, this section in the 1911 Annual Report was proof of the importance her father always gave to Arts and Science.

Yet, it was not until well after Murray's Presidency that the Arts had a building of their own. Walter Murray concentrated instead on building the Arts faculty with vigor.

"The progress of erection of the buildings has been slow," so Murray reported in 1911. The frustrations of shortages of material and workmen were evident early, and the resulting delays continued to be a problem. They were accompanied by large increases in cost over the estimates. Murray had to explain this to the government which fortunately was sympathetic and underwrote the increases. The Board of Governors decided in 1911 to authorize the construction of two homes, one for the President, and one for the Dean of Agriculture, as part of the university's initial building program. The architects, Brown and Vallance of Montreal, sent two plans for Murray's house, one a much more lavish building than Murray originally had contemplated. Vallance wrote Murray that his preferred design would be "a house such as we would like to see the University build for the President. This latter unquestionably would be in excess of any expenditure you would care to undertake."[14] The design was for a stone house; both Murray and the Board were attracted by the design and by the thought of using stone. Once the decision to use stone had been made, the Board discovered a local supply and thus was born the beautiful greystone used to adorn the main buildings of the university.

During the construction of the President's house, costs kept mounting, to Murray's acute embarrassment. At one point he tried to persuade the Board to prune one wing from the design in order to lower the cost and avoid any opportunity for public criticism. The Board overruled him, and the house was completed in 1913 at a cost of $42,000 (more than twice as expensive as any other house in the city).[15] Walter Murray and his family moved into the presidential mansion in February 1913, even though he confessed to the Premier that the money spent on the house was the one university expenditure he regretted.[16]

The house was built to enhance the prestige of the university, and the Board was determined that nothing should be spared. It wasn't. The stone structure overlooking the river would have been more appropriate in the architect's home city of Montreal. It was an anachronism in Saskatoon. Brown and Vallance were struck with the architectural possibilities offered by the river and envisioned the house rising from the riverbank like a castle on the Rhine. Their design metaphor was an apt comment on the finished result, for it was a regal mansion. Royalty has stayed in it, and the Murray family were to occupy it for the next twenty-four years.

The house had oak panelling and oak floors throughout, including the basement. There were servants' quarters on the third floor and a system of bell pulls in each room. It had seven fireplaces, one in each bedroom, which were absolutely essential during cold, prairie winters. Mrs. Murray protested during construction that the builders were making the house into a fortress because the windows were so small. They were enlarged. The house remained a building which dominated its environment and, because of its size and lavishness, was an obvious target for gossip. It was an imposing residence for the President of a Prairie university. Today it still stands as a showpiece of the university and the city.

Another frustration was annoying Murray around this period, and it was Murray-made. Three years after the Board of Governors approved the campus layout drawn up by Brown and Vallance and approved in September 1909, Murray persuaded the Board to hire Thomas Mawson, an English landscape architect. Mawson was to report on "the arrangement of the grounds, planting of trees, the location and making of roads . . . the location of buildings, with suggestions with regard to their arrangement both for landscape effect and for convenience."[17]

Mawson was a distinguished man in his field and naturally took this mandate as the carte blanche it was. He drew up an elaborate plan that disregarded existing buildings and those under construction, adding some forty buildings to the sixty envisaged by the Brown and Vallance plan. He even presented his plan to the Royal Academy where it was accepted for exhibition. It was not, and could not be, accepted by the university. The senior Mawson did not return to Canada, so the sorting out fell on his son's shoulders. After some less-than-complimentary exchanges between Walter Murray and Mawson Jr., the firm was apparently paid off for two hundred dollars. Murray summed up the matter in a letter to David Brown, the architect: "I can say this much, that if we had the thing to do over we would act differently . . . but that is in the past."[18]

During the autumn of 1908 Murray was vainly trying to persuade the Board and the government to locate the university at Regina and was busy with his extensive and tiring trip through the American mid-west, and central and eastern Canada. He still found time to complete his plan for the university, which he had outlined originally in his application for the Presidency. The plan as he conceived it in 1908 exists today almost as he had foreseen—a tribute both to the soundness of his educational ideas and to his imaginative leap into the future. He fleshed out his plan in November 1908, and the Board approved it early in April 1909. He wrote:

It seems to me that we may quite properly expect our University in time to embrace:

1   A College of Liberal Arts and Science, with Schools of Music, Art, Domestic Science, and Commerce.

2   A College of Agriculture with the Experimental Farm, School of Forestry, and Department of Veterinary Science.

3   A College of Education with its Practice Schools.

4   A College of Law.

5   A College of Medicine and School of Pharmacy.

6   A College of Dentistry.

7   A College of Engineering.

8   An Extension Department making provision for local Technical Schools, Correspondence classes, and lecture courses in local centres.

Murray also envisaged a university link with theological schools of various denominations.

> It would be an error of the first magnitude for our University to cut itself off from friendly relations with the theological schools of the province. While the University would adhere rigidly to the non-sectarian policy, it need not be indifferent or antagonistic to the religious interests. A community of theological colleges clustered about the University will not only receive much, but will also contribute much to the life of the University.

With the location determined, the agricultural question settled, and his plan approved, Murray next turned his energies to selecting faculty. For twenty-eight years, every faculty appointment was carefully considered and recommended to the Board by him. W.P. Thompson in *The University of Saskatchewan* writes of Murray's method:

> Before Murray recommended an appointment he always consulted widely with those who could be most helpful about candidates. For the first appointments his consultants had to be in other universities, but as he acquired staff of his own, their advice was sought regularly.[19]

His informal methods were successful, primarily because of his extensive network of contacts and his own ability to pick able people. W.P. Thompson was one. He served on Murray's staff for twenty-four years as professor, head of a department, and Dean. He was one of six faculty members selected by Murray who later became university presidents. In addition, Dr. Gerhard Herzberg, whom Murray assisted to leave Nazi Germany by providing a place for him at Saskatchewan, subsequently won the Nobel Prize. Another of Murray's choices, C.J. Mackenzie, the Dean of Engineering at Saskatchewan, went from there to be the President of the National Research Council and of Atomic Energy of Canada.

Murray's first four appointments in 1909 exemplified his careful methods. He hired George Ling from Columbia as the professor of mathematics. Ling served Saskatchewan with great distinction for more than twenty-five years as professor and as Dean of the Arts and Science Faculty. Edmund Oliver came to Saskatchewan as a professor of history. He soon established a distinguished reputation as a historian, as an educator in the University of Vimy Ridge during World War I, and later in theology as the principal of St. Andrew's College, the Presbyterian theological college. Oliver climaxed his career as Moderator of the United Church. Reginald Bateman, an eminent graduate of Trinity College, Dublin, was the first professor of English. His career, which began with such promise, ended with his death in France early in the First World War.

Arthur Moxon, a lawyer and former student of Murray's at Dalhousie, came as the first professor of classics. He then became a professor of law at the university and demonstrated his skills as a careful diplomat by first diffusing the angry opposition of the Benchers of the Law Society to the establishment of the law school at the university and in 1923 by winning acceptance for the school as the only training ground for lawyers in Saskatchewan. He served very successfully as Dean of Law until 1929, when he returned to private practice. Later, he was a member and Chairman of the University Board of Governors. Murray's evident "flair for judging men" brought distinguished scholars to Saskatchewan, and as evidenced in the careers of his first four choices, men whose versatility matched their scholarship.

Walter Murray stated in his 1909 Annual Report that "great care has been taken in making enquiries and no appointment has been made until those who made the recommendations were fully satisfied." He added his own selection standards: a distinguished undergraduate degree or equivalent from the "leading universities on this continent or in Europe," a proven record of success in teaching, and "industry, enthusiasm and high character."

In selecting faculty as in every other aspect of building the university, so much depended upon the President, but as Edmund Oliver wrote in his diary a few days before classes started in the autumn of 1909, "Murray is by far the strongest man of us all."[20] Saskatoon surpassed Oliver's expectations and clearly so did Murray. Oliver's description of Murray, the day he first met him, verifies this:

> Murray himself came in on the C.N.R. from Regina, a man presumably of some 45 [43] years, quiet in manner, knows exactly what he wants, exceedingly tenacious, with a statesman's vision. I wonder if he is not ultra cautious. . . .[21]

Oliver's opinion of Murray did not change very much over the years. At the beginning of 1912, he still talked of him as a man of vision and a statesman, and he still found him very cautious. Oliver's 1912 portrait adds a few more details: "[He is] possessed of high ideals, a warm heart, and an almost boyish appreciation of jokes and fun. He is troubled a bit with rheumatism and, I think, rather dislikes the climate. I am sure that he is trusted and loved by every member of the Staff and feared by none. We are all willing to speak our minds freely before him."[22]

Oliver was certainly right about Murray's attitude toward the climate. Murray's feelings were shared by his wife. The President brought his family west in September 1909 at a time when houses were difficult to obtain. Christina had been reluctant to move west, away from the Maritimes, her friends, and her family. She had considerable misgivings about moving to Saskatoon. By herself, she had to sell their house on Spring Garden Road, pack the family belongings, and board the train for a long and tiring rail journey accompanied only by three small daughters. Then, when they arrived in Saskatoon, they had to search for accommodation.

In late November or early December, they moved into a house in Nutana, near the Nutana Collegiate, which was then being built. The plaster in their new home was still wet when they moved in, and the house suffered by comparison with their home in Halifax. When Murray wrote his great friend Robert Falconer in December 1909, he was able to tell him: "We are into our house at last, and are becoming Saskatoonians, but not very enthusiastic. . . . Mrs. Murray seems to prefer the mud and slush of Halifax with all the delightful accompaniments to forty below in Saskatoon. It is difficult to understand how anyone could persuade him or herself that Saskatoon is not the finest place in the world."[23] The sarcasm bites.

Murray had little time to complain about the weather. He was too busy with the myriad tasks of creating a university. He recruited students, collected fees, bought library books (almost $1,000 worth of purchases was reported in his 1910 Annual Report, and this did not include the three hundred volumes of philosophical works he personally donated), let tenders and contracts, and bought the necessary furniture. Literally, no task was too big or too small for his attention. Years later, he was spotted sweeping the mat at the door of the College Building, which some careless maintenance man had failed to do. Walter Murray had not changed.

Seventy students—two were Saskatchewan born—comprised the first class of the infant university. Classes were given in French, Greek, Latin, English, History, Mathematics, and Philosophy, and the university's five professors, including its President, handled all the teaching. The students shared with their professors a buoyant optimism about their university, an optimism characteristic of youth. Delays and more delays in the construction of university buildings postponed the formal opening of the university until 1913, but the classes went on without interruption.

The first classes were held downtown, on the third floor of the Drinkle Building. Students and faculty had to take an elevator to the third floor, which enabled the university to proclaim proudly that it was the only Canadian university with an elevator.[24] Then, classes were shifted to two Saskatoon schools—the Victoria School and, subsequently, the newly built Nutana Collegiate—until the first university classrooms on the campus were completed, in time for the opening of term in 1912.

The auguries were good. When the cornerstone was laid on a hot sunny afternoon in 1910, a reporter noted that when the Premier spoke, "two tongues of flame sprang out of the northwest giving the university a spectacular baptism of fire."[25] The reservoirs of an oil company had exploded and provided a fiery backdrop to the ceremony.

The university grew rapidly both in student enrolment and faculty numbers. By the second year of operation, 108 students had enrolled, and this number grew to 382 by the fall of 1913. The faculty size was now 28 professors, 2 instructors, and 12 lecturers. The extension work of the university was widespread. The President's report for the year 1911/12 lists sixteen extension courses given in towns throughout the province, north and south. Murray had taught extension courses himself in his very first year at the University of New Brunswick. It was a tradition he successfully transplanted to Saskatchewan. Twenty percent of the university's expenditures in 1911/12 were devoted to extension work. It had not been possible to open the College of Agriculture in the fall of 1911 as had been planned, yet John Bracken was busy with his agricultural research on the experimental plots at the farm, and the extension department was fully operational. As the Advisory Council on Agriculture stated, "The time had been well spent during the winter."

While the university grew and prospered, Murray faced a number of problems during these early years directly related to the decision to locate the university in Saskatoon. In a word, these were the Regina problems. No doubt Murray's vigorous, public, and very partisan espousal of Regina as the only location for the university came back to haunt him because now he was forced to defend the monopoly claims of a state university located in Saskatoon. His fellow President, Tory of Alberta, wrote to him in August, 1909: "I hope you are not going to have trouble with the Regina people. I heard yesterday that they were taking steps to form professional schools down there. Surely the Government would deny them charters for any such purpose."[26]

The Benchers of the Law Society needed no charter. They controlled admission to their society and set the conditions and training required for entry into the legal profession in Saskatchewan. While Murray immediately set about planning a law school at the university, the Benchers, centred in Regina, opposed the scheme. They worked instead to locate the law school in Regina. In 1909, Murray offered Ira MacKay, a former student of his practising law in Winnipeg, a position as a professor of philosophy. But, in his letter, Murray mentioned his plan to establish a Law School and told MacKay he could go into the Law School if he chose. In Winnipeg, MacKay was aware of the Regina problem: "There is one fear which may arise out of the matter. Will the friends of Regina smell the scent too keenly if they see me on the ground?"[27]

Murray was fully aware of the risk of antagonizing the Benchers, but he believed that night lectures and daytime office work would not provide the same standard of legal education as would full-time attendance in a degree course in law at a university. It took four years before the law school opened at the university. During that time, Murray worked assiduously to win over the Benchers and defuse the animosity towards the decision to locate the university in Saskatoon.

In 1912, when he discovered that the Benchers proposed to create a Law School in Regina, Murray counter-attacked with an idea of his own. His proposal called for local schools to be placed in the more important legal centres, where students could supplement their office training with lectures; the law students would then come to the university for their final courses. The university and the Benchers would agree on the course of study and the examinations, and successful students would receive a university law degree and be admitted to the Saskatchewan bar. Murray absolutely refused to back down on the university's control of legal education. As he told Wetmore, the Chancellor of the university and the province's Chief Justice in 1912, "Should the Benchers take action and establish a School in Regina, I think the University will be forced to make a move for a School in Saskatoon. I think, however, it would be much better if the Benchers and the University could arrive at some understanding which would be satisfactory to both parties."[28] Wetmore agreed with Murray that some of the Regina lawyers were still fighting the Regina-Saskatoon battle over the university's location, and he sided wholeheartedly with Murray. He stated that he hoped the idea of a separate law school in Regina "will be fought to a bitter end, and both by the University and the Government."[29]

The Benchers decided not to engage in a head-on collision with the university over the formation of a university law school and in December 1913 formally welcomed its organization. The letter containing this news, however, contained a Freudian slip, referring to the University of Saskatoon instead of the University of Saskatchewan.[30] The Scott government approved the establishment of the law school at the beginning of 1913. Forty students enrolled the next fall in the first law class, but it took a number of years before the Benchers were completely won over. Murray, while regretting the persistent rivalry, was still optimistic about the long-term success of the law school. He wrote to Chief Justice Frederick Haultain in January 1913:

> It is too bad that the Benchers and the University cannot see eye to eye on the matter. Possibly after we both have experimented a little we may begin to realize the necessity for co-operation which at present seems impossible.[31]

The university did co-operate. Lectures by the Law School faculty, as well as active liaison and persuasion by Professor Arthur Moxon, Murray's former pupil and Dean of the Law Faculty, finally resulted in the closing of the Regina operation. But the task, when finally completed, had taken ten years to accomplish.

From his eastern vantage point, President Falconer of the

University of Toronto kept a close eye on Murray's relations with Regina and regularly wrote him encouraging letters. After receiving one of Murray's letters describing his efforts to win over the Regina Benchers, Falconer replied:

> Perhaps they thought that you were the spider and that they were the fly, and I gather from your letter that there is a little of the craft of the spider still in the University of Saskatchewan. I hope that you will get a fly, if it is not that particular one.[32]

The Benchers of the Law Society were only one aspect of the complex Regina problem confronting Murray and the university. Murray was sufficiently worried in October 1909, six months after Saskatoon had been chosen over Regina, that he wrote Calder, the Minister of Education, outlining his fears:

> This movement in Regina forces one to look ahead some distance. It is quite possible that in the future the government of the day may be forced to make a grant to the educational institutions that may grow up in Regina. . . . This Regina movement is not perhaps a very formidable obstacle today, but two or three of the men behind it, such as P. McAra and possibly Norman MacKenzie, and one or two others, are men who have considerable wealth and who are very determined; in fact, so determined that it may be difficult to distinguish determination from obstinacy. If the supporters of the movement are so skilful they can so inflame civic pride that they can secure a decent grant from the city, we may have in this province an institution like Brandon College while it is possible that some church may take advantage of the inflamed state of opinion in Regina to build up a church college.[33]

Murray saw the threat, but he was not willing in any way to compromise the essential principles of the state university to head it off. His university would embrace medical and other professional schools, and he was determined to snuff out rival operations in Regina or in any other centres, should they appear.

Murray's good friend, A.S. MacKenzie of Dalhousie, played down the importance of the Regina movement in a letter early in 1910, hoping to reassure Murray:

> I think the grouch of Regina can be ignored; they know it is not your doing and years are longer than in the East. Once you

show the University is doing excellent work, I'll bet they will send their children there.[34]

But Murray couldn't ignore it and it did not go away.

Those whom Murray regarded as enemies of the university were promoting separate schools of Medicine and of Pharmacy and a church college, in addition to a law school. Murray resisted each idea for a separate creation with the same tenacity, even though his cautious approach in creating university professional schools, especially in medicine, meant that no medical instruction took place at the University of Saskatchewan until the end of World War I, when pre-clinical work commenced. In 1910, Murray wrote that he did not expect to see a full medical school established at the university until Saskatoon itself had a population of at least fifty thousand. The key criterion was quality. As Murray said in connection with the medical school issue, "We are strongly of the opinion that we should do nothing unless we could do it well."[35]

A more serious threat, both to Saskatoon and to Murray's conception of a state university, was the plan of the Methodist Church to create a church college in Regina. From his experience in Nova Scotia, Murray knew as well as anyone what the effect of educational rivalries would be in Saskatchewan. If a separate institution rooted itself in the province's capital, then it might soon rival the fledgling university in Saskatoon. The prospect was an obsessive concern for Murray, and he used all his political talent to head it off.

In November 1910, writing to Robert Falconer, the President of the University of Toronto, Murray said of the Methodists: "Evidently their ambitions are as broad as our province and as high as the mountain in Hamilton."[36] But because the work in agriculture was proceeding so well and he could count on the farmers' support, Murray was optimistic: "Why then should we fear though the Methodists rage and Regina imagines vain things?" Murray's main strategy was to ensure that no government grant went to the Methodist College. He succeeded. Calder, the Minister of Education, promised him in 1910 "that it will be 'another government' and not the present one that will agree to grant any aid of any sort to denominational colleges."[37] The government stood by its principles, but so did the members of the Methodist Church. The Methodists had established denominational colleges across eastern Canada and had founded Wesley College in Manitoba. Now they planned to expand into Saskatchewan and were on the verge of doing just so. In this they were supported by a significant number of their members, especially in southern Saskatchewan but not exclusively there.

The government consulted Murray closely about the bill to incorporate the college, and Murray insisted the name be changed from Saskatchewan College to Regina College. He wrote to Calder, the Minister of Education:

> We can let it be known that we are benevolent in our attitude to them on the understanding that the purpose of the college is as outlined in their petition to the city council, and that they intend to become a feeder to the University and not a competitor.[38]

The venture went forward, and Regina College maintained an independent existence for twenty-five years before Murray finally managed to incorporate it into the University of Saskatchewan. To Murray, its separate existence was a constant reminder of the possibility of a rival university burgeoning in Regina, something he spent his lifetime trying to prevent.

When term opened in the autumn of 1912, Walter Murray was installed in his office in "The College Building"—it would be called that for many years—and he would occupy that office for the next quarter of a century. Throughout the term, plans were made for the second convocation (the first was held in 1912) and the official opening ceremonies which would take place at the same time. On May 1, 1913, seven women and fifteen men received bachelor degrees; Premier Walter Scott dedicated five university buildings in the presence of the Lieutenant Governor, members of the Cabinet, and a number of distinguished visitors, including Robert Falconer, Murray's long-time friend, who addressed the Convocation. It was an emotional moment for Walter Murray, the fruition of his dreams in creating a university. He basked in reflected praise as Falconer paid tribute to his accomplishments, and the audience responded with a prolonged ovation.

In private, he had still more occasion to glow. Premier Scott wrote to him, just after the Convocation, to say that he had been talking to a man from Toronto at the Convocation who said "that in his opinion Saskatchewan had a man at the head of its university superior to the head of the Toronto university, good as the latter undoubtedly is."[39]

High praise, indeed, and Scott obviously agreed with this judgment. Scott's only worry about Murray was that he was working too hard. At the Convocation the Premier had urged him to take a vacation, and a week later he wrote to remind Murray again:

This is not merely my own idea; we are all of the opinion that you have been sticking at the work too closely and zealously from the point of view of your health. Having been through the mill I am able to speak in a sense as one having authority. In this particular matter the old phrase about a stitch in time is especially applicable.[40]

Scott's concern was well founded for Murray did drive himself very hard, but now that the university was well launched, a summer holiday was possible.

The 1913 Convocation had a special significance for the people of Saskatchewan, as the *Regina Leader Post* pointed out. The opening of the University was another step in the realization of Saskatchewan's destiny within Confederation "and in assisting us to raise Canada into the rank of the great nations of the world."[41] The formal inauguration of the university in 1913 was a symbol of pride for the province, and an augury of a bright future for her people. Yet, neither Walter Murray nor the people of Saskatchewan had long to savour these dreams. Their musings were quickly forgotten the next year as World War I swept them up with all the force of a prairie cyclone. There was no escaping its impact.

■

Chapter 6

Murray's War

Boom to Bust

The early days of the University of Saskatchewan coincided with boom times for Saskatoon. In 1903, before the arrival of the Barr colonists, Saskatoon had been a quiet little hamlet on the banks of the South Saskatchewan River with perhaps a population of 400 people.[1] When the university was formally inaugurated in 1913, Premier Scott boasted to Lord Strathcona, then Canada's High Commissioner to Great Britain, about "a city of probably 30,000 souls, with half-a-dozen splendid public school buildings, a collegiate institute housed and equipped quite as well as any similar institution in eastern Canada and with the addition of a full-fledged University and Agricultural College turning out this year a graduation class numbering 29 and having during the term just ended a total attendance of 242—this all means a simply marvellous development."[2]

The boom had been frantic during the period 1910-1912, when the first university buildings were constructed. Speculation in land soared as fast as land prices. As with any boom, the question was when the bubble would burst. Walter Murray watched the boom with a cynical eye and a growing concern about the impact of a bust on his fledgling university. His satirical portrayal of Saskatoon's boom psychology in a letter to a Halifax friend contained underneath a foreboding of what was to come:

> Could I sell you a few lots? $5 down and $3 a month for the rest of your life, with the privilege of having the lots transferred in case of sun-stroke to the church or having your hospital bill paid should you injure yourself in any of St. Matthew's athletic sports. Lots are in an excellent locality quite near the University grounds within sound of the lowing herds, the bleating of sheep and the squealing of swine. The soil is 100 feet deep, capable of growing crops at any depth, with gophers on the upper story

and hard pan below. There is good water service, the power increased by a booster pump, Saskatoon make.[3]

The boom couldn't and didn't last. In its aftermath Murray's plans for the expansion of the university were bound to be affected, as he knew better than anyone else. Expansion depended on revenue from the government. When the boom collapsed in 1912, the Saskatchewan government had to retrench, but, amazingly, for a time the government continued to treat its infant state university with remarkable generosity.

The government approved plans for the addition of a Law School at the beginning of 1913, albeit with the injunction "that the undertaking shall be carried on for some time to come with the strictest possible regard to economy."[4] Murray was fully aware of the province's financial plight, and he was deeply grateful for the government's continued financial support. He had written to President Tory of the University of Alberta early in 1912 praising Saskatchewan's liberal treatment of its university even "when they have to cut the grant for public school education."[5] A year later Murray himself was gravely worried by what he saw. He described Saskatchewan's situation to Robert Falconer in Toronto:

> The province is face to face with a very serious condition of affairs. The farmers have been unable to sell their wheat, and what has been sold has brought very poor prices. The loan companies and the implement companies are pressing for payment and foreclosing right and left. There is much discontent in the country and it bids fair to increase rather than diminish.[6]

In spite of the economic crisis in the province on the eve of World War I, Murray pressed ahead with his plans for university expansion. He persuaded the Premier and the Minister of Education to approve the construction of a new residence and new buildings for Chemistry and Physics. The residence was tendered first in April 1914, but the others were victims of World War I. Nonetheless, in the first five years of the university's existence, Murray had presided over the expenditure of almost two million dollars for site, buildings, and operating costs.

Calgary College

Before World War I intruded on the University of Saskatchewan and Murray's life, he had agreed to serve on an Alberta commission to consider whether Calgary College should be given the right to grant degrees. The other two members of the commission were Murray's longstanding friends from his Maritime days, Robert Falconer, President of the University of Toronto, and A. Stanley MacKenzie, the President of Dalhousie. Falconer was named Chairman of the commission, but he accepted only because Murray was on it. Without a doubt, Murray was the key figure in a report which was as important in Murray's eyes for Saskatchewan as it was for Alberta.

Calgary, like Saskatoon, had expected to be the location of the provincial university once Edmonton had been chosen as the provincial capital. When Edmonton got the university as well, Calgary citizens petitioned the provincial legislature in 1910 for permission to incorporate their own university. The legislature responded by permitting the incorporation of Calgary College, but they denied it degree-granting powers. Murray was most anxious to aid his fellow President, Tory, of Alberta in resisting Calgary's claims so that no precedent would be set for Regina.

Murray had witnessed the rivalry of universities in the Maritimes, and he was utterly determined to prevent either the proliferation of universities in western Canada or the undermining of what he believed was the proper monopoly of the provincial state university. He had been remarkably candid in 1911, when he wrote Principal Gordon of Queen's urging him to reject the idea of affiliation with either the Methodist College at Regina or Calgary College.

> Now the object of the Calgary movement and possibly of some of the other movements is to gratify civic pride at the expense of the University. You know very well how intensely jealous the cities are of each other, and how foolish men who are wise in other matters become when an appeal is made to them through their civic pride. Opinions on higher education in the west are very chaotic. The average westerner looks upon the University with about the same feelings as he would regard a good packing plant. He is anxious to see it become a large institution and a profitable one to his community, but beyond that his interest ceases. He has no more compunction about throwing it over if it does not help his town than he has about transferring his bank account from one place to another. Of course there are many men who know the results of the unhappy divisions in the east, and are anxious to prevent a repetition here. The forces of evil, however, are strong. We hope that the eastern Universities will not make our tasks more difficult than they are.[7]

Murray's Maritime memories are evident in this letter. His concern about eastern assistance to western rivals of the state universities proved unfounded, but this letter helps to explain why he felt it was so important in 1914 to head off the creation of a second Alberta university. Once the commission was appointed in the spring of 1914, Murray defined for Falconer the key issue confronting them as "the extent to which the province can support two competing universities." His own preference was clearly evident before the commission met—the establishment "of a University college in Calgary in affiliation with the provincial University."[8]

The commissioners could not arrange to meet before November, and then they held public meetings both in Calgary and Edmonton. Their report concluded that it was not financially feasible to create a separate University in Calgary, either privately endowed or as another provincially supported institution. Murray's well-known views about the evils of competing universities took up a significant portion of the report, although the examples were carefully chosen from the United States. The commissioners quoted the President of the Carnegie Foundation in words that for Murray were suitable for engraving:

> The establishment of more than one institution of higher learning by the State Government has been almost always a source of political and educational weakness, and it has resulted in nearly every case in the waste of State money and in unwholesome rivalry.[9]

In what was a foregone conclusion, the three commissioners rejected the idea of creating another university in Calgary, and instead suggested the establishment of an Institute of Technology and Art. The institute would grant diplomas in applied mechanics, an early version of the modern community college. Murray's suggestion of an affiliation with the provincial university was also incorporated into the final report. Murray had good reason to be pleased with the report. Its acceptance by the Alberta Legislature gave him an important precedent from a neighbouring province to help him resist any similar movement in Regina. Murray's work for this Alberta commission was much more than educational altruism; it was part of his ceaseless struggle to maintain the educational monopoly of the provincial state university and thus prevent the battles he had endured for so long in the Maritimes.

The Round Table Movement

The onslaught of World War I pushed all educational battles into the background. Murray's personal commitment to the British Empire had never wavered. Prior to the war, he had made special efforts to foster contacts between Saskatchewan and groups or individuals from the rest of Canada. This communication was largely to counteract the dangers of intellectual isolation for his tiny faculty in Saskatoon. One such group which flourished in the pre-war years in Saskatoon was the local branch of the Round Table Movement, with Murray providing both a link with the East and its intellectual leadership.

The Round Table Movement grew out of the desires of a small group of British Empire activists who saw imperial union as the ultimate goal for Britain and her Dominions. By 1910, active Round Table discussion groups had sprung up throughout the Dominions and Britain. Toronto was their Canadian focus and the home of the most influential Canadian imperialists. But the organizers, both Canadian and British, were anxious to win over western converts and Walter Murray was potentially an important one. He was a close friend of Falconer, an active imperialist, and a former pupil of Sir George Parkin, a lifelong imperialist and secretary to the Rhodes Trust. Murray's contacts in the West put him in an ideal position to sway other Westerners.

Murray organized a discussion group in 1911 which functioned until the end of World War I. The Saskatchewan group never assumed a prominent role in the movement, and they were undoubtedly seen as peripheral by the directing authority in London. But, largely through Murray's initiative, the Round Table recommendations for constitutional change in the British Empire were discussed in detail by the Saskatchewan professors and their comments returned to London. They at least had the feeling, even if it was an illusion, of participating in affairs of state that preoccupied intellectuals and politicians from London to Auckland. Murray reported in 1911 that the Round Table magazine was "eagerly read" in Saskatoon,[10] and the next year he commented that the imperial question "has grown wonderfully in interest to us out here and I believe it will become a very important one to the west shortly."[11]

Murray's own interests in imperial matters went beyond leading a discussion group. He had followed the debates on Imperial Union from the 1890s, and his own notes suggest he was in favour of closer connections between the Dominions and Britain, especially in a period when the danger of war loomed on the European horizon. Murray fitted James Eayrs' description of Canadian Round Table members as "those who favoured imperial federation as the ultimate if not immediate solution of the problem."[12] With his historical interests, Murray reached back to the eighteenth century for historical precedents. He examined the imperial union plans of

Benjamin Franklin and Adam Smith, seeing in these plans the
forerunners of the organic union ideas current in the pre-war debate.
Murray believed that union, if it came, would have to serve the dual
purpose of defence and trade. Quoting Edward Burke that
"government is a contrivance of human wisdom to meet human
needs," Murray argued that the pressures pushing Britain and the
Dominions closer together would determine the actual form of
imperial union should it occur. If the need was trade, he felt an
organic union would be created; if it was defence then there would
have to be central control of the armed forces and defence policy as
well as a need for more tax revenue. In 1912, Murray sensed the
priority had to be defence because of the growing threat to world
peace from Germany and Japan.

In the summer of 1912, he assessed the mood of the Canadian West
towards the Empire in a remarkably prescient article foreshadowing
the enthusiastic support of the West for the war effort after 1914. His
article entitled "Western Canada and Imperialism" which appeared
anonymously in the Round Table magazine attempted to synthesize
a western Canadian viewpoint on imperial matters. It began with a
favourite Murray theme, the effect of the immigration of different
ethnic groups on the formation of a western Canadian viewpoint.
Murray agreed that, once in the west, people looked at the world
differently. "I believe that old-world opinions and sentiments count
for little in the new land." He went on to underline that the true
westerner was a radical, and was made so by the every-day challenge
of existence. "The conditions of life are so novel and so different that
he soon feels like a plant torn up by the roots and placed in different
soil and under changed skies." Whether as farmer, mechanic, or
businessman, the westerner had to develop new techniques, dictated
by the features of the land and the society in which he found
himself.[13]

But Murray was conscious of the war clouds massing in Europe
and their effect on the Canadian prairies:

> The westerner's greatest enemy is war. Today he may not
> believe this, tomorrow he will. The supply of men to fill his
> towns, to till his lands, to build his railways, will dry up if a
> great European war breaks out, and more particularly a war in
> which Britain is involved. The heavy immigration from the
> British Isles to Canada would almost disappear.

So would the supplies of capital. Murray realized that the price of
western wheat would soar initially, yet insecurity, greater risks
because of war, and added difficulties of transportation might nullify

the possibility that war would mean more money for the wheat farmer.

Given these likely effects of war on the west, Murray went on to contrast the imperialism of western Canadian businessmen with that of the eastern Canadians. The westerner was an imperialist because his business interests made him one. His wheat and cattle were produced primarily for European markets. Because his imperialism was based on economic interests, the westerner, according to Murray, wanted effective and efficient defence measures.

> If then peace can be assumed only by Canada's active participation in the burden of the naval defence of the empire, the westerner will not be satisfied with make-believe policies and trifling measures. . . . He will not quibble about ways and means, but will insist more emphatically on efficiency—on doing something worthwhile. He will not be terrified by the magnitude of the project, but will rather be fascinated by its far-reaching consequences. Nor will he sit down and carefully consider every penny of income and outgo before making the venture. He will launch forth on a grand project with a big faith that everything will somehow turn out all right, provided that nothing is spared to make things go.

Murray's article was written at a time when the Round Table movement was trying to remove the naval defence question from Canadian party politics. They had suggested a compromise between the Liberal position of establishing a small Canadian navy and the Conservative one of contributing to an imperial navy in return for a greater voice in imperial defence.[14] The attempt at compromise failed, as did the other Round Table initiatives on imperial union.[15] Murray's contribution thus had little, if any, impact, but it was further evidence of his strong loyalties to the British Empire. These loyalties would surface again during World War I.

Officer Supernumerary

Murray plunged into World War I with the same vigour and singleness of purpose that he had displayed in building the university. As his daughter later acknowledged, Murray fought the war from Saskatoon. Less than three months after the outbreak of hostilities, he had a recruiting program instituted at the university. Writing to Major Hill, who was in charge of recruiting in Saskatoon, he stressed that the university "encouraged the members of its staff and students to offer their services."[16] The positions of those who entered military service were kept open, they were given half pay, and an additional allowance was provided for the wives of married men.

Students who enlisted were given credit for one year's work. Murray wanted to postpone the enlistment of certain faculty members until teaching replacements were obtained, but he saw this as only a temporary thing. In any case, there was a surplus of volunteers in the autumn of 1914. Meantime, the university arranged military instruction and drill for its staff and students who were "preparing themselves for further emergencies."[17]

The university's role as a recruiting depot was not unique; other Canadian universities, most notably McGill, were similarly engaged, but Murray's personal activities as a recruiting agent throughout the war were remarkable. His first recruits went to the Universities Companies, which trained at McGill, and went overseas as reinforcements for the Princess Patricia's Light Infantry. By the spring of 1915, seventy men had enlisted from the university. Murray continued to steer recruits to McGill through the summer and fall of 1915 until five companies had been recruited. The Officer Commanding was pleased with Murray's work. "I appreciate the descretion [sic] you have shown in recruiting in Saskatoon. They are a fine lot."[18]

By the summer of 1915, however, Murray along with others on his staff was growing restive because of the bad news from the front lines in Europe and his helpless frustration at not being able to do more. His spring optimism that the war might be over by the end of the year had disappeared into prairie dust. There was no victory in sight and greater sacrifices would be required. Murray wrote an old Halifax acquaintance, who was now a Lieutenant Colonel, asking his advice on what the university could do because "the average military officer here is either ignorant, indifferent or so bound up in red tape that he is unable to give us an opinion which we are able to receive in confidence."[19] Murray even hinted that he was willing to join up if the army would let him. The advice Murray received was to apply to the Militia Department for authority to organize a Saskatchewan contingent of the Canadian Officers Training Corps. He was not encouraged to enlist himself.[20] Murray immediately acted on this suggestion and offered two, and possibly three, companies for the Corps, to be formed after enrolment in the autumn. By then, the University Senate had made physical drill, including military drill, compulsory for all students. The university's efforts to organize a C.O.T.C. foundered a bit because of the lack of qualified officers to lead it, but this was soon overshadowed by a still more ambitious plan.

At the end of October 1915, the Canadian government increased the authorized number of Canada's armed services by 100,000 men to a total of 250,000. By the beginning of 1916 this figure had doubled. Such an expansion meant an enormous demand for additional manpower. When the secretary of the Manitoba C.O.T.C. suggested the formation of a Western Universities Battalion to the Presidents of the four western universities late in November 1915, he received a very favourable response. Murray played a principal role in organizing the Battalion and in providing the Saskatchewan Company. Each university was responsible for one company of the Battalion.

The organization of the battalion was underway in early January 1916. It was carried through with remarkable dispatch and also with some unusual military procedures. The University Presidents met and allocated the battalion officers proportionately among their institutions. Murray arranged for E.H. Oliver, the Principal of the Western, Presbyterian College, to be designated chaplain and for Reginald Bateman to command the Saskatchewan Company. Bateman was the first professor of English at the university. He had gone overseas with the first contingent, served in the trenches, and was a sergeant when the battalion was born. When it sailed for England in the autumn of 1916, he was a major. Two other faculty members, C.J. Mackenzie and F.J. Freer, were selected by Murray for commissions as lieutenants. Somewhat more than normal military speed was required for their admission to officer training, but Murray arranged it. He also appointed the Battalion's medical officer.

Because Bateman was at the front when the Battalion was created, and did not return until the Saskatchewan Company was recruited, all the responsibility for organization fell on Murray's shoulders. At the same time, he was the Secretary and Co-ordinator of the Committee of University Presidents in charge of the Western Universities Battalion. Much of Murray's work in the early months of 1916 was military in nature, organizing the Battalion and recruiting the Saskatchewan Company. The detailed arrangements even extended to the type of trousers to be worn and the badge of the unit (Murray wanted a grizzly bear). All these issues had to be settled, often after exchanges of telegrams, by the University Presidents. Murray certainly was, as he described himself, the "Officer Supernumerary."[21]

Murray himself virtually recruited all of the Saskatchewan Company. He even wrote the press handout to advertise the battalion and to stimulate recruiting. The release went to Saskatchewan papers across the province, from Regina to Prince Albert.[22] There was an underlying competition among the four universities to produce the quota of men they had agreed upon. By the middle of March, Murray claimed that he had "80 men in sight and 12 more for the Ambulance

Corps," although for a brief time he was disappointed with the slow pace of recruiting.[23]

There were problems in recruiting the men. With the rather small enrolment of the University of Saskatchewan, it seemed unlikely the full complement of the Saskatchewan Company could be filled. As a result, it was decided to recruit "university type" men from outside the university. A considerable number of these were recruited. Murray informed a correspondent in 1917, "We sent, however, nearly 250 graduates and undergraduates, and through the university 400 others of university type have been secured for the army."[24] Not all the 400 went to the Saskatchewan Company. Some went to the Ambulance Corps and others to the University Companies at McGill for which Murray continued to recruit. The Commanding Officer of the University Companies was unhappy at the appearance of a western rival and did his best, without success, to discourage it.[25] Murray, however, continued to recruit men for the University Companies until mid-August, even though his main project remained the Saskatchewan Company. By April, he was confident the Saskatchewan complement would be filled through the hard work of recruiting agents, who had fanned out from Saskatoon on the railway lines to round up volunteers.

Murray's vigorous recruiting roused some anger from parents with sons at the University of Saskatchewan. An undated letter simply signed "A farm boy's mother" pleaded that she had an only son needed on the farm. "Can that boy not serve his country just as well here as if he were at the front? Now is the University doing its duty in trying to get all they possibly can to enlist, regardless of the thought that any of those boys has any other duty?" The letter alleged that it was drilled into the boys that they should enlist. "I heard one boy remark 'they make you feel like two cents at the University if you don't enlist.' "[26] Just at the time recruiting for the Saskatchewan Company was getting into full swing at the university, another parent complained:

> I am an old man, 60 years of age. I have a half-section of land with power and implements to work. Realizing that the younger generation of farmers need more agricultural education than the preceding one, I sent my son (on whom I entirely depend to help me with my work) to college for the winter. . . .
>
> Now he says he must either enlist or give up his studies and come home. He says the place has gone "crazy" over enlisting and from all accounts I think he has used the right word. What

with pickets standing at every street corner hailing young lads as they go on their way and silly girls waving white feathers, no other word would describe conditions. To my mind conscription would be ten times more honorable. I do not consider it a fair deal on your part to allow the agricultural students to enlist until you find out at least if they can be spared from the farm. . . . To my mind the agricultural students can serve King and country as much on the farm as in the trenches.[27]

To this vigorous denunciation of the university's recruiting policies, Murray replied:

I have not urged any students to enlist, and in not a few cases have I dissuaded them from going. . . . You need not be afraid about a fair deal so far as I am concerned. Every student who comes in to enlist is asked whether he has his parents' consent. The Minister of Militia has made provision for allowing soldiers to assist in putting in the crop. I agree with President Reynolds of Manitoba who told his boys that everyone should be either on the farm or at the front, and that some could probably serve their country better on the farm than at the front.[28]

No doubt it was true, if narrowly interpreted and somewhat rationalized, that Murray had not urged any students to enlist, but the university, under his enthusiastic leadership, certainly encouraged both staff and students to do so. Just a week before he answered the complaint about recruiting, he had happily reported to Tory, the President of the University of Alberta and Chairman of the Presidents' Committee for the Western Universities Battalion: "Today the students are beginning to enlist and there is quite a buzz of excitement. I do not think there will be much doubt about securing sufficient numbers."[29] Murray was also aware that the recruiting was upsetting students and interfering with their academic program. He wrote that "some of the men want to go on at once to full-time. They have become so unsettled by the recruiting that they simply cannot do justice to their studies."[30]

The complaints of the parents really echoed Murray's own words, but academic considerations no longer had top priority. He was so deeply involved in the organization of the battalion, as well as the recruiting, that the university, and his responsibility as president, were relegated to second place. During the winter, spring, and summer of 1916, all matters relating to the recruitment and the organization of the Saskatchewan Company passed across his desk.

In June, the battalion was mustered in the heat and dust of Camp Hughes, Manitoba. From then until it left for England late in the fall, Murray was a frequent visitor. E.H. Oliver, the chaplain, in letters to his wife, mentions Murray's visits in July, August, and October. He also sent parcels of books and phonographs, and he paid for an oyster supper for the men before they departed for England.[31] Murray, along with Tory from Alberta and MacLean of Manitoba, was present for a formal parade of the battalion at the end of its Manitoba training. Oliver told his wife that a dust storm blew up while Murray was there and he "had a chance to eat some more Camp Hughes sand."[32]

Following the departure of the battalion, no time was lost by the university presidents who immediately set about planning reinforcements for the battalion. Murray was in Ottawa at the beginning of January 1917 where he interviewed the Minister of Militia and the Adjutant General. All went well in Ottawa, but the battalion was broken up in England almost on its arrival. It needed no reinforcement drafts as it became "a funnel through which reserves are sent to France."[33]

The decision to break up the battalion came as a bitter blow to the men and to their universities. As Oliver wrote to his wife: "Sentiment for universities counts something with the men, but it does not count in all places. . . . The 196th was a Battalion, the finest and the best that ever came across. It is hard to keep up much enthusiasm for a funnel."[34] The University Presidents, and Murray in particular, shared the men's feelings. His emotional attachment to the unit and to the men who had enlisted in it remained for the rest of his life. When he wrote the chapter on the First World War for A.S. Morton's history of the university some twenty years later, he included the following assessment of the battalion: "It had made the Western University men war conscious, and had united them in a brotherhood of arms as nothing else could have done. It provided much good officer material when it was badly needed."[35]

After the disbandment of the Western Universities Battalion, Murray's career as an army recruiter also ceased. He had succeeded in creating high expectations in Ottawa which he could no longer fulfill. Two years later when the Chief of the General Staff telegraphed him about a proposal to outfit immediately a Canadian University Tank Battalion, Murray replied that he doubted whether any students would be available. Those over twenty either had been conscripted or had volunteered for the Flying Corps.[36] In any case, by 1917, Murray no longer had the time to act as a recruiter. His energies were absorbed by another national cause, the advancement of scientific research.

Agriculture and the N.R.C.

Scientific research was not a new thing for the President of the University of Saskatchewan. He had long been a strong proponent of the need for it, especially in agriculture. For several years he had been pressing the case for postgraduate training in agriculture, which Murray regarded as a national priority. When the Conference on University Presidents first met in 1912 (he was appointed its secretary) he raised the problem there. He also approached Milton Burrell, the Minister of Agriculture, on the same topic. "I believe the Science of Agriculture in this country whether in the College of Agriculture or the institutions for research will not come into its own unless some satisfactory provision is made for higher instruction in that subject."[37] Murray saw a big and growing need for postgraduate education in agriculture. He had been seeking men for his agricultural faculty and had been struck by the inadequate training available. Now he sought the help of the Minister of Agriculture to fund scholarships for postgraduate work. The Minister was polite, but only that.

A few months later Murray returned to the attack. "It is a platitude to remark that the prosperity of the country depends on the prosperity of Agriculture. . . . I believe one dollar spent on improving agriculture here would yield five dollars in the general business of the province."[38] The Minister agreed with Murray's multiplier, but he did not provide any money. Murray was ahead of his time with the idea of Dominion funding for agricultural scholarships.

Walter Murray was not the man to give up on a project that was so important for his own university, his province, and the country. He had sent John Bracken to the western United States for a refresher course as soon as Bracken accepted an appointment in Agriculture at Saskatchewan. If the Department of Agriculture was not helpful, other avenues would have to be explored. The next year he was busy suggesting to Macdonald College what the two institutions could do on their own by arranging a sort of postgraduate exchange. These persistent efforts to establish postgraduate work in agriculture helped to make Murray known to academics and politicians alike across Canada. The Committee of University Presidents appointed him to head a committee on postgraduate work. Murray was also actively engaged in promoting agricultural research at Saskatchewan. Bracken commenced his work on crop rotation and tillage methods almost as soon as the land was made ready on the university farm. The little plots mirrored the problems and needs of the prairie farms which Murray knew.

The brief of the University of Saskatchewan to the Royal Commission on Technical Education and Industrial Training in 1910 reflects Murray's awareness of agricultural problems and his desire to promote scientific research. The writing style and the content of the submission show Murray's hand and mind. "The conservation of the fertility of the prairies is not only of national but also of imperial importance." He went on to argue that the training needed to solve the agricultural problems in order to safeguard what was both a national and imperial food supply was a national responsibility.

The brief then turned to the question of research. It set out in outline form the basis for a federal research body, an idea which also was ahead of its time in 1910:

> The importance of research for industrial development is now recognized by even the most unprogressive of nations. To foster it is a national duty. . . . What is needed now is the organization of a great institution for scientific research at Ottawa and the establishment of a number of smaller institutions throughout the Dominion. The central institution should aim at being complete and of the highest grade. The local institutions should be adapted to the problem peculiar to their locality and should cooperate with the central institution where tests of a national character, involving great diversities of conditions, are required. . . . This institution (the central one) would be both an agency for research and a bureau for collecting research results throughout the world."[39]

He published his views on scientific research in a letter to the editor of *The Canadian Courier*, written when the University's brief was being prepared. In it, he stressed that a vital ingredient of a new national policy had to be a Dominion-wide approach to scientific research. "The appeal to Science for direction and assistance in the work of national development is our greatest need." He urged the creation of laboratories across the country and of the means to disseminate the results of research. He summarized his program by saying:

> A New National Policy should build up laboratories, organize scientific bureaus, strengthen and increase schools of science in order to preserve the fisheries, to conserve the forests, to exploit the mines, to enrich the farms, to turn the wheels of the factories, to cheapen the cost of living, to protect the public health, to place within reach of all the instruments of health,

happiness and prosperity. For knowledge makes for national power, national prosperity and international peace.[40]

It was not until World War I that the federal government began thinking in these terms. By then the need for scientific research to solve some of the pressing problems of western agriculture was urgent. One of the most serious problems was the wheat rust that ruined the western wheat crop in 1916; it reduced the crop by half, with the resultant loss of more than a hundred million dollars of prairie-farm income. Just as grave was the loss of food in the middle of war. Wheat rust did not appear for the first time in 1916. It had been known on the prairie for a quarter of a century. Fortunately, a scientist on the staff of the University of Manitoba, Professor A. Reginald Buller, had begun to investigate it. In June 1917 he sent his famous paper, "The Rust Disease of Wheat," to three men: Walter Murray, President MacLean of the University of Manitoba, and Dr. J.H. Grisdale, the Director of the Experimental Farm in Ottawa.

At Murray's urging, the first Rust Conference followed in Winnipeg in August 1917. This meeting helped to launch the rust research project, an organized program of research designed to rid the western prairies of this blight. While not involved in the research himself, Murray played a key administrative role in launching the project and supporting it. He even tried, without success, to have the National Research Council publish Buller's paper "as an illustration of how the State, by endowing or assisting Science, can advance the important industries of the country. . . . I am quite convinced that this bulletin would be very effective in convincing the public of the value of spending money on scientific investigation."[41]

Murray had campaigned for some years for greater government involvement in scientific research. He was not involved in the preliminary discussions which preceded the launching of the Advisory Council on Scientific and Industrial Research in 1916, which later became the National Research Council. Nor was Murray a scientist or an industrialist, the type of man Sir George Foster, the Minister of Trade and Commerce, claimed he wanted to appoint to the Council.[42] Why then was Murray appointed to the Council as one of its first members?

No doubt Murray's attitude and activity in support of scientific research influenced Foster when he sought a western representative for the Council. Foster had known Murray's father as a family friend from New Brunswick, and he knew Walter as a boy. But Murray's name also was familiar to agricultural scientists, the Minister of

Agriculture, western leaders, and Members of Parliament, as well as university authorities both in the east and west. In addition to "proper geographical representation," the Minister wanted "to ensure the sympathy and co-operation of the West in the general scheme."[43]

Murray was Foster's first choice as western representative on the Council. Murray was understandably reluctant at first because he was not a scientist, but he yielded to Foster's persuasion, no doubt seeing this as a further opportunity to contribute to Canada's war effort and to implement programs whose need he had long recognized. Murray's personal attributes for the position were evident to H.M. Tory, the President of the University of Alberta, himself a scientist and later the President of the National Research Council: "Your skill as an arbitrator and in smoothing out diverse judgements will be invaluable and, further, there is no man in the west whose judgement all of us would rely on as yours when it comes to a question of fair play and goodwill."[44] It was a complete vote of confidence by one of his most important western colleagues. Murray thus became the lone western voice on the Council.

With characteristic imagination and drive, Murray went to work. He immediately organized a meeting of western university chemists in Saskatoon at the end of December 1916. The subjects discussed included postgraduate assistance for scientific research, library facilities in western universities, the advisability of closer contact between western Canadian industry and the western universities, and what western scientists could do in order to ensure the proper development and conservation of the western lignite fields. Murray made sure that the problems raised were placed on the agenda of the first meeting of the Council. Plant and animal diseases headed his list, but it also included tar sands, lignite coal, and water supplies. Interestingly, the list still remains current two generations later.

Murray kept the western university presidents informed of the Council's activities, highlighting the consideration being given to problems in their areas. He urged the need for, and arranged, a tour of the western provinces by a Council delegation headed by its Chairman, A.B. Macallum. This was not only to discuss western needs but to make the eastern-dominated Council aware of them and of their importance to western agricultural and industrial development. Murray's concern for his constituency extended to British Columbia, as he was careful to write to the President of the University of British Columbia. "They all recognize that British Columbia had a great number of very important problems to deal with and they are all anxious to meet the needs as thoroughly as possible."[45]

Murray's work as the western representative on the newly formed Council was very time consuming. Frequent meetings meant that he was away from Saskatoon almost more than he was there. He confessed to Wesbrook of U.B.C. early in February 1917 that travel to and from meetings of the Council had taken him away from the university for one month out of the previous two.[46] Added to this was the time he spent on his constituency work, his administrative involvement in the wheat-stem-rust program, and on the soil survey of Saskatchewan that would demand his attention for the next twenty years. How did he find time to run the University of Saskatchewan?

Others were asking this question in 1917. Members of the Board of Governors in March thought Murray could not give as much time to the Council as he had without serious interference with his duty to the university. He was advised "to withdraw at an early date if the demands continue."[47]

That is startling and severe criticism of any chief executive. Obviously, members of the Board would not have spoken out unless they regarded the situation as serious. This is all the more surprising, given the short time that had elapsed since Murray's appointment to the Council and the fact that this was a national appointment during wartime to a Council concerned with Canada's present and future welfare. Were there other elements of criticism hidden underneath? Had Murray perhaps placed the university and his presidential functions subordinate to another cause or causes? In March 1917 it would have been unthinkable for the Board to criticize Murray for spending too much time and energy on war activities to the neglect of the university, but criticism of the time he had spent on the Advisory Council may have been a convenient stalking-horse. What was the real objective of the Board? Possibly it was simply to bring their President to the realization that important as the war effort was, his first duty was to the university he headed.

When the Advisory Council was transformed into the National Research Council in 1917, Murray continued as a member. He served until 1931 when he finally resigned. His long service was only surpassed by that of his close friend, A. Stanley MacKenzie, who resigned the same summer, a few months after Murray. There is no record of any criticism from his university following the 1917 complaint.

The War's Impact

The war had a profound and lifelong impact on Walter Murray. Like many others, he romanticized war. The university presented a scroll to each university recruit who sailed with the second contingent in the spring of 1915 with the following words: "We ask each man to accept from us as a token of lasting remembrance a watch strapped to his wrist in a manner befitting the days of chivalry, and may this be to you an incentive to emulate the valiant deeds performed by Arthur and his Knights of Old." For Murray, these men were Saskatchewan's young knights going off to do battle for the Empire. Murray's romantic view of war was not shared by the provincial auditor who disallowed the use of university funds for gifts of watches and safety razors.

Twenty years later Murray still retained rose-tinted memories of the war. A message to the graduating class of 1934 refers to the war: "There were moments when the courage, fortitude, self-sacrifice and immortal comradeship of men attained heights beyond the most daring flights of imagination." In contrast, the four years of the Depression had witnessed "the world at its worst."[48]

Commencing as soon as the Saskatchewan men arrived overseas, Murray wrote to them and they to him. As one said, "I thought you would probably be glad to hear of the erring sons from Saskatchewan who wandered forth to find the Holy Grail."[49] He certainly was. Murray's correspondents embraced everyone from the faculty to the university herdsman. One of them, Private Glower, labelled him Saskatchewan's "intensely patriotic president."[50]

Christmas cards and parcels were sent to each man in the name of the university. These and Murray's letters helped to reinforce the already strong sense of camaraderie among the University of Saskatchewan soldiers. For them, Murray was the symbol of their university, an alumni link that assumed a much deeper meaning for men in the trenches of Europe. To Murray, they were the university's sons, and the fatherly relationship, sincere and reciprocal, was one that neither Murray nor his "boys" ever forgot.

The relationship became even more poignant when the casualty lists began appearing. Murray informed Falconer in 1916 that "from the seventy-five men who went overseas before June there are about thirteen deaths."[51] Of 330 men who went overseas, 67 professors and students died, a casualty rate much higher than that of the army as a whole. At each Convocation, Murray read the casualty list, weeping publicly for his dead students and staff, many of whom he had recruited personally.

Murray's enthusiasm for the war effort and his obvious identification with the men who enlisted turned him into a zealous recruiter. Slowly, the man who had been known for his calm, objective judgment and as a conciliator became committed and partisan. His recruiting efforts, first for the Universities Companies and then for the Western Universities Battalion, were augmented by his membership in the Citizens Recruiting League. Murray was moving towards advocating compulsory service. The Recuiting League asked the government by resolution dated May 10, 1916, to induce unmarried men of military age in the civil service to enlist. Five months later Murray confessed to his old friend, A. Stanley MacKenzie, President of Dalhousie: "I am not greatly enamoured of the men who could have enlisted and have not."[52]

Murray's disillusionment with the Liberals in Ottawa for opposing conscription reached its peak in 1917. A lifelong Liberal, breaking with the party was not easy for him, and he did it only because of his overriding belief that everything had to be sacrificed to the war effort. He undoubtedly shared the feelings of E.H. Oliver who wrote to his wife at the end of May 1917: "I could not support a Government or a party that hesitates to send some of the funkers over."[53] When the Conscription Act was introduced, Murray was one of its strongest supporters. He wrote to one of his faculty members serving in Europe: "It would delight your heart to see the way in which certain individuals are yielding to the argument of the law after their strenuous resistance to your argument of the spirit."[54] Clearly Murray was equally delighted.

By the fall of 1917, Murray's commitment to conscription and the need for an all-out effort to win the war impelled him to cast aside the non-political posture he had deemed essential and obligatory to keep the university separate from party politics. He publicly campaigned for the Union Government in a speech for the Unionist candidate in Saskatoon. The Saskatoon *Phoenix* described it as an "impassioned appeal for Canada's brave sons" and commented that Murray "displayed a depth of emotion that was unusual for him."[55]

Murray told the people crowded into Saskatoon's Third Avenue Methodist Church on December 4, 1917, that in his view this was "the greatest issue the Canadian people have ever faced. Confederation was a great issue; it caught the imagination of our fathers, but that was a slight issue in comparison with the issues of today, which are of life, and death, honor and liberty." Canada had to sacrifice more for victory. The greatest need was for additional manpower, and only conscription could provide it. His address had the tenor of a patriotic sermon. The audience loved it and applauded him at length.

Nevertheless, the decision to enter the political campaign in 1917 was an agonizing one for Murray because it represented a breach of his own principles. He sent a letter of resignation to the Board basing it on his political involvement. The Board executive referred it to the full Board in February, and it was rejected. This was the only time in Murray's career as President that he violated his own creed and entered the political arena. He justified it as a necessary part of the fight to defeat Germany.

Murray later used the story of his involvement in politics in 1917 to justify his policy of discouraging faculty members from actively participating in provincial or federal election campaigns. He recounted that when the Board of Governors met in 1918 to consider his offer of resignation, "they were very deliberate and in no hurry to overlook the intrusion into politics."[56] His own justification for this rigid policy of non-involvement was the protection it offered to the university from the evils of political patronage. Murray believed the state university had to adopt the same political neutrality as the civil service. His conduct in 1917 was the exception to this rule, but when he defended his actions, he did so on the grounds that national, not party issues were at stake.

The war also caused Murray's openness towards European immigration to narrow, although this changed again after the immediate dangers of the war period had vanished. In a speech to the Regina Canadian Club in 1910, Murray had advocated an attitude of sympathy and co-operation towards immigrants in order to build a unique nation enriched by European traditions.[57] By 1917, he was urging the virtues of loyalty to Saskatchewan's immigrants in threatening tones:

> We Canadians will not tolerate hyphenated citizens—citizens who use Canada when it suits them and who, when troublous times arrive, serve other countries and other kings. Such Canadians are traitors to Canada and will be treated as traitors.[58]

Murray wanted the immigrants to put Canada first, to attend Canadian schools, to learn English, and to forget the nationalist divisions and ethnic rivalries that had split Europe.

Murray realized that Saskatchewan needed continued immigration, but in a brief on western immigration to the Dominions Royal Commission in 1916, he argued for greater selectivity. In it he specified the risks posed for Canada by the nationalist propaganda stirring up the Ruthenians and Ukrainians in Europe.[59] Yet Murray also urged a more enlightened immigration policy with measures to help the immigrant adjust to western Canada after arrival and to learn the western farming techniques necessary to survival. He anticipated that the largest number of rural immigrants in the post-war period would come from central Europe, and these would pose the biggest challenge of assimilation. In order to ensure success, Murray called for a combination of federal and provincial programs to help the newly arrived immigrant integrate into Canadian life.

The war sharpened Murray's awareness of the dilemma posed by Saskatchewan's depending on immigration to create the type of province he wanted. His concept of nationality embraced an ardent patriotism for Canada and the British Empire, and during the war, both elements became for him vital ingredients for citizenship. When J.A. Calder, Saskatchewan's Minister of Education in the early days of the university, joined the Union Government in 1917 as Minister of Immigration and Colonization, Murray wrote to him requesting his help to bring soldiers' wives and families from Britain to Saskatchewan after the war. "I am sure it is not necessary to emphasize the value of this kind of immigration. It is the very best that we could secure for Western Canada. We want all the English immigration that we can get and as little as possible of mid-European."[60] After the war, Murray's opinions on immigration altered substantially, but as long as the war lasted it affected his outlook towards Saskatchewan's immigrant population. Nevertheless he was prepared to help Russian refugees by offering free tuition and summer employment to help students meet expenses.

Murray had another opportunity to go overseas, had he wished. H.M. Tory, President of the University of Alberta, was appointed to head the "Khaki University," or the University of Vimy Ridge, to give it the official title, a university designed for Canadian soldiers in England and on the continent. Before Tory left for England in the summer of 1917, he sought Murray's advice and his participation. From England, Tory continued to importune Murray to come over and help as his deputy. The wooing of Murray went on through the fall of 1917 and the year following.[61] Murray dragged his feet, but he never turned down the request clearly and definitely. When Tory cabled him in November 1918 asking if he could come over right away, Murray replied, "Your cable was a very great temptation. I don't know when I wished as much to accept an invitation. It is the opportunity of a lifetime." But he begged off on the grounds that the state of the university would not permit his absence.[62]

As early as the spring of 1917, Murray took up the question of education for returned soldiers. Already on the campus there were "nearly two score taking the course and we have also had a few others who have not been sent here by the hospital commission."[63] Murray was the President of the National Canadian Conference of Universities for the year 1919 and, as such, was responsible not only for arranging the meeting but for negotiating with the federal government regarding returning veterans. The universities wanted federal grants for veterans' education, but none was forthcoming. Even if disabled, veterans were excluded from educational assistance by legislation. Murray had raised the issue at the 1917 NCCU Conference, but neither he nor other university presidents were successful. At Saskatchewan, Murray instituted a special program for veterans, exempting them from fees, permitting them to register at any time during the academic year, and putting on special classes for high school matriculation subjects. Even by 1918, special vocational classes had been given to 286 veterans, and the eventual total surpassed 1,000.

The fall of 1918 brought the disaster of the influenza pandemic to Saskatchewan. The university ceased classes, after the imposition of a strict quarantine, for nearly seven weeks. Emmanuel College became a hospital, and the Murrays used their home to care for the volunteers who attended the sick in Emmanuel. One of the twelve volunteer nurses was Christina Murray, the President's oldest daughter. As Murray later described it, the temporary hospital "was crammed from attic to cellar."[64] At one point 130 patients were being cared for by the volunteers, six of whom caught the 'flu. They were nursed in the Murray home, and all recovered.

Toward the end of the war, Murray seemed to be overcome by a mood of pessimism and political cynicism. His bitterness at what the politicians were doing was one reason he campaigned passionately for Union Government, but once it was elected he did not hold out high expectations for its performance. He had no time, however, for meditating about national politics. He was constantly busy, trying to minimize the disorganization to university classes caused by the returning veterans or coping with the 'flu epidemic.

What he really needed was a rest. He had always driven himself beyond normal levels, and the war was no exception. He had probably attempted too much, but he never would have admitted it. The closest he came was to confess in a letter to E.H. Oliver that "the snap has gone out of things in the last year or two, and I think we are all suffering a little from frayed nerves. Why we, who are so far away from the scene of trouble in France, should be affected, one cannot understand, but the fact is there."[65] There was to be no rest. The veterans had to be looked after, and the 'flu victims had to be nursed. Yet it was a problem he did not see, festering within the university, which would grow and bear down upon him in the year following the war that would cause the most serious crisis of his professional and personal life. For Murray, the war's end brought no relief.

■

Chapter 7

A Crisis of Loyalty

In March 1919, S.E. Greenway, the Director of Extension Work at the University of Saskatchewan, met the Provincial Treasurer, C.A. Dunning, in Regina in the absence of the Premier and made several very serious charges about the operation of the university. He accused Murray of falsifying a return presented to the Saskatchewan Legislature in 1913 and of misappropriating public funds. Dunning recorded that Greenway had told him of great dissatisfaction among faculty members, and that there was a general lack of confidence in Murray's administration, and a lack of loyalty to him as President. Dunning subsequently asked Murray and Rutherford, Dean of Agriculture, to meet with him and informed them of the charges made by Greenway. At Murray's request, Dunning then wrote to him detailing what Greenway had said.

Murray was shocked not only by the charges but by the fact that Greenway had gone over Murray's head to the government without first discussing them either with himself or with the Board of Governors. Greenway was out of town when Murray returned from his meeting with the Provincial Treasurer, but Murray immediately wrote to him, indicating how bitter he felt about Greenway's action. "The assassin stabs and leaves his victim to find out if he can who did the deed and why it was done. That sort of thing cannot be tolerated in any responsible organization."[1] Murray informed Greenway that his "damaging" statements about both the University and the President would have to be cleared up on Greenway's return from Victoria. Thus began a crisis that rocked the university for over a year, caused Murray to have a nervous breakdown, and ended with the dismissal of Greenway and three other professors.

Although Murray had no forewarning of Greenway's charges, they were the culmination of a series of problems which had caused dissatisfaction both inside and outside the university and had helped to create a climate of opinion in the province that all was not right at the provincial university. Faculty discontent had arisen in 1918 over salaries. The three faculty members—Hogg, McLaurin, and MacKay—who were eventually dismissed along with Greenway, comprised a faculty committee pressing for increased salaries. When the Board responded by paying war bonuses, Hogg then led a campaign to have the faculty refuse the cheques.[2] Finally, the university took its case for better salaries to the provincial government, seeking additional funds, and the Saskatchewan government approved the introduction of the University of Toronto salary schedule at Saskatchewan. The salary problems had been alleviated by 1919, but the scars of the struggle still remained.

Another grievance within the university concerned the allocation of money for research. This particularly affected the head of the Chemistry Department, Professor McLaurin, who had devised a scheme to obtain from straw a gas that he enthusiastically projected would be the solution to the prairie energy needs. McLaurin was also involved in promoting a furnace to burn lignite coal. As head of the Chemistry Department, Professor McLaurin's opinion carried weight with boards of trade and the public. C.J. Mackenzie, a colleague of McLaurin's and later President of the NRC, remembered him as an entrepreneur whom the Board of Trade loved. "They were interested in his straw gas thing."[3]

So effectively did McLaurin capture the public imagination and use public support to promote his schemes that both the NRC and the provincial government found it expedient to give support to the straw-gas research. The provincial government gave the university $25,000 for research in 1918. $10,000 of this amount was allocated to Professor McLaurin, but he wanted more. In spite of the support Murray had shown for his research, both through the NRC and in the allocation to it of the largest portion of the provincial research grant, McLaurin saw Murray as an obstacle standing in the way of his obtaining sufficient research funds. It was later revealed that McLaurin had a financial interest in two companies formed to exploit the results of his research.

Given Saskatchewan's position as the provincial university, the provincial Cabinet was well aware of its internal quarrels and even before 1919 had discussed possible solutions. One was a change in the appointments to the Board of Governors. Murray obviously felt under pressure since the criticisms were really directed at him. He wrote at length to Premier Martin at the end of December 1918, indicating his willingness to see the government increase its appointees on the university board. In this letter Murray wryly remarked:

One of the reasons for the change that I have heard is that it is supposed to be highly desirable to have a strong curb put upon the autocrat who is at the head of the university. I was not aware of the fact that I had been autocratic; in fact, I thought that I had been too easy-going; but probably when people do not get what they wish, they think that those who oppose them are autocratic and wrong.[4]

Murray knew that some of his decisions had been unpopular, but he was certainly willing to contemplate changes in the structure of the Board if that was what the government wished. The Premier, for his part, wanted to avoid any charge that appointments to the University Board of Governors were political. He believed this might occur if the government increased its appointees, but he saw the need for changes in the people on the Board.[5]

The possibility of changes in the makeup of the university Board of Governors surfaced in a debate in the provincial legislature at the end of January 1919 when W.R. Motherwell, the Minister of Agriculture, implied that current Board members were too busy to fulfill their functions, and as a result, the university president was carrying too heavy a burden. During his speech, Motherwell also called attention to "the parsimonious salary structure," which he found "past comprehending."[6] This marked the first time since Murray assumed the Presidency that a Cabinet Minister had criticized the administration of the university in the Legislature. It was particularly galling to Murray since Motherwell's comments, he felt, were aimed directly at him.

That same day the Premier wrote to Murray suggesting an amendment to the University Act which would enable the government to replace the Board members appointed by Order-in-Council. Murray strongly opposed the terms of amendment on the grounds that it would give the Legislature power to vote the Board out of existence any time it wished, and it would be a clear, public signal of the government's lack of confidence in the current Board. If the government was seen to have no confidence in the Board, Murray pointed out to the Premier, this would mean "very serious dissatisfaction with the conduct of the University itself."[7]

Murray went on to make clear to Martin how much he had been stung by Motherwell's speech which "will, no doubt, set the people asking questions and imagining vain things. I may say that it has set me asking certain questions; and if it really meant what it might mean, that the management of the University up to date has been so bad that a reform of the Board was absolutely necessary, then a change in the President is still more necessary." Murray then dealt point by point with each of the criticisms of the university; salaries, research grants, and an unfounded allegation that Methodists had been ignored in university appointments.

There was also a fourth criticism: "The University is not progressive, more particularly in the matter of buildings." Murray sensed that some Saskatoon businessmen were tired of his conservative approach, which he defended to the Premier. "I believe it wiser for the University to keep well within the just expectations of the Province in matters of expenditure, than to go extravagantly beyond them and incur suspicion and distrust, so that when needs are pressing and great, and we ask for large and liberal contributions, our recommendation may be taken at face value." Murray admitted the university might do more in publicity to "boost" Saskatoon, but he told the Premier that the ox plodding along drawing the plow accomplished more work than the bull that bellows and throws dust over his back in the centre of the field. His metaphor of the ox clearly revealed the man and his philosophy. Murray's long letter obviously caused the Premier and his Cabinet to have second thoughts because no more was heard about the proposal to amend the University Act. Yet the rumours of dissatisfaction could not be stilled.

In February, the university became embroiled in a public controversy over a proposed site for the Provincial Normal School, which was to be built on the University grounds. The provincial education authorities deemed the site offered by the university unsuitable, and a public argument ensued. Two of the people taking public positions against the Board were Professors McLaurin and Hogg. The latter was head of the Physics Department and, as Murray was later to discover, had provided much of the ammunition that Motherwell used in his speech in the Legislature. Finally the Normal School was built several miles from the University, but the dispute alienated sections of the Saskatoon public and teachers.

Other influential critics of the University also surfaced. The chairman of the public school board was so violently critical in a telephone call that Murray felt obliged to write a point by point rebuttal, revealing each criticism to be groundless. It was not easy to give rational answers to allegations such as that "the law school was a farce."[8]

Murray's troubles were further compounded by his social isolation from influential sectors of Saskatoon society. He and his wife confined their social life to the campus and its people. They had so few social contacts with the business, professional, and social leaders of Saskatoon that these groups might well have concluded that the

Murrays avoided them. The isolation was not deliberate. According to Murray's daughter, Dr. Jean Murray, her parents devoted themselves entirely to the university. She could only remember one couple from the groups noted above who were ever entertained in the Murray home. Her mother considered afternoon teas "a waste of time," although university staff and graduating classes were regularly invited for tea.[9]

The separation of town and gown was unfortunate for Murray. Some of Saskatoon's leading citizens remembered Murray's strong support for placing the University in Regina, and others believed he was not sufficiently aggressive in expanding the university. Certainly there existed a number of people in Saskatoon critical of the university and its administration.

Greenway's charges struck Murray, therefore, not as an isolated incident, serious though that would have been, but as the latest of a series of attacks against the administration of the university and in particular against its President. Murray was both extremely sensitive to the accusations and vulnerable because they were not the first.

His strategy was to counterattack immediately. He had asked the Provincial Treasurer to write a letter specifying Greenway's charges, but even before Murray received it, early in April he called a meeting of the University Council, comprising all the teaching faculty. Here he outlined Greenway's charges, particularly the allegation about the majority of the faculty being disloyal to the President, and asked the Council "to settle the question of fact whether there was or was not disloyalty."[10] Murray then withdrew. Greenway was not present to speak for himself, but since Murray was convinced Greenway's charges were a device to force a confrontation, he decided to bring the affair into the open himself before the University Council. After a lengthy debate, the Council adjourned for two days so that everyone could give further consideration to the matter and be present for the vote.

When the Council reconvened, Murray received a solid vote of confidence from the faculty, who declared they were loyal to him. All the faculty voted for the resolution, except four who abstained. Murray was delighted with the support he had received, but he was now more determined than ever to deal with the small faction of conspirators he believed was responsible for the university's recent difficulties. In long letters to his old and intimate friends Robert Falconer, President of the University of Toronto, and A. Stanley MacKenzie, President of Dalhousie, Murray described what had happened and how he planned to resolve it. He told Falconer: "For some time I have known that there has been an active propaganda on the part of certain members of the University, which has had the very definite object of bringing certain changes in the administration. The propagandists number not more than two or three."[11] Murray, certain that the malcontents wanted to get rid of him, in turn decided the time had come to deal with them.

> [The debate in the University Council] and certain subsequent events have brought to a clear focus the centres of disaffection, and to some extent, the substance. I have a feeling, however, that matters cannot rest here. We must carry the things through to a finish. The disease must be uprooted. As it appears to me, the personal factor has made it clear that it is not a question of difference of opinion on policy or administration; but something more disturbing than that, and therefore we cannot go on as we have in the past.[12]

Murray acted quickly and decisively. The debate in the University Council had isolated the opposition and forced them to take a stand in public within the university. The President then took the matter to the Board of Governors and asked for a full investigation. He wanted the inquiry "begun promptly and carried through with dispatch." He knew what he was doing, and he told Falconer, "I am prepared to accept full responsibility and to pay the price if necessary."[13]

Both Falconer and MacKenzie immediately replied, offering moral support and giving the same advice: Don't back down. Falconer said, "I suppose that it is the long continued underhand machinations of those who have been opposed to you coming to light. Now that it is all out you will be somewhat relieved. An out and out fight is better than concealed suspicion, but as you say it is now a case of either you or them. One University cannot hold both."[14] MacKenzie advised: "Once you are freed from any onus of improper dealing, strike, and strike hard. Have the ulcer brought into the open, and when the Government sees the rottenness and insidiousness of it, they will concur in your performing the necessary Surgical operation."[15] Falconer and MacKenzie had long been aware of the campaign against him. But they also knew Murray, and because of what Falconer described as Murray's tendency to "put in a large measure of mercy with every set of justice," they each separately tried to steel his resolve to carry the fight through to a finish.

Murray brought the matter before the Board of Governors at the next meeting held April 21, 1919. He reported the charges made by Greenway, the resolution passed by the University Council, and as well, his own suspicions. After Murray had withdrawn from the meeting, the Board agreed to investigate further. The Board Secretary was authorized to write each faculty member indicating that the Board believed dissatisfaction existed among faculty regarding the administration of the university and requesting a statement in writing "indicating clearly whether you are satisfied or not with the administration and management of the University, and if dissatisfied, your reasons for being so."[16] Those who expressed dissatisfaction were invited to meet with the Board on May 2, for "a full and free discussion." Murray wrote to Falconer after the Board meeting that he had "nothing to regret or complain of, but the matter is not disposed of and will not be until the probe has been inserted more deeply."[17]

During the war a variety of issues, besides those already discussed, had surfaced within the university, each of which added to the discontent among some faculty with the way the university was being run. W.P. Thompson, in his analysis of this crisis, summarizes all the contentious points under ten headings. These included things like salaries, research grants, Greenway's accusations, and the location of the normal school, but there was also criticism of the way the university was being run including the composition of the Board of Governors.[18] Many of these controversies pitted Hogg and McLaurin against Murray. When Greenway levelled his broadside against the administration, Hogg and McLaurin, believing in the truth of his accusations, demanded either a ministerial or a judicial inquiry. Thus, by the beginning of May 1919 the situation within the university warranted investigation. Both the President and the small group of faculty members opposing him staked their careers on the outcome. The time for compromise solutions had passed.

W.P. Thompson, who was a member of the faculty at the time, suggests there was another element to this affair, the character of one of the professors, J.L. Hogg, and his apparent bitter enmity toward Murray. Thompson says of him:

> Hogg was the most active and aggressive in attempting to exploit all the criticisms. . . . He was a very ambitious man whose real purpose was apparently to supplant Murray as president. That statement cannot, of course, be documented. But it was the firm belief of many of the faculty at the time. He was prepared to use any means to belittle and injure the President.[19]

Murray had laid out his strategy very openly in his letters to Falconer and MacKenzie, letters written before he received Dunning's written statement of Greenway's charges and before he presented his case to the Board of Governors. He wanted immediate action. There can be no doubt of his determination to eliminate the malcontents by forcing them to resign, the sooner the better. With the strong moral support of his two closest friends among Canadian university presidents, he pressed on.

Unfortunately for Murray, his plan for a quick resolution of the crisis soon began to unravel. The Board of Governors took charge of the investigation because Greenway's accusations were directed against Murray as President. Having placed the issue before the Board, Murray then participated in Board discussions only when invited to do so. There was no question where the Board's loyalty lay. To a person they were anxious to support the President, but the Board also wanted to conduct a complete investigation before deciding what to do. This meant delays as letters were sent, individual professors interviewed, and long Board meetings held during which Board members wrestled with the complexities of the thorny dilemma in which they found themselves. Murray's plan also greatly underestimated the ability of the discontented professors first to drag out the process and later to muster public support for their position. No decisions were reached for two months, and as the crisis worsened, so did Murray's health.

When the Board of Governors next met on May 2, 1919, the members had in front of them letters from all but four of the thirty-one faculty expressing confidence in Murray's administration. Murray wrote to Falconer, following the meeting, that "a great many" of the respondents had written effusively about his contributions to the university. Of the four who hadn't replied, one sent a "non-committal note" and two had been out of town. Murray added, "I believe it is the intention of the Board to follow this matter up, and to act after they have gone further."[20]

At the same meeting Greenway appeared before the Board. After a full discussion he admitted he had been wrong in his charges that Murray had misappropriated public funds. He handed a letter to the Board saying there were no grounds for further investigation of his complaint and denying he had ever imputed "dishonest actions or motives" to Murray.[21] Greenway expressed his willingness to resign if the Board so desired, but the Governors took no action on this at the May meeting. The Board did not meet again until June 16. By that time three professors still had not replied to the Board's letter sent to all faculty members on April 22. Two, Professors Hogg and McLaurin, were heads of departments, and the third, Professor MacKay, was a member of the Law faculty. McLaurin and MacKay had refused to attend the May 2 meeting, but all three men were requested in writing to come to the Board's June meeting.

Walter Murray still held tenaciously to his view that the Board must conduct a complete investigation and require the three men to appear. Murray placed his own position before the Board in a blunt memorandum.

In view of all the circumstances leading up to Mr. Greenway's statement to the Hon. Mr. Dunning, the public rumors of dissatisfaction of certain members of the staff with the administration of the University, the action of the University Council and now of the declination of certain members reported to be dissatisfied, either to appear before the Board or to express their opinions in writing, I have been forced to the conclusion that unless a thorough investigation is held and all the members of the University holding responsible positions, such as heads of departments, to be summoned before the Board and examined and such action taken as the evidence so secured justifies, I cannot any longer remain responsible for the proper discharge of the duties of President. Certain members have more than once given expression to dissatisfaction of a serious import and when an opportunity to discuss these matters with the Board has been given, they have declined to appear or have taken no notice of the Board's letters. I hold that every member of the University is in duty bound to answer every request or notification of the Board and to comply with its requirements as far as possible.[22]

In effect, Murray told the Board to act by obtaining the resignations of the dissidents, or he would resign. This was not a change from his attitude in April, but his memorandum to the Board in June had the tone of an ultimatum. If the Board did not fully support him by conducting a full investigation he made it abundantly clear that he would resign. The Board continued to stand by the President and press on with its inquiry. Yet, it was an investigation which was proving to be as frustrating for Board members, who could not pin down the facts of what had occurred, as it was exasperating to Murray, who wanted rapid action. The Board's frustration stemmed from the attitude of passive resistance adopted by the remaining faculty members. Professor Hogg finally appeared before the Board at its June meeting, after being given the alternative of presenting himself or resigning, but he refused to make any statement or to answer questions. Professor MacKay also had not answered the Board's original letter. The Board adjourned until early July, after instructing its Secretary to inform both men that either letters or statements from them were to be in the Board's hands before the next meeting.

Murray was briefly optimistic about finding an acceptable solution after a long conversation with Professor McLaurin. He drafted a memorandum to the Board clearing up two of the issues affecting only McLaurin, but the other problems remained.[23] At the July Board meeting, Professor Hogg appeared and requested the appointment of a tribunal with representation from the Board and from people unconnected with the University. The Board turned down his request, and Hogg refused to make a statement to the Board, arguing it was not an impartial body.

Murray, knowing the Board was considering some form of dismissal of four professors, had prepared a memorandum on tenure for Board members.[24] He stated he believed in making "the tenure of academic appointments as attractive as possible" After alluding to controversies over academic dismissals in the United States during World War I, he went on to say:

> It is now generally recognized that freedom to think, to learn and to teach is vital to the life of a university. This academic freedom is at times interpreted to permit activities in speech and deed that make for a change in the form of the personnel of the Government of a university. Open, frank and fair criticism of policies should, in academic as well as in political government, be recognized as legitimate and as a necessary corrective. Every governing body should always be ready to listen to such criticism and to profit by it.

Murray indicated how, in the University of Saskatchewan as in other universities, there was plenty of opportunity for what he called "the proper expression of criticism." This was the nub of the President's position. "It is the duty of every member to make his objections known through the proper channel and of every official to receive with courtesy and to give just consideration to representations made to them." Had the criticisms come through these channels, Murray implied, he would have dealt with them openly and fairly. But the dissident faculty had not chosen that route:

> There is an insidious criticism that resorts to intrigue and insinuation and never comes into the open. Such criticism breeds an atmosphere of suspicion and jealousy, saps public confidence and ultimately weakens and paralyzes, if it does not destroy the institution which permits it to continue unchecked. Every man has the right to express his opinions of the administration of the institution in which he serves, but that carries with it corresponding responsibilities. He must be prepared to justify his criticism or take the consequences.

In Murray's eyes, the four faculty were guilty of intrigue. Because they had either been unable to back up their criticism, or had refused to do so, they could not be permitted to remain. Murray had elaborated a gentleman's code of honour, which he lived by and which he expected others to honour. Murray's strict, Victorian morality did not countenance what he labelled "insidious intrigue." His view of tenure and his reasons for dismissal would not stand up in today's university world, but in 1919 his own Board had no intention of permitting those faculty who, from the Board's perspective, were undermining the legitimate authority of the university, to escape.

Murray withdrew from the Board meeting when the Board resumed its discussion of the case. The Board, loyal to its President, came to the unanimous conclusion that it would be in the university's best interests if the four faculty members left. Each was offered a period of leave with pay on the condition of submitting his resignation at the end of the leave period. When Murray returned to the meeting, he expressed his approval of the Board's action of forcing the resignation of his opponents.

Shortly after the Board met in July, Murray left for Ottawa to attend a meeting of the National Research Council. His close friends, and certainly his family, had begun to worry about his health. His wife hoped that a real holiday in Nova Scotia would restore him, but no one, not even Walter Murray himself, realized the extent of the damage to his fragile health caused by the worsening university crisis. He went from Ottawa to Halifax without his wife or family, to stay with A. Stanley MacKenzie and enjoy both rest and vacation.

There he received the news, in his wife's words, "that the murder was out."[25] The four professors had refused the Board's offer of paid leave to be followed by their resignation and had openly challenged the Board of Governors, seeking a public investigation of the university and its administration. The University of Saskatchewan Act provided that the Board could not dismiss staff except on the recommendation of the President. Walter's wife was very worried that he would interrupt his holiday and return to Saskatoon. She also doubted whether her husband would have the stomach to recommend that the professors be fired. She and A. Stanley MacKenzie shared the same worry that a failure of Murray's will at the last moment might jeopardize the issue. From Saskatoon, Christina wrote to her husband to stiffen his backbone:

> Above all things stay where you are. Send your recommendation but don't come back till you are better. I know how you feel about using the sword but I can't see how you can

get out of it. It must be done. These men are not sparing you and all question of their feelings must be given up by you.[26]

Walter had come to the same conclusion: there was no other way out for him. He wrote to the Board from Halifax on July 25 regretting "that the absence of that cordial co-operation and mutual confidence between certain members of the staff and their colleagues, essential to the well being of the University, and the small prospect of any improvement, make such action necessary." Realizing that his recommendation to fire the four really meant "the accused passing judgement upon his accusers," he placed his own resignation at the disposal of the Board should they desire it.[27]

The Board had no intention of dismissing Murray, but at the next Board meeting it acted on Murray's recommendation and fired the four faculty members. It had been a very hot summer in Saskatoon, as Walter's wife had emphasized in her letters to him, but the firing of the Four fanned a prairie fire whose heat soon began to curl around the toes of the provincial government. Murray, now in his home town of Sussex, New Brunswick, could not escape, either. He told his wife he was willing to return to Saskatoon at the Board's request, but he wanted nothing more to do with the professors.[28]

When the confirmation of the firing reached him on August 12, far from calming him, it seemed to worsen his condition.[29] Murray had watched Premier Scott of Saskatchewan suffer a serious nervous breakdown in office and now found himself facing an agonizing dilemma. In a private letter to Rutherford, his Dean of Agriculture, Murray bared his soul. "I must make the choice of keeping on and going to pieces like Scott or asking release or leave of absence with proper treatment."[30] He felt he would be letting down the university, the Board of Governors, and everyone but his family if he did not return. He even contemplated resigning. "To resign is to give the public the impression that I do not approve of the action of the Governors—a very serious thing. For they have done the only thing to bring permanent peace to the university. Yet my inability to pull them thro' will be ample reason to seek another President."[31] Murray's own sense of inadequacy began to overwhelm him. In a letter to his wife the next day he confessed, "It is most humiliating. In the midst of a very critical situation I, the key man, fail to come to terms with force and decision. So much depends upon it."[32]

Murray was suffering a nervous breakdown. Three days later he wrote to James Clinkskill, Chairman of the Board of Governors. In shaky handwriting and muddled thought, quite different from his usual clear style, he composed the first of two resignations he would send in the next three days.[33] Murray's brother, a medical doctor, acted as soon as he saw him, sending him to Montreal for professional treatment and wiring the Board of Governors. The Board quickly granted Murray a three-month leave. Clinkskill, the Board Chairman, insisted to Murray's brother that Murray take a complete rest.[34] He wired Murray personally suggesting a trip to Britain as a rest cure, saying there would be no difficulty in extending his leave for another two months.[35] The next three weeks Murray spent in the Royal Victoria Hospital in Montreal.

Happily the breakdown, although severe, was amenable to treatment. Within a week there was a noticeable improvement. The doctor reported to his brother: "Prof. Murray is improving rapidly. He has lost practically all his fears and is sleeping like a normal person. He still has an aversion to meeting people but that is lessening every day. It should not be long before he has complete control of himself."[36]

After his release from hospital, Murray returned to Sussex, New Brunswick to continue his recuperation. His wife had remained in Saskatoon, but now she was anxious to join him. Christina and the children had written regularly to cheer him up with news of friends and home. His old friends like Falconer wrote to reassure him. For a time it appeared his recovery would be quick. By early October, Murray had plans to attend Convocation at Queen's then visit Montreal, Toronto, and Ottawa before going back to Saskatoon, but only if the doctor agreed. Walter had at least convinced himself he had recovered completely.

His judgment was not that of his doctor, his family, his friends, or the Board of Governors. The doctor evidently vetoed Murray's proposed return. Murray's guilty conscience, greatly aggravated by his medical condition, pressed on him. He had written his wife from the Royal Victoria Hospital: "I feel that I should be back in the mess. It is very unfair to leave the burden upon Ling and the others. It will be pretty tough work to keep head to the storm."[37] In fact, Walter had no cause to worry about the administration of the university in his absence. Ling, the Dean of Arts and Science, was functioning very effectively as Acting President; classes began without incident, and enrollment was up. Falconer wrote to pass on Ling's advice: "Though he [Ling] does not wish to do the work of the presidential office a day longer than duty requires, he is strongly of opinion that you should not return to the university before Christmas. This partly in order that matters may be settled without your being there; partly because he feels that you ought to have a thorough rest."[38]

His proposed travels had been encouraged by an invitation from Queen's University. Queen's, forgetting they had previously granted him an honorary Doctorate, offered him another. The Principal had to retract it after discovering the mistake. He wrote Murray, "I suppose behind the offer there was the memory rather of recent than of past events and a certain desire to express sympathy and appreciation just at this particular time."[39] Murray also had received an informal offer of a post as Superintendent of Education in Nova Scotia. However, attractive as this was, he did not want to leave Saskatchewan under a cloud, and he did not want to desert the Board after they had supported him so loyally.

The Chairman of the Board of Governors wrote Murray again at the end of September to tell him the Board would not permit his return "till you have had a complete rest and are thoroughly fit again. Don't think of any date for your return, just keep your mind easy, get well and we will all be the better pleased."[40] The Board and Murray's colleagues realized what a toll had been exacted by the eleven years of unremitting labour that Murray had given to building the university and to his other activities. They unanimously recommended a long period of rest. Finally, Walter's family and friends persuaded his wife to join him in New Brunswick and take charge of his convalescence. Before she left Saskatoon she tried once again to reassure him about the state of affairs at the university. "Everything is as quiet as can be as far as the trouble is concerned and the old spirit of good fellowship seems to have returned to the University."[41] She clearly was anxious about Walter's health. She joined him by the middle of October, and they left together for Boston.

She had good reason to be anxious. Walter's recovery progressed slowly, and both Walter and Christina knew he was still not his old self. Neither the Chairman of the Board nor Murray's wife could keep him isolated from the university. Murray's secretary along with Professor Moxon, his loyal friend and colleague in the Faculty of Law, each kept him up to date on university and community activities with long letters full of detailed analysis and commentary. Murray could not keep aloof, either. His letters reveal his desire to be back, as instructions were sent about the annual report and the preparation of financial statements. Typically, he even sent a contribution for the orchestra for the students' Hallowe'en dance.

The Board of Governors, in the middle of November 1919, extended Dean Ling's appointment as Acting President and at the same time extended Murray's leave until February 1920. Murray had planned to be back in Saskatoon by the end of November, but his medical condition would not permit it.

A letter his wife wrote to Premier Martin late in December tells the full story:

> We have spent many weeks in a vain search for health. After three weeks in Boston, two in Toronto, and one at the Kirkfield Inn, we returned to Toronto on the 16th intending to leave at midnight the 17th for Ottawa and then to Saskatoon. But just as we were about to leave for our train, Walter was forced to acknowledge that he was not well enough to go. The next morning I persuaded him to see the doctor, and after a very thorough x-ray examination lasting five days, he was operated on last Thursday. His trouble turned out to be a very bad appendix and adhesions. . . . Dr. Starr says that he has been absorbing poison for a very long time, and that he will probably feel like a different man after this.
>
> I think his anxiety to get back to work made him try to avoid this operation, but I am glad it is over as I was afraid something serious was developing. This last attack was the fifth one since the middle of October, three not severe at all, but two quite bad ones.[42]

Christina was right. Murray was a different man after the operation. He was back in Saskatoon by the middle of January, and by the middle of February 1920 he wrote President Tory of Alberta that in "the last few days I have been more like I was before the war."[43] His recovery was complete. He would remain President of the University of Saskatchewan until 1937, and never again did he require a medical leave of absence.

The six months that he had been away had been eventful for the university. As soon as the dismissal of the four professors became known in the summer, a public controversy began to brew, with the Board of Governors and the administration at the centre of it. The professors were prominent public figures in the city and the province. McLaurin had just been elected vice-president of the Canadian Institute of Chemists, and Hogg was a member of the Saskatoon Public School Board. Greenway was the director of the extension department and thus probably known to more people in agriculture societies and municipal councils than any other person on the university staff. The Saskatoon *Star-Phoenix*, reporting his dismissal, said of him: "His single aim has been to preach the gospel of Happiness through Work, to rouse the rural manhood and womanhood from the stagnation and curse of Drudgery, through Craftsmanship to Art."[44] Dr. Ira MacKay had a devoted following among the young lawyers who had graduated from the law school. John Diefenbaker was one such. He claims in his *Memoirs* that he and Walter Murray had "come into each other's firing lines on a number of occasions, both when I was a student and over the years, one equalling the other in the expression of unreticent opinion."[45]

The young graduates requested that a special meeting of Convocation be held to discuss the dismissals. Only fifteen signatures were required for the meeting, and these were easily obtained. Twenty-eight actually signed the petition, many of them, like Diefenbaker, young law graduates. They wanted Convocation not only to examine the dismissals but to discuss "all other questions of organization, administration or policy" connected with the university or its departments which might have a bearing on the dismissals. Their request was really for a full-scale open inquiry into the operation of the university. Justice Emmett Hall, another of the signatories, recalled in an interview: "It was the law school that was carrying the torch in a sense. This was largely because of MacKay . . . as a lecturer he was fantastic."[46] Convocation consisted of the Chancellor, the Senate, and all graduates of the first University Convocation which, because of the way the University was created, included all university graduates living in the province as of 1908. The powers of Convocation were strictly limited to making recommendations to the University Senate, but it was a public forum in which the issues could be debated. The University Chancellor duly, but not hastily, convened the meeting on November 20, 1919.

By now, the Premier's sensitive political nose told him the university situation was potentially troublesome, and he moved with dexterity to contain it. Throughout the spring and summer, D.P. McColl, the Board Secretary, had kept the Premier fully informed of each stage of the investigation. Martin had heard of the move to have Convocation meet, and he wanted to make sure the meeting had enough supporters of the administration to fend off the attacks of the young graduates. He wrote to his political crony George McCraney, former Member of Parliament for Saskatoon:

> The difficulty with such a meeting is that only a few persons will attend and the few will likely be largely of one mind. Perhaps the representation may be confined to men who live in Saskatoon and I think if such a meeting is held that some of you in Saskatoon who are of a more moderate mind should be there and I think some effort should be made to get representatives from other parts of the Province to attend. As you can readily understand, I do not wish to interfere but I wish I were in a position where I could. The danger is that any action on my

part would be misconstrued and perhaps would do the institution more harm than good.[47]

There was no question where the provincial government stood on the issue. The Premier wrote to Murray personally to tell him of the strategy for the Convocation meeting and of his assessment of the likely outcome. "What the men whose services have been dispensed with hope to gain by endeavouring to stir up trouble I cannot very well understand because ultimately there can only be one result and that is that they will be entirely discredited in their conduct. They have shown their disregard for properly constituted authority and anyone who does this finally loses the sympathy of the public."[48] Murray also received reassuring notes from the Deputy Minister of Agriculture and from the Chairman of the National Research Council. Macallum visited Regina late in August and met Premier Martin and Dunning, his Treasurer. He reported to Murray that both were "extremely sympathetic" towards him. "Both seemed to locate responsibility upon Mr. Hogg, whom they accuse of trying to get the Presidency by displacing you."[49] Dunning was even franker in a confidential letter to Murray. "The Bolsheviki are exploding their ammunition quite fruitlessly as far as most sober thinking people are concerned. Some effect is apparent among the alumni in Saskatoon itself, but in no other part of the Province is any effect visible." Dunning added, "I want to tell you that I find on every hand among the most responsible people of the Province the keenest sympathy and support for you, the more so as people are beginning to realize that the trouble has its foundation in disloyal conspiracy of the worst kind. . . ."[50]

Murray himself, unless requested to by the Board or the Chancellor, had no intention of taking part in Convocation even if his health permitted, which it did not. But he did foresee with equanimity the possibility of Convocation recommending a public investigation and told his wife that "if an investigation is ordered by a properly authorized body there can be no objection to going into the trouble as fully as may be desirable."[51]

Murray's colleagues on the university staff were even more determined not to let the Convocation meeting get out of hand. C.J. Mackenzie, the Dean of Engineering, promised Murray that "a few hot headed partisan graduates are not going to run this show."[52] A number of the University staff who had expressed their loyalty to Murray in the spring now wrote to him personally to tell him of events in the university and to reassure him of the outcome of the Convocation meeting. His friends and colleagues rallied to bring sufficient supporters to Convocation in order to defeat the cry for a royal commission. Even before Convocation met, the two sides were taking public positions and drawing in members of the Saskatoon community.

Soon a Saskatoon holy war was in being, as ministers joined in. Charles Endicott, the Minister of Grace Church in Saskatoon, used his pulpit to attack the university administration. Dr. E.H. Oliver, the principal of the Presbyterian College of the University, countered with an emotional speech at another Saskatoon church, praising the University and especially its President: "And Saskatchewan must not forget what it owes to such a man. For he has contributed mightily to the nation's morale."[53]

From Boston, Murray wrote to his Acting President, Dean Ling, just prior to the Convocation meeting. He was sure Ling would arrange for staff members who wanted to participate in Convocation to do so without cancelling all classes. Murray expressed optimism about the outcome but reiterated very plainly his own position: "If the Government should order an investigation and if the investigation should call for reinstatement it will of course mean the retirement of the President, who will not recommend the re-appointment of men already dismissed. . . ."[54]

Nearly two hundred graduates and faculty appeared for the Convocation meeting on November 20. The debate lasted from ten-thirty in the morning until nearly eleven that night. Moxon recounted to Murray that "Convocation was a unique gathering, where the threads, or rather currents, of feeling were so confused and the tension was so high, it was hard to get a good idea of what it was really trying to accomplish. Nothing went exactly as we expected. . . . It was a mixture of an emancipation meeting and an English House of Commons discussing Supply."[55]

On the motion to establish a Royal Commission of Inquiry, there was a clear division between the recent graduates on one side, and the faculty and original convocation members on the other. The motion was defeated 105-83, which was a triumph for the combined political organizing powers of the provincial government and the university faculty and administration. Probably not even a three-line whip could have produced more votes for the administration. Justice Emmett Hall, who was there along with Diefenbaker, alleges the first resolution was defeated by a muster of original Convocation members who appeared late in the day. "They hadn't heard the debate, but they sure voted."[56] The numbers and solidarity of the younger graduates reflected more than a generation gap. As W.P. Thompson concluded after examining the proceedings: "In the circumstances the very substantial vote in favour could be interpreted as a real demand for a formal inquiry."[57] A second motion deploring the manner of dismissal of the four professors passed 99-79. Murray's secretary sent his wife a long, rambling account of the meeting. "The great feature for rejoicing that I pick out is that there was practically no personal sparring and no attack on anybody. In fact the loyalty expressed by the Four and their following in the President was almost ludicrous, all things considered, and I think they almost overdid it."[58]

Murray's closest friend among his colleagues, Professor Moxon of the Law Faculty, tried to keep Murray's name out of the debate, but it proved impossible. He confessed later, "The Governors' backs were not strong enough to carry the load."[59] Moxon intervened to state emphatically that Murray had signed the recommendation to dismiss the four professors. The administration had acted together even though some of the arguments at Convocation suggested this was not the case. Thus the vote against an inquiry was seen as a vote of confidence in Murray. If the vote had gone the other way, it might have been interpreted publicly as a lack of confidence in the President.

The long public debate at Convocation in November did not end the affair. Instead it encouraged the dismissed professors to mount a wider public campaign for the sort of inquiry they wanted. The professors proceeded to exploit their advantage vigorously. They desired a commission composed of one labour representative, one agricultural representative, one businessman, and two educators. Premier Martin began to be deluged in December by a series of resolutions demanding an inquiry. These were sent to him on behalf of teachers' organizations, agricultural societies, homemakers' clubs, the Saskatoon Trades and Labour Council, the Y.M.C.A. of Moose Jaw, and church organizations. In the little town of Rouleau, Saskatchewan, for example, the Agricultural Society, the Homemakers' Club, and the Methodist Church all sent resolutions supporting a public inquiry to the Board of Governors. One of Martin's supporters reported to him the province was beginning "to seethe."[60]

The campaign centred in Saskatoon where a Citizens' Committee was formed in defence of the dismissed professors. In a manifesto issued in December, this Committee articulated four basic principles which they believed had been violated by the Board of Governors.[61] Two were rights claimed by all British subjects: the right of an accused to know the charges against him and to confront his accuser, and the accused's right to a fair hearing. The other two were the belief that no one, especially in a public position, should be dismissed without prior warning, and the fear that the Board's action constituted a threat to the tenure of office of all teachers in the province.

The four professors managed to mobilize considerable public sympathy for their position, and the political controversy this caused could no longer be publicly ignored by the government. Nor was the political climate the easiest in which to contain a burgeoning crisis. The Winnipeg General Strike had shaken the west the previous spring, a west which was still trying to recover from the war. Words like "Reds" and "Bolsheviks" were bandied about in Saskatoon to describe the dissident professors, not because they were socialists but because they were seen to be threatening one of the province's leading institutions by their public demands. The well-publicized resignation of a fifth faculty member in December as a protest against the Board's actions only added to the public clamour.

Premier Martin, convinced the campaign was solely due to what he called "deliberate propaganda," at first obstinately resisted any idea of a public inquiry, and especially the demand of the Citizens' Committee for an inquiry composed of people from outside the province. He wrote to one of the campaigners, Reverend Endicott: "I believe that the campaign which is being carried on at the present time is doing more harm to the institution than anything else possibly could do because every effort is being put forth to create in the minds of the people a feeling of distrust in the institution."[62] Martin's distaste for any overt government interference in university affairs gave way before the pressure of public opinion. The government, through an Order-in-Council, invested three King's Bench judges with the powers of a visitor, a British convention incorporated into the original University Act, and in this way a full judicial inquiry was held in Saskatoon between March 23 and April 9. While acceding to their desire for a public inquiry, Martin thus neatly side-stepped the Citizens' Committee's demand for an inquiry board that was either broadly representative of the protesting groups or composed of educators, preferably from outside the province.

Walter Murray was recuperating from appendicitis while the public agitation was stirring up a political blizzard, but after his return to Saskatoon in January 1920 he commented on Martin's solution in a letter to Adam Shortt, the former Queen's political scientist and long-time Murray acquaintance:

> ...they have revived some musty Acts and found that the Visitor of certain institutions is the King, who acted through the Lord Chancellor, and the Legislature passed an Act investing the

King's Bench with the powers of Lord Chancellor so far as it pertains to the duty of Visitor. So we are expecting a Visitorial investigation in the near future. One begins to appreciate the feelings of men who are in doubt whether they will be hanged or not, but are kept in suspense about their probable fate. I think, however, that things are turning our way, although there is a good deal of talk.[63]

Murray's dry wit is evident, a sign of his health and his optimism. Murray's pen was even sharper in a letter to President Tory of the University of Alberta, describing the tactics of the professors:

We arrived back in the midst of an attempt to stampede the students, rush the Agricultural Societies and bully the Government and the Legislature. It has all failed. Then the Poison Gas was turned on the Graingrowers but the wind blew in the other direction and they escaped without a whiff.[64]

Murray was convinced that the judicial inquiry under visitorial provisions was a trap into which the professors had stumbled unwittingly. He was right. Murray learned that the judges could inquire into the motives of the Board and whether they had exercised their powers properly, but they would not render judgment on the wisdom of the Board's action. This, of course, restricted the judges' scope and made a judgment in favour of the Board more likely. He personally had no qualms about facing a public inquiry.

The details of the various parts of this complicated dispute were all revealed before the judges. Even the Provincial Treasurer was called to testify about the original meeting with Greenway which triggered the crisis. Dunning told the inquiry that after visits from both Greenway and Hogg criticizing the administration of the university, the mayor of Saskatoon had seen him and urged the government to do something about the university: "The state of things is rotten up there."[65] The mayor's intervention made up Dunning's mind. He then called in both Murray and Rutherford, the Dean of Agriculture, to inform them of the various allegations. When Murray took the stand on April 6, he reiterated what he had told the Board of Governors the previous summer. It was in the best interests of the university that the four be dismissed because of a lack of co-operation on their part and their inability to get along with other staff members.[66] Even when he recalled the affair much later in his life, Murray remained convinced that jealousy and thwarted ambition were at the root of the discontent evidenced by three of the professors, Hogg, McLaurin and MacKay.[67]

The judgment of the visitors was a complete vindication for Murray and the Board of Governors. The judges found that "a state of affairs in the University had been created such as made it impossible that these men should remain any longer in the service of the University." They upheld the actions of Murray and the Board in dismissing the professors and took Murray's side completely over the loyalty issue. "It is difficult to understand why a man who is loyal to the president of his own institution should fail him at a time of need, or hesitate to vote loyalty to his chief if the loyalty exists."[68]

Murray had no doubt whatsoever about what he had done, and the judges' decision was a most welcome confirmation of what he had believed all along. Now that the verdict was in, he wasted no time in mounting a publicity campaign to counter the reports of the dismissals which had been circulated to newspapers and periodicals both in Canada and the United States by friends of the professors. *The Canadian Chemical Journal,* in an editorial of January 1920, had severely criticized the university for dismissing the professors "in the same manner and with about the same degree of thought that would be given to the dismissal of a foreigner from a street-cleaning department."[69] Murray sent copies of the judgment to the editor of this journal (who, however, refused to print it) and to any others that had reported the affair. As he told his friend, A. Stanley MacKenzie, "We are very willing the world should know all there is to know."[70]

Extracts of the judgment went to *The Nation* and *School and Society* in New York. The only thing constraining Murray's publicity drive was a desire not to make it more difficult for the dismissed faculty to find other employment. Murray was not vindictive and did not want to embarrass the men any further. He even wrote to the Acting Principal of McGill, saying he would welcome "with relief" the appointment of one of them, Ira MacKay, to McGill's faculty.[71] MacKay was appointed to McGill and went on to a distinguished career there.

Murray's crises were over. For the ensuing seventeen years of his presidency, he would never face another breakdown nor another university crisis resembling that of 1919. His Montreal doctor wrote to him in August warning that "the 'devils' will surely torment you at times, but you have beaten them off in the past and can do it again."[72] Dr. Mundie's letter also contained a prophecy. "The University scheme is yours and you are going to carry it out to completion." There was no outward sign from 1920 on of Murray's "devils" tormenting him. With his crisis behind him, he threw himself once again into the task of building the University of Saskatchewan. The doctor's prophecy was fulfilled.

■

above:

Early board members tour American universities, Walter Murray, D.P. McColl and John Dixon, 1908.

left:

Turning the sod for the University of Saskatchewan, James Clinkskill, Chancellor Edward Wetmore, and Walter Murray, 1908.

left:
Mrs. Christina Murray

below:
The Murray children,
Christina, Jean and Lucy

top:
Berry picking at Big River

above:
*Mrs. Murray disliked tenting
at Big River*

above:

Murray reading the names of
the students who died in
World War I at the dedication
of the Memorial Gates, 1928

left:

Murray examining an oven
on a Ukrainian farm during
the Community Progress
Competition, c1931

left:
The Murrays at the Emma
Lake Art Camp

below:
Walter and Christina Murray,
two honourary doctorates of
the University of Saskatchewan, 1938

above:
Walter and Christina Murray at a Christmas party for children, c1935

left:
Fosberry's painting of Walter Murray, 1938

Chapter 8

Presbyterian Reformer

Walter Murray's devotion to the Presbyterian Church was as great as his dedication to the University of Saskatchewan. The two institutions were inseparable branches of his educational mission. Together they consumed his intellectual and physical energy. All his adult life Murray immersed himself in church activities at both the local and national level, but none took up more time than the cause of church union. Walter Murray worked as hard and as long as any layman in the Presbyterian Church to create the United Church of Canada. From the time he embraced church unionism with all the zeal of a new convert until the union was achieved in 1925, the unionist cause became an all-consuming personal crusade. His goal was no less than the formation of a New Jerusalem in Canada. He struggled for over twenty years to reach it, but the triumph was one he savoured the rest of his life.

Ecumenism had been part of his life from early childhood. His grandfather, a dour follower of the Free Kirk, instilled the tenets of Presbyterianism in him, but these were fused with the less rigid outlook of Anglicanism inherited from his grandmother. From this dual heritage emerged a potent missionary vocation which found outlets long before he moved west to Saskatoon. Dalhousie, where he taught for sixteen years, was a Presbyterian College with an ordained minister as its Principal. Christian beliefs were inculcated into the students by the professors as a regular part of the academic program, and Walter Murray played a full part in the transmission of Christian theology.

He was a regular lecturer at the popular Y.M.C.A. Sunday afternoon lectures held at the College. In 1894, for example, he presented a series of lectures on character sketches of Old Testament figures.[1] Appreciative students and townspeople regularly filled the hall for Murray's talks. The student paper summed up one of his performances by saying, "Professor Murray is always listened to with pleasure and close attention."[2]

Murray's theological reputation was such that he was called on continually to give summer workshops for Sunday school teachers throughout the Maritimes or to lecture at conferences arranged by the Maritime Presbyterian Church. In August 1901, he spoke to a gathering of Presbyterian Ministers at St. John's, Newfoundland, and the following summer he took part in a ten-day workshop organized by the Presbyterian College of Halifax.[3] He managed in some summers to combine a vacation with church work, as in 1906 when he taught at a church summer school held in Glace Bay, Nova Scotia.

He also wrote regularly for church publications such as the *Teacher's Monthly,* part of the home series of the Canadian Presbyterian Church. His own work on child psychology won him an international reputation in Presbyterian circles. The American Presbyterians invited him to prepare a teacher training course of six lessons on child study in 1904, and that same year the Canadian Presbyterian Church approached him to write a book from articles he had published in *Teacher's Monthly.* This was the origin of *Studies in Mind Growth,* an 18,000 word booklet published in 1904 primarily for Sunday school teachers. It proved both popular and lucrative; he earned royalties from it until World War I. The booklet was published in Britain in 1909 in a special English edition and issued as well in the United States. When the American Presbyterian Church asked him in 1916 to rewrite it, Murray had to refuse because of lack of time.

After moving from Fredericton to Halifax in 1892, he soon became an elder of St. Matthews, the oldest Presbyterian church in Canada. His connection with St. Matthews lasted until he moved to Saskatoon, and it was as a commissioner of the Halifax Presbytery that he began to participate regularly in regional and national Presbyterian Synods and Assemblies. At St. Matthews he was involved in many aspects of church activity from conducting Bible classes for young men to preserving the old records of the church, which went back to 1769. Out of his archival work grew an interest in the history of the church. In 1903 he read a paper on the early years of St. Matthews to the Nova Scotia Historical Society, later published in the *Collections* of the Society. He was unable to complete the paper for publication before he moved west, but it appeared in 1912 in its original, if somewhat fragmentary, form.[4]

The paper spanned the era from the founding of Halifax to the end of the American Revolution, a period Murray characterized as one of "Congregationalism flavoured with Presbyterianism." He was intrigued by the congregationalist influence of New England on

Nova Scotia prior to the American Revolution. In his paper he traced the evolution of St. Matthews and how it had been affected by New England religious currents. As he said, "I believe that one cannot understand the history of the old congregation, of many names and diverse peoples without seeing in its life the strong and deep current of Puritan ideas and customs that flowed from the shores of New England."[5]

St. Matthews gave him far more than an opportunity to chronicle the early religious history of Halifax. It was in Halifax and as a member of St. Matthews that he became converted to the idea of a larger church union. Five years before he decided to move west himself, Walter Murray had thrown his enormous energy into what would become the longest campaign of his life, working out the details of a new Church of Canada and persuading his fellow Presbyterians to accept it. Here, too, St. Matthews provided a precedent. Murray's study of its earlier years, when it was in fact a unionist church, sparked the beacon of unionism within him.

In 1905 Murray carefully analysed the need for union among the Presbyterian, Methodist, and Congregational churches. The key element for him was the transformation of the Canadian West due to the huge influx of immigrants. Before 1901 the churches had managed, though barely, to keep pace with immigration, but after 1901 they had fallen badly behind. The three churches together could not provide sufficient missionaries, churches, and ministers for the burgeoning west, and competition among them worsened an already serious problem. Murray also had done a cost analysis of the ten religious colleges operated by the three churches and concluded that only five were really needed. To his Scottish background, this was an intolerable waste. He argued that national needs demanded efficient co-operation, but at the same time there should be as little disturbance as possible for the individual congregation. His philosophy of liberty for local congregations combined with efficient co-operation at higher levels did not change throughout the long struggle to achieve unity. He did not minimize the obstacles, including deep-rooted ethnic differences among Scots, English, and American descendants in the three churches. Yet, overriding these differences, Murray saw clearly the pressing need for religious unity.

Although by no means the first to think in such terms, by 1905 he visualized "a Canadian Church, a United Church of Canada, united for the work of the church in Canada." He prophesied that the sectarian divisions of the nineteenth century would soon disappear in a larger union. Names like Burgher, Anti-Burgher, Kirkman, Free Kirker, Wesleyan and Methodist Episcopal would vanish into history, subsumed into a United Church of Canada. Murray's immediate goal was union of the three churches, but like others he hoped the union concept would embrace all of Canadian Protestantism and a true Protestant Church of Canada would be created.

Murray lectured on the possibility of church union at Dalhousie early in 1906 and reiterated the needs of the Canadian West.

> The demands for union are many, but perhaps none is so pressing as the call for concentration of energy among the church in providing religious ordinances for the great West. At the present time, the tide of immigration is flowing so strongly into Canada that the various religious denominations, each working by itself cannot meet the demands for Home Missionaries. Moreover, the obstacles once supposed insuperable are now seen to be insignificant. Doctrinal differences in the negotiating churches have been reduced to few, and prejudice, so long a barrier to union, is yielding to reason.[6]

Murray's solid convictions about the urgency of church union strengthened after he moved west in 1908 and saw for himself the religious needs of the emerging prairie communities. He reiterated his earlier views in 1912, commenting on a manuscript history of the background to the union movement prepared by one of his faculty members, the historian of the West, Dr. A.S. Morton.[7] Murray was delighted with the quality of Morton's study, but he argued that Morton had omitted what for Murray was a key point—the mandate of Canadian nationalism to develop the West, not just with people and material goods, but with a lasting spirituality. Without union, the missionary effort would be ineffective. Murray contrasted the mergers in business leading to higher profits with the churches' search for religious efficiency through union. The former might be undesirable, but the latter serving non-material ends was essential if the church were to accomplish the religious work urgently required on the prairies. Murray never wavered from this position. For him western conditions dictated church union.

Murray joined himself to the reform-minded Presbyterians who sought to reverse the fissiparous tendencies of the religion their Scottish fathers and grandfathers had brought over to the new land. The union of the provinces into a Dominion of Canada in 1867 assisted in creating conditions in which the four major strands of the Presbyterian churches in Canada could unite. This occurred with the creation of the Presbyterian Church in Canada in 1875. From then until the end of the century, Canadian Presbyterianism enjoyed both an unprecedented stability and continuous growth. Nevertheless, the challenges of the emerging West, industrialization, and issues like temperance caused Presbyterians, as well as Methodists, to think of a new church to embrace all the Protestant denominations. Of these challenges, the most acute was the new West. In 1898 Presbyterians had broached to the Methodists the possibility of co-operation in western missionary work. Four years later, in 1902, the actual union enterprise was launched when the Methodist General Conference called for committees to be appointed from each of the Methodists, Presbyterians, and Congregationalists to discuss the possibility of organic union.

Murray's optimism in 1906 about the success of Church Union was understandable, if naive, because he had just returned from a very constructive meeting of the Joint Union Committee in Toronto. In 1904 the three churches had appointed representatives to a Joint Committee on Church Union, which met for the second time in Toronto shortly before Christmas, 1905. Murray was present at both meetings and served as the Presbyterian convener of one of the five subcommittees struck to work out the terms of union. Each subcommittee had the same ratio of Presbyterians, Methodists, and Congregationalists, 2:2:1, among its 40 members. The subcommittees dealt respectively with doctrine, polity, ministry, administration, and church law. Murray's task, as one of the Presbyterian convenors of the polity subcommittee, was to develop an acceptable political structure for the new church: defining the constitution, setting out the duties and powers of the different church courts, and planning the organization of the new congregations. As the secretary of this subcommittee, Murray summarized in seventeen pages what became the nucleus of a new church constitution.

Many of his own ideas were incorporated in it, and these rested on his own fundamentally democratic view of church organization which fused local congregational liberty within a larger church structure. He believed that Presbyterianism had moved closer to Methodism as its missionary role, particularly in the Canadian West, had become more pronounced—a desirable trend which he predicted would continue. He set down his beliefs in a note appended to a paper he prepared for the Maritime Local Committee of the Joint Union Committees in 1906:

> The similarities in the politics of the two churches are many and fundamental, the differences largely matters of detail. Both Churches are democratic in principle; yet the machinery of the Methodist Church permits a more effective supervision and

subordinates more completely the preferences of localities and individuals to the general interest of the church. The Presbyterian System is more deferential to the individual. The Methodist form of Church Government leans more to Episcopacy, the efficient oversight of the official; the Presbyterian more to Independency. These differences are the legacies of the past. The more completely these Churches adapt themselves to the needs of the Present in the Home and Foreign Mission Fields the greater the likeness in their organization and methods of work.[8]

For Murray, the key to merging the structures and traditions of Presbyterians and Methodists was to adapt to contemporary needs.

The 1905 report was circulated in each of the three churches along with a digest of procedures in the Methodist and Presbyterian churches that Murray had prepared for the 1905 meeting. During 1906 Murray then prepared a much more detailed position on polity for the maritime local branch of the Joint Union Committee, which was commended by all his unionist friends. Falconer wrote to him: "I have gone through your draft with a great deal of care and admiration; it is very clear as well as comprehensive."[9] Murray's draft on church polity was incorporated without substantial change into the report of the Joint Union Committee which met again in December 1906. Thus, Murray played an influential role in drafting the constitution of the new church, a task completed by the Joint Union Committee in December 1908. Thereafter, he concentrated his activities on converting his fellow Presbyterians.

For some, the advantages of union were apparent. Financial saving was a powerful argument, as one of Murray's correspondents recognized. "I am bound to admit that the argument of cheapness is having quite an effect. Many of our people say it will be cheaper under Union—the burden will not be so heavy on us. . . ."[10] Optimism prevailed in the early days. Falconer wrote to Murray after a debate in the Presbyterian Assembly in 1906 "that no strong rational arguments against union can be produced."[11] Reports from Presbyterians in the West indicated almost unanimous acceptance of Union. The optimism derived from the enthusiasm of the union converts who believed they would quickly convert their churches to the cause. Nowhere was this optimism so misplaced as in the Presbyterian Church. From 1908 to 1925 the divisions over union split the Presbyterians into two warring camps. There was no doubt where Murray's own allegiance lay, and for him the most difficult of the tasks on the road to Union was to persuade his fellow Presbyterians to adopt Unionism. Because of his commitments as

President of the University of Saskatchewan, he was not able to devote as much time as he wished to church affairs from 1908 to 1913, but he was involved and followed developments very closely.

Within his own university he avidly promoted the Presbyterian Church and the unionist cause. He had hired Edmund H. Oliver to teach History in 1910, and the following year, after Oliver had been approached by the University of Alberta to join their theology faculty and had turned it down, Murray promised him the Principalship of the Presbyterian College as soon as it was created.[12] He then initiated the campaign to build what eventually became St. Andrew's College. He told Oliver the time was propitious to launch "an aggressive campaign on behalf of a Presbyterian College in Saskatoon" in order to establish a claim which the University of Alberta would respect and also to prevent it from being built in Regina. The Lutherans were also planning to construct a College, and Murray wanted to make sure the Presbyterians secured a prime site. Besides, as he noted in August 1911, "a good harvest and the elections out of the road should make people ready to consider and give."[13] The Presbyterian Synod of Saskatchewan duly endorsed the project, and St. Andrew's became first the Presbyterian and later the United Church theological college at the University of Saskatchewan.

Walter Murray's desire to house a Presbyterian College within the university he was creating stemmed not just from a desire to give the Presbyterians a leg up over their rivals but also from his own strong religious and educational beliefs. Murray saw a Presbyterian College within the university as a powerful stimulus for missionary work in the province and a recruiting agency for potential ministers from among the student body. In advocating the establishment of church colleges as an integral part of state universities, he was consciously breaking with the secular state-university philosophy of the American Midwest which divorced religious education from the state university. Murray's view was: "The new State universities in Western Canada, while non-sectarian in principle, desire to surround themselves with institutions representative of the churches. If the churches come while everything is in the formative stage, they will find it easier to secure the desired atmosphere."[14] For the churches, establishing a church college as part of the state university offered a unique advantage. Murray threw out an irresistible challenge to his fellow Presbyterians in an article he wrote for *The Presbyterian*, describing the proposal to establish a new theological college at the University of Saskatchewan. "At no place in the Province will it be possible to come into closer contact with every provincial interest than through their representatives in the student body. Can any great church afford to neglect this unrivalled opportunity of leaving its impress on the young men and women who will be leaders in its work in every corner of the province?"

As Murray well knew, the Presbyterians, prodded by him, were not likely to ignore such tempting bait. He also had to combat a still strong sentiment in the church that Winnipeg was the controlling centre for Presbyterian activities on the prairies. He pointed out how Saskatchewan was resisting what he called Winnipeg's pretensions and argued strongly for the existence of provincial jurisdictions in religious work as in other areas.

Nine years later, in 1921, he elaborated more fully his philosophy of the integration of church colleges into a state university. Believing that a university should represent all interests, he constructed four pillars to support the inclusion of church colleges:

a   Religion is the deepest and most far reaching of all interests. Therefore the University cannot cut itself from the religious life of the people.

b   The best traditions of University life may be traced back to religious associations. The Universities are the children of the churches.

c   Sound traditions in sport, sane views of life, of the relations of students to each other, and to the Community, must spring from a wholesome moral outlook which in turn is strengthened by religion.

d   The Y.M. and Y.W.C.A.s, the religious services, the life and conduct of sincere theological students deeply influence student opinion.[15]

Murray equally insisted to the church that it must not ignore the university. Future church leaders would receive the best preparation for the challenges of national life from association with students; co-operation between clergy and laity could best be assured by training the leaders of both together; with the leadership of the country increasingly coming into the hands of university graduates, the church had to ensure that its own key people received a university education. Some of Murray's arguments in favour of church colleges were definitely elitist, possibly a throwback to his absorption of the public school educational philosophy of Edward Thring, but he succeeded in his aim. His own state university definitely embraced the concept of religious colleges.

Pre-occupied though he was with the daily, often maddening, difficulties of constructing a new university, Walter Murray kept in regular contact with the Presbyterian unionists. He had played an influential part in shaping the structure of the new church, but now a larger task loomed—persuading his fellow Presbyterians to accept union.

The General Assembly of the Presbyterian Church received and approved the proposed basis for the union of the churches in 1910, but it could not proceed with the actual union until the individual presbyteries had voted their assent. Presbyterians themselves would decide the fate of church union by ballot in their individual congregations. The vote itself dragged on over the winter of 1911 and eventually produced an overall majority of nearly 70% in favour of union.

Walter Murray was as anxious as anyone in his church about the outcome of the vote. He scrutinized the results with exacting care. Even before the vote was completed, with the western presbyteries' results still to come, he predicted an overwhelming majority in favour of union. He proclaimed that "union seems to be almost a certainty" even if the earliest it could be implemented was 1913.[16] This public confidence masked an inner nervousness, for throughout the 1911 voting in the West, he hovered like the anxious leader of a political party waiting for the voting results to come in, as the slow process of voting by presbyteries snaked its way across the prairies. Murray wrote a number of prominent western Presbyterians to keep abreast of the returns, and then after he personally had compiled them, he sent the results to the editor of *The Presbyterian* for immediate publication.[17] He also made sure that the leading papers of the West had the Presbyterian voting tallies by personally sending them to the editors of the Saskatoon *Phoenix*, the *Moose Jaw Times*, the *Regina Leader*, the *Manitoba Free Press*, the *Calgary Herald* and both the Edmonton *Journal* and *Westland*. Once Murray discovered the strong desire of western Presbyterians for church union, he wanted to publicize this as widely as possible to sustain the unionist momentum. He continued work on analysing the election returns, comparing them both with the results of voting in the Canadian Presbyterian Church in 1874 and also with the federal election of 1911. His analysis was designed to place the 1911 Presbyterian vote in the most favourable context for union as well as to counter arguments by anti-unionists.[18]

From 1912 on, western Presbyterians were all for immediate implementation of church union. The brakes were being applied in the East. Murray's heart was with the West, but until 1914 he still hoped it would be possible to bring a united Presbyterian church into union with the Methodists and Congregationalists. As long as this hope remained, Murray stood in the front ranks of those who were willing to delay implementation as they searched for an acceptable compromise.

Murray did not confine himself to analysing the vote in the Presbyterian Church. The Union Committee within the Church, which had propelled the cause of union for the previous seven years, seemed to fall apart on the eve of the vote. The Convenor of the Committee died, and the Committee's Secretary moved from Toronto to Vancouver. Walter Murray wrote a series of letters to key members of the Committee and to the Moderator of the Church to find replacements and keep the Committee going.[19] He succeeded in his rescue operation, but he was forced to admit the following spring to a correspondent that "the union movement is sadly lacking in leadership, and many of us have been too scrupulous about keeping out of the fray in deference to the protests of the non-unionists, while they have taken every opportunity to put their side of the case before the people."[20]

While Walter Murray had avoided a blatant pro-Unionist propaganda campaign during the 1911 vote, he had skilfully presented the potential benefits of union for Saskatoon as typical of the advantages of union for the prairies in an article for the *Presbyterian Witness*, read by Presbyterians all across Canada. Knowing its readers, Murray stressed the practical side. "Give us Union and we can provide accommodation for every Presbyterian and Methodist and Congregationalist in the city in a convenient church. Without it there seems a probability that for some time as in the past groups of from twenty to two hundred will be turned away from the evening service in some buildings."[21] Murray was preaching to the converted in the West, but he did not win any new converts in the East, where the split within the Presbyterian Church was most pronounced.

When the Presbyterian Union Committee met in the spring of 1912 to assess the result of the vote, they found themselves in a weakened position and on the defensive. Their own leadership had been patched together, and they were facing a situation which offered no clear choice. They anxiously debated whether the vote in favour of union was sufficient to press for immediate implementation and reluctantly decided that unity within the Presbyterian Church took precedence over church union. This decision, as Murray later acknowledged, was an error since it gave opponents of church union more time to launch an offensive and left Presbyterian supporters of church union dangling.

It also left the Methodists and Congregationalists in an ambivalent situation. Both churches had endorsed the union proposals and now awaited a green light from the Presbyterians. Walter Murray had the task in June 1912 of explaining the Presbyterian dilemma to the Methodists. He did so in a lengthy letter which optimistically stressed the likelihood of bringing almost all the Presbyterians into a united church through a process of conciliation. The future would prove him and his fellow Unionists wrong, but Murray's belief in conciliation rested on the 1875 union of the Canadian Presbyterian Church in which negotiations, after a divided first vote, had led to near unanimity on the second ballot. Nevertheless, Murray's letter to Chancellor Burwash of the Methodist Church had an apologetic tone:

> I hope your church will not become impatient with us. We can quite well understand how irritating our actions must be to you, but we are placed in a very awkward position. We do not wish to bring about union by leaving a quarter or a third of our people outside of the united church, for we believe that patience and caution and consideration for the minority will in the end bring nearly all of them into union with us.[22]

Murray realized after the Presbyterian General Assembly in Edmonton in June 1912 that a second vote would be necessary, and this meant another substantial delay. He still felt, however, that the Presbyterians could be persuaded, and a year later he attended the next Presbyterian General Assembly held in Toronto hoping to succeed. A reporter covering the Assembly characterized him as an advocate of the "new thought." The *Toronto Daily Star* summarized Murray's position: "President Murray would go to the people again and get an overwhelming mandate for church union. It is a 'stateestical' speech and therefore highly convincing. The Assembly applauds it to the echo."[23]

Yet Murray's views were changing and his patience waning as the opposition to union within the Presbyterian Church strengthened and took on a more strident tone. Could he persuade all his fellow Presbyterians that Canada was changing and their church had to change with it? No longer could a church that aspired to be national in scope be the private preserve of a homogeneous group of transplanted Scots. As he said in a letter to the *Presbyterian Witness* early in 1914:

> Scottish conditions do not hold in Canada; nor do they hold in Nova Scotia any more than in Manitoba. . . . Our children may

witness a Presbytery of the United Church of Canada with a
Bodrug in the Moderator's chair, a Glowa at the Clerk's desk, on
the motion of Pyndykoski and with the recorded approval of
Ephraim Perich making application for the reception of the
Rev. Angus Neil MacTavish of the Presbyterian Church of
Scotland.

A union, whether 'chemical' or 'mechanical' or 'organic' is
taking place in the national life of Canada and the Presbyterian
Church true to her national traditions in Scotland is struggling
to adjust herself to the needs of the Canadian nation.[24]

The Presbyterian General Assembly of 1915 ordered that a second
vote be held in each presbytery on the question of union. Murray's
desire for a second vote was fulfilled, although the result was
disappointing. In spite of the fact that a large majority voted in
favour of union, slightly more than in 1912, there was a significant
increase in the number of those voting against. The 1915 ballot, far
from healing the divisions within the Presbyterian Church, widened
them to an unbridgeable chasm.

Walter Murray had observed this trend, evident particularly after
the formation of the Presbyterian Association for the Federation of
the Churches in 1911. The rallying of the "antis," as Murray and
other unionists referred to them, made the Unionists more militant,
and Murray was no exception. By 1914, even before the second vote,
his position had hardened considerably. He saw the choice then as
one between paying the price for Union in the loss of those opposed
to it, a price he was now willing to pay, or through further delay,
throwing away the opportunity for church union perhaps for a
generation or more. In a long analysis of the Unionist position in the
summer of 1914, he appeared as a veteran crusader, with a ringing
call to arms:

I believe we must be prepared to slough off the sentimentalists
and the 'stand patters' and to proceed. We will lose in all
probability about one-third of the men who have been in the
limelight of the battle against union, and possibly more of
those who dwell in cities and have accumulated wealth. On the
other hand we will gain in esprit and enthusiasm, and we will
receive some of the benefits that came to the Free Church at the
disruption. I do not believe that our entry with eighty percent of
the members into union with the Methodists and Congregationalists will weaken our influence in the United Church. On
the other hand, it seems to me it will make us stronger, for we

have faced an issue squarely and made a decision that has cost us much.[25]

He was too severe on his opponents when he branded them incapable of taking on the tasks that he saw as urgent priorities for a national church: "The regeneration of the city, the evangelization of the heathen and the Canadianization on Christian plans of the foreigner. . . ." He was also wrong in his prophecy of the future of a separate Presbyterianism: "Presbyterians in Canada within a generation will take on the character of the Wee Free, or the Auld Licht, or the Original Succession or one of those interesting historical institutions which remain as curious relics in the land. There is no life or spirit it seems to me in the forces which gather behind the old church." But his clarion call was unmistakable. "I expect that the majority for union will not be much, if any, greater than the last time; but if it is as great as it was before, I think we should have no hesitation in bringing the consummation about as quickly as possible."[26] From 1914 to 1925, Murray was both a spokesman for the West in the church union debates, determined that union would succeed even at the cost of losing some adherents, and an indefatigable political tactician in the struggle to achieve union.

The religious needs of the West were uppermost in his mind. Following the completion of negotiations on the basis for union of the three churches in 1908, a movement towards union churches had grown up. This was particularly popular in western Canada, and by 1914 the three negotiating churches—Methodist, Congregationalist, and Presbyterian—established an Advisory Committee to assist these fledgling union churches. Walter Murray acted as one of the Presbyterian representatives on this committee. When Murray attended the first meeting of the Advisory Committee, he found the union churches in the West angry and frustrated by the Presbyterian divisions. Even though Murray's attitude was less compromising towards his fellow Presbyterians, at the same time he was trying to restrain the militants in the union churches who argued that it was not necessary any more to wait for the formal authorization of the Presbyterian General Assembly and the passage of legislation to create a united church; a movement of union churches across the country would accomplish the same result. Murray strongly opposed this, and his work with the union churches in the West, especially during the war, encouraged them to continue but helped them to avoid a radical break with their parent churches.

The 1915 vote left the Presbyterian unionists in a more acute quandary than they had been after the 1912 vote. The majority vote was very strong, especially in the West, but the minority vote had grown substantially and was concentrated in the East. Canada was now embroiled fully in World War I. What should they do? Murray's good friend and close ally in the unionist fight, Robert Falconer, wrote to him at the beginning of 1916 with a shrewd and detailed statement of the unionist predicament:

> A number of us have been thinking with a good deal of anxiety as to the issue now that that Union vote is in. You will have seen that many are assuming that it is now all up with union and that the Assembly will do only one thing—reject union. It may be also that the Presbyteries will settle the matter by advising against and so keeping up the barrier. But that is what most of us here wish to prevent. The Presbyteries ought to give the Assembly a free hand, for it will have more information than any Presbytery and will have had longer to consider the consequences one way or the other. The vote is as you know, East against West. The comfortable old congregations in the East that would never discover any practical differences in their own affairs if union were effected and which know nothing of Western conditions are putting a cold hand upon the struggling West. It seems to me that the new Union churches of the West will in all probability turn to the Methodists rather than to us, and that we shall be regarded as hopelessly sectarian, and deservedly so, if a minority so artificially stimulated is to check our own development.[27]

Murray was definite in his stand after the 1915 vote. The presbyteries should be left alone. It was now up to the General Assembly to act before a movement for unionist churches or a western church caught fire. But in Murray's eyes, the West now was experiencing more serious problems because of the war's effects. The supply of student ministers had fallen and contributions were down, but for him there was a still more alarming question. Racial animosities had definitely been aggravated by the war. Murray saw religion and education as tools for the national assimilation of ethnic minorities. He and Edmund Oliver, the Principal of the Presbyterian College at Saskatchewan, had begun to campaign for church union on grounds of patriotism and Canadian nationalism. Political and sectarian differences weakening Canadianism were to be opposed; a national church appealing to all Canadians was the answer. This was the message he sent to Falconer in a letter which was expressly written for publication in *The Presbyterian:*

I believe that the church that would accept the Basis of Union or a similar basis and appeal to the west as a distinctly Canadian church would sweep the country. Great as is our pride in our Scottish descent and our Presbyterian ancestry, it is as nothing to our passion for Canada. The war has intensified our sense of peril and has accustomed us to make sacrifices.[28]

Before the Presbyterian General Assembly convened at Winnipeg in June 1916, Murray was part of an unofficial conference of western Christians who met in Regina in May. They drew up an appeal to the General Assembly stressing the need for unity and co-operation. Farmers' co-operative movements were singled out as "having a most pronounced educative effect upon the thinking of our people."[29] Local union churches were seen as the religious equivalent of the farmers' co-operative.

After his disappointment over the vote in 1915, Murray was delighted with the Winnipeg General Assembly's overwhelming majority for union, and he was content to wait until the end of the war to see the necessary legislation passed. But he and his fellow Presbyterian unionists were not prepared for the strength of the campaign launched by the Presbyterian opponents of union in the autumn of 1916. Murray had been instrumental in naming Robert Falconer as the convenor of the Presbyterian Union Committee in June 1916, and the two worked together during the fall to neutralize their opponents. The Unionists arranged to buy controlling interest of the main Presbyterian journal, *The Presbyterian*, for $15,000 to keep it out of the hands of the "antis." Murray, although financially strapped himself, contributed $100 and helped to raise more money for the purchase.

Murray was equally active in writing articles for *The Presbyterian*, countering the arguments of his Presbyterian opponents. These articles were directed primarily at defending the actions of the Winnipeg Assembly and trying to put the record straight.[30] At Falconer's request, he wrote an article on the reasons for union from a westerner's point of view. In it he reiterated his earlier themes of community interest, the spirit of co-operation, and the need for assimilation. He was more explicit about the impact of racial animosity than he had been before.

In western Canada one person in every three speaks another tongue than English; in large districts not one in ten of the adults knows English. In such places the English speaking people saw themselves not only outnumbered but divided up into petty groups by religious differences. They found the alien nationalist clinging as passionately to his religion as to his language, and they felt that national considerations drove them to seek union in religious matters with their neighbours. . . . Rightly or wrongly, the western Canadians' hopes of national supremacy are centred in the school and the churches. They will not tolerate sectarianism in their schools and they like it little better in their churches.[31]

The message was unambiguous. Patriotism required church unity.

Following the end of the war, the Presbyterian Church delayed any further consideration of church union until the General Assembly of 1921. After another heated debate between pro- and anti-unionist factions, the Assembly authorized church union by a 4-1 margin. Murray's enthusiasm for the union cause remained undiminished, and he continued to be one of its foremost Presbyterian partisans.

Writing in the first issue of the United Church's *The New Outlook* in 1925, Murray sketched a brief memoir of the union movement and hinted at the disarray among Presbyterian unionists in the later war years after the decision to delay the consummation of union until the end of the war: "At each delay the union craft lost impetus and drifted aimlessly until the war and some of its confusion was well over."[32] Murray himself had been embroiled in the problems of his own university, which led to his nervous breakdown in 1919. He had neither time nor energy for church union until 1920, when once again he threw himself into the fray with renewed vigour. Most of his spare time from 1921 to 1925, and some he could not afford to spare, was given over to the cause.

He made a special point of attending the Presbyterian General Assembly in 1921 to speak once again for church union. His postwar union campaign began before the Assembly met early in June with an anonymous article on the new alignments of prairie churches published in the *Manitoba Free Press*.[33] He had tried to publish it in the *Presbyterian Witness*, but neither the *Witness* nor *The Globe* would accept it for fear of stirring up more union controversy just before the General Assembly met.[34]

Murray's theme was that denominational loyalties were weakening before the religious challenge of the time, just as party loyalties had given way to Union Government in the midst of the crisis of war. The connection of political with religious events was a favourite theme for him, even though in this instance, as in others, his conclusion proved wrong. Denominational loyalties, especially those of the militant Presbyterians in eastern Canada, were strengthening.

Murray's example, however, was western Canada, and here he was on firmer ground. Nearly seventy union ministries had been created in the West by the summer of 1921. Murray saw in these the hope for the future, a wave which would sweep over rural Canada just as the United Farmers Movement was doing, another political parallel he used to support his case. The triumph of this union movement for Murray signified a united effort to battle vice and drunkenness and to encourage education. Equally important, he saw union churches in the West as valuable tools for instilling Canadian nationalism in an immigrant population of differing ethnic backgrounds. If the union movement failed, Murray feared the western union churches would "sink into parochialism and be indifferent and neglectful of those great currents which sweep through the national life, ennobling and enriching all who are caught in them."[35] He also warned the Presbyterian Assembly that defeating church union would pit the West against the East, "a serious matter both for the church and Canada."[36]

With the ratification of church union by the Assembly, Murray embarked on what became the final phase of the long struggle to achieve union. The Presbyterian minority who opposed church union now fought a rearguard battle to preserve the Presbyterian Church independent of a new United Church. Murray still saw a faint possibility of a reconciliation between the divided wings of the Presbyterian Church, and had there been any overtures on behalf of the anti-unionists, he would have jumped at them. There were not and Murray, along with his fellow Unionists, had to chart a course towards the goal of a Union Church that would minimize the effects of the split among the Presbyterians and attempt to carry as many Presbyterian congregations as possible into the new church.

Late in 1921 he wrote Dr. Pidgeon, the Convenor of the Joint Union Committee, with suggestions for its agenda. The first item had to be a conference to settle the policy of the three partner churches towards the new union congregations in western Canada. He also suggested the appointment of a committee to examine carefully the legal and legislative implications of church union and to recommend the steps which needed to be taken. Murray argued that this could and must be done without appearing to challenge the Presbyterian opponents of union.[37]

These two suggestions were accepted. A Committee was appointed to revise the terms for local union churches which had been drawn up originally in 1917, and Walter Murray was made its chairman. It met in September 1922 and accomplished its task, enabling these fledgling union churches to carry on their work while the contest over church union reached a climax. Murray was also a member of the legal subcommittee which set in motion the legislative changes required to create the new church.

The Unionists were preparing quietly to establish their united church without realizing their opponents, still determined to preserve an independent Presbyterian Church, were gathering their forces. Late in 1921 Murray continued to advocate a policy of moderation towards the "antis" and still believed, naively, that the split would not embitter relations. He wrote to Dr. Pidgeon:

> I have a feeling that moderation and wisdom, but firmness will win out. By firmness I mean tenacity by holding to our object. Wavering might serve to strengthen their attempts, but unless I am very much mistaken, there is less bitterness than there was, at least intense bitterness.[38]

As the Unionists prepared for a meeting of their Union Committee in the autumn of 1922 to discuss the legislative proposals they had been working on, they became aware that the Presbyterian Church Association was organizing a coast-to-coast campaign to counter the union movement. A national office was established in Toronto, and what the unionists saw as a propaganda campaign directed against them was getting underway. This forced the Unionists' hands. Murray's friends, including Dr. Pidgeon, the Convenor, urged him to attend the Unionist meeting. Pidgeon even sent a handwritten letter with a strong personal plea: "To me your help and personal counsel are simply invaluable and I feel far more deeply than I can say the strength it brings to me."[39]

It proved impossible for Murray to attend the meeting, but he and the other unionists now prepared to mount their own propaganda campaign. The battle was not over, as Murray now realized, yet he remained optimistic. "There will be not a little passion and many things said might be left unsaid but if we keep our tempers, the final result will be eminently satisfactory. The general public think the question is dead but the violence of the attacks of the Antis will indicate that there is considerable life 'in the old dog' yet."[40]

Murray's help was enlisted to recruit Principal E.H. Oliver of St. Andrew's College at the University of Saskatchewan to direct the unionist efforts for the first five months of 1923, leading up to a Presbyterian General Assembly. Pidgeon and Murray's old friend,

Robert Falconer, both pressed him to release Oliver to tour Ontario in order to combat the "languidness or indifference on the part of many laymen" towards church union.[41] Oliver turned down the request but agreed instead to deliver a series of addresses in the East. Murray wrote that one of Oliver's reasons for rejecting the idea was a belief that a westerner would be unacceptable for the task. "There is a great tendency to decry and discount what the west says on any national matter."[42]

If Oliver could not escape the involvement in this renewed propaganda war, neither could Murray. He was asked to write a number of pamphlets and articles for the Unionists early in 1923 and he complied with every request. The strongest was a tract trying to head off the idea of still another vote in the Presbyterian Church on church union.[43] In this he listed all the reasons against another ballot, concluding "it would be utterly useless, for it would in no wise settle the question. The active opponents of Union do not recognize any vote for Union as valid."[44]

The pamphlet ended with another of Murray's nationalist sermons. Church union was in the national interest, and opposition to it was quite simply unpatriotic.

> So far as Canada is concerned, unity of organization is essential to the national life. The immense distances, sparse population, and vast, void spaces, all tend to separate the people, and any movement that fosters the spirit of national unity and will promote and intensify the national consciousness is of the highest value and should receive universal support. There are class and sectional unions that tend to national unrest and disintegration **but the union of the churches is in the highest and largest sense constructive and beneficent.**[45]

As the pressure of the struggle waged by the two camps of the Presbyterian Church intensified in the first half of 1923, Murray was hard put to respond to all the demands on his time. He was consulted about the legislation that was being drafted, and he received impassioned pleas to attend vital meetings of the Unionist Committee.[46] The illness of his brother and his university responsibilities kept him from the Unionist meeting in April, but he was present at the next Presbyterian General Assembly in June 1923 at Port Arthur as one of the unionists' most forceful and persuasive speakers. Again the vote in favour of union was carried by a large margin.

Once the Unionists had overcome the hurdle of the Presbyterian General Assembly, there remained the task of getting legislation passed in each provincial legislature and in the federal Parliament to create the new church. The Presbyterian non-unionists were no less determined to protect their own interests, and it was by no means clear how the congregations would divide between the opposed camps. Murray was a key figure in the Saskatchewan provincial campaign along with two ministers, Dr. Wylie Clark and Dr. Murdoch MacKinnon, and his close colleague and friend, Principal Oliver of St. Andrew's College. Murray chaired this Church Union Legal Committee for the province.

The strategy of the unionists was to have the legislation passed first in the prairie provinces, where the least resistance was anticipated, in the hope that this would build a momentum and influence the debate in Ontario and Quebec, where passage of legislation was much less certain. Saskatchewan was the second province to pass the enabling legislation. Murray was congratulated on his "singular achievement in Regina. That the Bill passed the Private Bills Committee without essential amendment in the face of Premier Martin's attack and Judge Robson's and Judge Farrell's persistent fillubustering [sic] is . . . something to be thankful for."[47]

The success had not been accidental. Murray and his Committee had mounted an intensive lobbying campaign of all members of the provincial legislature. Murray drafted the letters which were signed by the Secretary of the Unionist Committee and, in addition, he wrote a number of personal letters to key members, appealing to their political rather than to their religious instincts. To one, he wrote, "Union has made great advances on the prairies; outside of the towns and cities there are few strictly Methodist or Presbyterian congregations. It will be a disaster if all congregations that have brought about local union in the hope of larger union, should be forced to revert to the old condition of groups and cliques and competition in church matters."[48]

He also took care at the same time to write to influential Saskatchewan federal politicians like Senator Calder and W.R. Motherwell, Minister of Agriculture. Calder was a reluctant convert, but he had agreed with the force of Murray's argument that church union was essential for the west. Murray had warned him, "If it does not go through we will find the rural congregations in the west break up and become almost secular congregations and the whole country will drift back to an indifference of religion that will leave its mark for generations."[49] In these appeals to politicians, Murray argued that the social and moral fabric of rural prairie communities was at stake in the church union controversy. Whether or not the politicians inclined to Murray's view, in the end they were prepared to vote the necessary legislation in Regina and in Ottawa.

After the legislation was passed, it was left to individual congregations in the Presbyterian Church to decide whether they would join the new United Church or remain with the Presbyterian Church. Murray threw himself into the cause of trying to win over doubtful congregations with the same missionary zeal he had displayed from the earliest days of the unionist movement. He volunteered to go to Edmonton if he was needed; he was invited to visit Calgary in December 1924, and he spoke in Prince Albert early in December. He and other Unionists failed after intense efforts to win St. Paul's Church in Prince Albert, but he was prepared to answer any call even when the cause appeared lost.

Neither in the West nor in Ontario did the results meet the Unionists' expectations, but Murray's own assessment in a letter to Robert Falconer stressed the positive.

> The cold weather is cooling Church Union on the prairies. We have had two or three surprises in Saskatchewan, but on the whole matters have turned out as well as we expected. . . . The results in Western Ontario and Pictou County are considerably worse than we expected, although reports that come through private individuals are cheering to the extent that in many of these congregations the active working forces are for union.[50]

Murray shared in the spiritual joy of the religious service held on June 10, 1925 in Toronto to celebrate the consummation of what he regarded as the greatest religious union in the country's history. He felt both triumph and relief, yet his work for the unionists did not end in 1925. He was named to the Dominion Church Property Commission in 1927, which was charged with dividing the contested assets between the Presbyterian and United Churches.

Here he faced difficult technical and legal issues. What were the assets of the church colleges and how could they be divided? Murray's solution was to request a statement of assets and liabilities for each one, valued as of June 1925, and then divide them. While being fair to both sides, he had also to be watchful of the interests of the United Church. Finally, the contentious and difficult task of separating the assets was accomplished. Murray's particular job on the Commission had been to decide the division of mission and extension funds and college endowments. He could not satisfy everybody, and some of the Commission's decisions were controversial, but considering the bitterness preceding union, the settlement of the outstanding claims was a relatively peaceful process.

With the achievement of church union, Walter Murray's church commitments were greatly reduced. His national role as a pioneering missionary working to build a new Canadian church was over; he had accomplished his goal. His involvement had been deep and intense, his contribution large and vital. Now his participation in church matters was less, but he was still actively involved. He continued to serve on the Education Board of the United Church for theological and other colleges, he chaired the Board of Governors of St. Andrew's College in Saskatoon, and his advice continued to be sought by ministers seeking a change in pastorate and by churches seeking a minister. As his close friend Clarence MacKinnon wrote in 1926, ".'Old habits cling closely and when in trouble we all turn to the 'good Walter'."[51] His powerful support was ready at any time to defend church colleges when they seemed to be vulnerable. During the Depression he helped to convince the United Church not to abandon its colleges at the new universities on Canada's prairies.

His years in Saskatoon were closely associated with Knox Church, just as his Halifax years were linked with St. Matthews. He was an elder of Knox from 1911 to his death in 1945 and a member of the Board of Trustees for more than twenty years. When he died in 1945, the Session and Congregation paid tribute to the church's "oldest, most faithful and active member" and recognized "the persistence, tolerance, understanding and statesmanship so ably employed in . . . the bringing into being of the United Church of Canada."[52] The baptismal font in Knox is dedicated to the memory of Walter Murray. With his love of children and his devotion to his church, nothing could have pleased him more or have been a more appropriate symbol of his lifelong work.

■

Chapter 9

The Sunny Years

The decade of the twenties dawned as bright and clear as a prairie morning for Walter Murray. His breakdown was behind him and would not recur in any way for the rest of his life. Moreover his recovery was complete from the surgery for the removal of his appendix. No doubt the cure and the recovery were aided by a long rest of more than nine months. He had come back to Saskatoon in January 1920, but he did not return to his desk and take up the duties of President again until September, when the new university session commenced. It was an active period of rest. Murray corresponded with other university presidents on university salaries and arranged a new scale which the Board of Governors approved the following October. He remained a member of the University Board of Governors and of its executive. But the break from the day-to-day administration of the university, which Dean Ling managed for the year, was just what Murray needed to recover fully his physical strength and intellectual energy. In 1920 Murray was fifty-four. The war and the crisis were over. He was free once again to take up the task, central to his life, of building the University of Saskatchewan.

The picture of Walter Murray as a man involved in all aspects of the university's work and deeply interested in the community and its people was caught by a reporter from the *Winnipeg Tribune* who sketched a portrait of him in 1925.

> I first saw Mr. Walter C. Murray, president of the University of Saskatchewan, in his peculiarly cluttered office at Saskatoon— cluttered mainly with books and pictures and serried volumes of annual reports on everything in Canada, with samples of school equipment, curious handwork from some immigrant settlement—a vivid miscellany, significant of an active, interested and sympathetic mind.

> As he talks in his quiet but vibrant and slightly nasal voice the thought is likely to come to you that he has long ago forgotten

that there is any such person as Walter Murray. He has but one passion and that is a passion for the work of others. Anything anybody is doing interests him intensely—whether it be a child's first scratches with pen or pencil, or a vast scientific investigation involving years of effort. He is Saskatchewan's deepest well-spring of enthusiasm. Quick to recognize and praise good work, even if his silences are fruitful of suggestions for more and better work.[1]

Murray was also freed from the mental agony of the crisis which had consumed his time and led to his breakdown. Both he and the Board of Governors had been completely exonerated by the judicial inquiry. From 1920 until his retirement, neither his reputation nor his authority as president was seriously questioned. He could concentrate completely on building the university. This embraced not only adding to the physical plant but expanding departments, adding new faculties, and extending the work of the university in the larger constituency of the province.

The main parts of the building program had been approved prior to the war but postponed on account of it. Murray had pressured the government in 1918 to start the long-delayed Physics Building. It was completed in 1921, the first of the university's postwar constructions. In 1925 the Engineering Building burned down. Out of necessity it had to be replaced immediately. Because it was under-insured, there was an extra cost to the university and the government of $200,000. A Chemistry Building, completed by the middle of the decade and "the most lavish of the early University buildings," was an obvious source of pride for Murray.[2] Other additions included the observatory and the memorial gates which he described as "the two most beautiful structures on the campus."[3] Without generous government support this building program could not have been undertaken. Yet Murray was frustrated both at the slow pace of construction and particularly at the lack of any finances to build an Arts Building. He complained in his Annual Report of 1924-25 that the Saskatchewan government's support for the university's building program was much less than Alberta and Manitoba had provided for their universities. The lack of an Arts Building was a constant burr to Murray since it appeared to reflect both on his own and the university's priorities.

It had been an integral part of his vision for the university from the very beginning. He had visualized the university as a place where the Humanities and Sciences, especially Agriculture, provided a mutually reinforcing education for the people of Saskatchewan. The government had been quick and generous in providing the funds necessary to build an agricultural facility, but the Arts had not been looked after. Murray hinted at his frustration in his Annual Report for 1920-21 saying, "The Arts Building, the crown of our present group, has long been hoped for and partially promised."[4] In his mind and with his own solid background in the Humanities the idea of the Arts Building as the crown of the initial building scheme of the university was a natural reflection of his own educational priorities. Yet the long-promised Arts Building did not materialize during his lifetime. His failure to get it built was the greatest personal disappointment of his presidency, but it had not been for lack of effort on his part. He had pressed the Board on numerous occasions to begin construction, but each time external circumstances intervened. Twice during the 1920s and 1930s the time appeared propitious. But the first time the funds earmarked for it were used to rebuild the burned Engineering Building. Finally in 1930 it seemed at last that the building would be constructed. Plans were approved and tenders submitted, but the Depression intervened. There was simply not enough money to pay for it, and the project was postponed again. Sadly for him, Murray's crown faded into a mirage.

Murray long remembered Premier Scott's quotation from Benjamin Disraeli in Scott's address at the formal opening of the university in 1913 that "nothing so truly represents a people as a public building."[5] The buildings of the University of Saskatchewan were a source of pride for all the people of the province. In constructing them Murray sought functional efficiency and architectural excellence. He told the university's architect in 1924 that the buildings "have won the admiration of every visitor."[6] One visitor was Murray's longtime friend and former colleague from Dalhousie, Archibald MacMechan, who wrote a column for the *Halifax Herald* in 1927 describing a train trip across Canada in which Saskatoon and its university were an obvious highlight. The university "has a noble situation on the high bluff overlooking the river and it possesses the finest complex of buildings of any university in Canada." He named Walter Murray as the man responsible for this and concluded, "It is not given to every man to erect such a mausoleum for himself."[7]

For Murray the buildings were important, and he worked very hard on the details connected with their construction. However, he did not view them as a personal monument, much less as a mausoleum. They were important only to serve his larger purpose—they were to stand as the home of higher education in Saskatchewan. Their beauty, stability, and permanence symbolized what Murray hoped would be the enduring characteristics of the province's university.

His credo for education was simple and clear:

1 What is best for the pupil? How can he be assisted in making the most of his talents?

2 How can the largest return in wealth, population and industry be obtained for each dollar spent on education. . .? We educate our children for their own sakes. If a boy or girl can become a good painter, a good musician, poet, author or scholar, or has a genius for science or invention it is his right to have the opportunity to make the most of his talents.[8]

Painter, musician, poet, author, scholar, scientist and inventor—for each his vision provided a plan, a place, and an opportunity to develop. This required new colleges, schools, and faculties as well as departments with appropriate accommodation and staff.

Murray's vision had a greater chance of fulfillment during the 1920s than at any other period of his presidency. It was an expansionist era, and the pressure for growth came not only from one man's personal vision. Enrollment increases forced the pace of expansion. Before the 1920s, the university's peak enrollment had been reached in 1915-16. By 1920-21, the figure had nearly doubled, and by the end of the decade it would double again.

The enrollment growth and the university's expansion at the beginning of the 1920s coincided with a period of depressing economic conditions. Murray wrote:

The conditions here are worse than I have ever seen them. And the most disquietening feature of all is the loss of hope. . . . Farmers who have never experienced trouble for the last ten or twelve years, now say they are practically left with the original land and some of their equipment; cleaned out they report. Many will be forced to leave their farms; quite a number are doing it voluntarily. . . .[9]

Privately, he acknowledged to President Tory of the University of Alberta that the provincial universities were "making demands in excess of the capacities of the Provinces to meet them."[10] Without an early improvement in the prosperity of the West, the universities would be forced to moderate their expansionary plans. The same message came to Murray from Premier Dunning, who pointed out at the beginning of 1923, "This is scarcely the time for expansion. . . ."[11] There may have been concern about "difficult times," but new buildings had been built and building continued.

Economic conditions greatly improved during the latter half of the decade. Grants for operating expenses increased substantially in this period, but the building impetus slowed down. The only major building erected was Field Husbandry. Funds for buildings and equipment actually declined considerably from the spending pattern of the earlier years. As an example, for the year ending June 30, 1929, the total expenditure for buildings and equipment was $61,556.45. This very modest sum was for an exceptionally prosperous year in Saskatchewan. Murray's timing in capital projects was unfortunate. By the time the provincial economy had recovered in the latter part of the decade, the initial thrust of university expansion had faded.

The enrollment explosion by itself put great stress on the administration of the university. During the crisis of 1919 both Murray's supporters and his opponents had questioned whether he could and should carry the burden essentially on his own shoulders. The response of the Board of Governors was to appoint a business manager to relieve the President of much of the onerous detail necessary to the operation of what was now a large and complicated institution.

Even this change had to be broached indirectly to the President. Donald MacLean, the Board's lawyer, asked C.J. Mackenzie, the Dean of Engineering and a cousin of Murray's, to negotiate with him. Then and later, Mackenzie was noted for tact, diplomacy, and negotiating skill. He enjoyed Murray's complete trust. On a Sunday morning he reported back to MacLean, "Murray had seen the light."[12]

The man appointed, Colonel F.M. Riches, was a war veteran and former teacher. He proved to be a successful and long-serving administrator, but his choleric temper did not always make things easy for Murray. In 1926 Riches quarrelled with the Saskatoon postmaster over the responsibility of the farm foreman for mail delivery to the farm workman. The issue went to the president, who soothed the ruffled feathers and made sure the mail was delivered.[13]

Riches was diligent in his search for economies. Whether he succeeded in a population control and economy program with guinea pigs remains unclear, but he tried. In 1928 he informed Murray: "We have in the Animal Diseases Laboratory approximately 300 guinea pigs. I understand that 100 would be sufficient if influenza should break out in the department. These guinea pigs cost over $50.00 per month to feed and take one-third of the janitor's time to feed and clean. The total cost is not less than $75.00 per month."[14]

Riches was equally vigilant in monitoring the oversights of faculty members. In 1927 he forwarded a report to Murray about lights found burning and a red-hot electric stove in Professor Morton's office at

8:15 p.m. on a Saturday evening. "This is the second time in two years that this stove has been left burning and in view of the inflammable nature of much of the material stored in the professor's office with the library adjoining, I am reporting the matter to you."[15] The inflammable material in part consisted of ten years' work on Morton's *A History of the Canadian West to 1870-71*, which was published in 1939.

The farm operations, the maintenance of the buildings, and the operation of the university book store were some of the burdens removed from the president's immediate concern. Riches and Murray formed a successful team. This meant that Murray could devote his considerable energies to the university's future without undue concern. The guinea pigs, the farm workers, and the red-hot stoves as well as the lights would be looked after.

Freeing Murray of some of the onerous administrative burdens was one of the Board of Governors' actions arising from the public controversy that accompanied the firing of the professors in 1919. There was another matter that surfaced and was of great concern to the Board. It became evident that the administration of the university, the Governors and the President, did not command the support of influential sections of the Saskatoon public. Murray himself was partly to blame for this.

Mr. F.F. MacDermid, Q.C., who had practiced law in Saskatoon from 1908 and was still active in 1978, explained the problem:

> It was well known in Saskatoon that Murray favoured Regina [as the site for the university]. This prejudiced his standing with the group that was most active in promoting Saskatoon, the mayor, leading businessmen and the political leaders. Murray made little or no effort to cultivate this group in the years that followed. He was deeply involved with the university group and the church group but not with the social leaders. . . . The simple way he lived affronted the social elite.[16]

Perhaps it came as a shock to members of the Government and members of the Board of Governors who were from places other than Saskatoon to discover that the Saskatoon community was less than wholly supportive of the university administration. The Governors evidently decided to do something to improve this. In May 1921, the Board Chairman, James Clinkskill, hosted a very large luncheon at the university. The Rotary and Kiwanis Clubs were there "en masse," and the directors along with a number of members of the Chamber of Commerce as well as representatives of the Canadian Club were his guests. Before giving the visitors a tour of the university, Clinkskill used the opportunity to praise the university president. When he averred that the Board had made no mistake in their selection, "the audience greeted this remark with considerable applause."[17] Murray, however, did not alter his habits. Again the judgment of Mr. MacDermid:

> Murray built a fine university. At the end of his term it had the best reputation of any in the west. Murray did not change after the row. He continued to move in the university and church circles and did not cultivate the social group. He was never careful to keep in with the leading women, nor did his wife.[18]

This was confirmed in interviews and in conversation with Murray's daughter, Dr. Jean Murray. The Board attempted through public relations to do what Murray either would not or did not do.

Professional Schools

One of the essential elements in Walter Murray's philosophy of the state university was the inclusion of professional schools. He had elaborated his ideas in a Convocation Address at the University of Manitoba in 1913. "A University may be likened unto a tree whose trunk is the Liberal Arts, whose taproot is Research, and whose branches are the professional schools. From the Liberal Arts and Sciences it derives its stability; from the taproot of Research its vitality; and its utility is manifest in the professional schools."[19] Murray went on to argue that the rivalries of cities and the rush of professions seeking incorporation under provincial statute created confusing conditions which could be untangled only by making the state university in each province the agency for testing and licensing professional practitioners. This would be the first step. The second and more important step would be for the state to ensure there was an adequate supply of professionals in each profession—medicine, law, dentistry, accounting, pharmacy and architecture—through the creation of professional schools within the state university. Murray gave this address in Manitoba, but his words were aimed at Regina. He ended with a special plea to western Canadian lawyers:

> Is it not high time that the training for the legal profession ceased to be a clerical apprenticeship, and became a rigorous, comprehensive and exhaustive study of legal principles and their application—a study not one whit inferior to that of medicine? The highest interests of the profession no less than those of the public demand that the school of law should take its place beside the schools of medicine, of engineering and of the

other professions within the university and come under the fertilizing influence of the pure sciences and the liberal arts.[20]

He was really striking out at the rival claims of Regina where the Benchers of the Law Society had decided to establish a Law School "notwithstanding all our arguments and pleadings," as he wrote to his friend, A. Stanley MacKenzie, Principal of Dalhousie.[21]

But the Government in 1913 had also authorized the formation of a Law School within the university. Murray then envisaged a long struggle taking "perhaps ten years for our school to get to the top."[22] The root of the rivalry was of course the decision to locate the provincial university in Saskatoon, a decision which infuriated a number of people in Regina, many of them lawyers. Organizing and carrying on a law school in Regina served the dual purpose of keeping the control of the profession where the largest group of the province's lawyers was located and possibly preventing the University of Saskatchewan from establishing a viable school.

The latter aim failed. Walter Murray was both determined and persuasive. He also managed to staff the University Law School with competent teachers, headed by Arthur Moxon who became the School's first Dean and one of Murray's closest allies in the university. Moxon developed the Law School and co-operated with the Regina Benchers so that in the ten years predicted by Murray, the problem of the rival law schools in Saskatchewan had been resolved.

Murray proudly announced to the University Convocation in 1923:

> Perhaps the most notable event of the year has been the action of the Benchers of the Law Society in turning over to the University Law School the responsibility for all legal instruction and in requiring students who article hereafter to attend a recognized Law School. This action centralizes Legal Education at the University and enlarges the scope of its usefulness. Henceforth the examinations for admission to the Bar will be under the joint direction of the Law Society and the University.[23]

He went on to point out that with the affiliation of the provincial Law Society to the university, each of the province's ten incorporated professions was connected to the university, fulfilling Murray's aim of embracing the professions within the state university. He did not have to fear any longer the threat of professional societies competing with the university. The growth of the professional schools during the 1920s followed the establishment of degree programs. Degree courses in Pharmacy began in 1921 and in Accounting in 1917, although the first degree in Accounting was not awarded until 1923.

Murray's own family background equipped him well to understand the complexities of how to provide the proper medical education in Saskatchewan. He was the son of a country doctor who had first apprenticed and then had travelled to New York to complete his medical education at the forerunner of the Columbia Medical School. Walter Murray's family memories undoubtedly influenced his strong conviction of what constituted a proper medical education.

Even before the 1920s, Murray had tried to obtain external financial aid to establish a medical school in the university. He applied to the Rockefeller Foundation in 1919. In the memorandum of application he stressed that "the need for a Medical School in the University of Saskatchewan at Saskatoon is great."[24] He then went on to set out the reasons. Provincial laboratory facilities for testing and research were inadequate as was the number of doctors, especially in rural areas of the province. Many rural women who travelled long distances to hospitals were found "to have suffered from neglect at childbirth." Both the people and the livestock of the province required adequate facilities. Murray pointed out that "it is inevitable that these plains should supply large stocks of animal and plant foods. In these conditions diseases attack animals and plants, sometimes with great virulence." These were the arguments justifying his proposal to locate within the university "a Health Institute for the Province where the best laboratory facilities should be available for the investigation, prevention and eradication of those diseases that attack man and his sources of food supply." Murray also alluded to the problem of immigrant rural communities which had difficulty attracting graduates of eastern medical schools. Non-English students could not afford to travel east for medical training, but if "Western men," as Murray put it, "could begin the long and expensive medical training at home, where the convenience is greater and the cost less, they would without doubt finish it elsewhere, if necessary."[25]

Plans already had been made. Fourteen acres had been reserved for a community hospital to be supported by both the city and the university. Bacteriological and Pathological laboratories had been built, and a professor of Bacteriology had been appointed. In 1919 Murray did not envisage a complete Medical faculty because he informed the Rockefeller Foundation that the subjects of Medicine, Surgery, and Obstetrics would "not be attempted." Even though support from the Rockefeller Foundation was not forthcoming, Murray went ahead in the 1920s with plans for pre-medical classes.

At the Convocation of 1927, he announced that a Medical School had been created in the hope that more Saskatchewan students would enter medicine and return to practise in rural areas where practitioners were desperately needed. His own diagnosis was clear and, in a sense, prophetic.

> Until a system of State medicine makes more adequate provision for the needs of our rural communities we should do all that we can to encourage Saskatchewan men and women to prepare themselves for service at home since they are familiar with our conditions and take pride in our province.[26]

He still opposed the introduction of a full medical course at Saskatchewan because the hospital facilities were not, in his opinion, adequate "for all the requirements of clinical work." "What we do, we wish to be well done. We can offer as good courses for the pre-clinical years as any Medical school."[27]

In keeping with his views on the university creating health facilities for both humans and animals, Murray planned for a Veterinary School at the University, although he did not live to see its actual appearance. Writing to his fellow President, Tory of Alberta, in 1924, Murray set out Saskatchewan's bargaining position, as approved by the University Council and Senate, in any future expansion of professional schools on the prairies. Saskatchewan would not compete with Manitoba in Electrical Engineering or with Alberta in Mining. Medicine would be restricted, and Alberta's monopoly in Dentistry would be respected as would Manitoba's in Business Administration. What Saskatchewan wanted in return was to have a Veterinary School for the prairies.[28]

Five years later he developed the argument more fully, again writing to Tory who was now the President of the National Research Council. Murray wanted the backing of the chief federal scientific body for his cause. "I think Saskatoon is the logical place for the development of special veterinary work on the prairies. We have built and equipped a laboratory for Animal Diseases and have a staff of three veterinarians and a technician. . . . I do not think that any other place on the prairies has given as much attention and has made equal provision for the study of animal diseases as we have and consequently if one place is to be preferred to another the preference should be given to Saskatoon."[29] In another letter Murray emphasized that Saskatchewan was the logical place to focus western research on animal diseases.[30] The groundwork for the future school had been done. It was left to a later generation to bring this element of Murray's vision to fruition.

Education was the other profession which Murray laboured hard to bring under university control, but he was not able to achieve what he desired. Murray had introduced and taught the first Education courses at Dalhousie. He had also frequently written for the leading education journal in the Maritimes. He came to Saskatchewan convinced that the training of teachers was a function only the university could perform. In November 1908 he proposed and the University Senate adopted a plan for the academic structure of the university. Listed as number 3, and preceded only by Arts and Agriculture, was "A College of Education with practice schools."[31] Even before Murray presented his plan to the Senate, he had told his wife of his determination to take over the training of teachers completely and totally. Part of his failure to achieve this must be laid right on his own desk.

He did not succeed in winning over the key officials in the Department of Education to his plan. His ideas, which he made no secret of, undoubtedly made him enemies in the Department of Education. Augustus Ball, the longtime Deputy Minister in the Department, and the Hon. Sam Latta, Minister of Education in the 1920s, were two of Walter Murray's least favourite people.[32] In this struggle Murray had no one to rely on other than himself to carry on the negotiations.

When he tersely announced the formation of a College of Education to the 1927 Convocation, there was a scarcely disguised tone of disappointment.[33] The university intended to supplement, not duplicate, the work of the Normal Schools. That was not what Walter Murray wanted, but it was all he could accomplish. The Education Department successfully fended off the best efforts of the University of Saskatchewan to wrest control of teacher education from it during Murray's tenure of office and well beyond. Next to his failure to provide an Arts Building, the inability to obtain for the University of Saskatchewan the training of the province's teachers must rank as one of the key personal disappointments of his presidency.

Art

The postwar era gave Walter Murray an opportunity he had long wanted, to develop the Fine Arts at the University of Saskatchewan. His Annual Report of 1921 lamented the lack of paintings and sculpture on the campus and made a strong case for the lifelong civilizing effect on students of literary and artistic influences gained at university. "It is difficult to overestimate the value of Literature and the Fine Arts in giving that tincture of Culture that distinguishes the gentleman from the savage."[34] He urged the university to embark on a program of art collection and leadership in the Fine Arts.

> Hitherto, the University has followed, not led. It has manifested a benevolent interest in the Provincial Festivals and has hoped for fine paintings. It is well for us to remember that the University must lead in the recognition of the Fine Arts, not only as instruments of culture but as the expression of the highest forms of human genius.[35]

Almost immediately he set about procuring for the university those "hoped for fine paintings." Some measure of his activity and his success is evident from the excellent catalogue of the university's permanent art collection, published in 1980. This lists approximately five hundred paintings of which twenty percent (or more than one hundred) were acquired during Murray's presidency. He purchased many himself. As the catalogue notes, "The president enjoyed a great deal of discretionary power and Dr. Murray was able to proceed on an enviably individual basis. His interest in art was more than nominal. . . ."[36] It certainly was. Murray's acquisitions enabled the university collection to constitute "an almost continuous record of artistic production in this region from its beginnings."[37]

His search was not confined to fine paintings alone. He delighted in finding and encouraging promising artists. A Maidstone rancher, Gus Kenderdine, arrived in Saskatoon one day in 1921 with two paintings which he took to the Tyrie Art Shop. The owner, an Englishman, had a sharp and discerning eye for talent, and he saw this in Kenderdine's work. He telephoned Walter Murray, who had a long talk with Kenderdine. This resulted in Kenderdine being given space to paint among the rafters in the attic of the new Physics Building.[38] From this beginning can be traced the development of the university's art program, the creation of the Emma Lake summer artists' workshop, and the environment that spawned a distinctive Saskatchewan artistic community.

Murray later gave a public tribute to Kenderdine's art in 1936, revealing an intimate acquaintance and knowledgeable appreciation of the artist's contribution:

> He has taken subjects of little interest to the passerby; the rough trail, the flat prairie, the tangled underbrush, the log house of the homesteader and with skilful draftsmanship, play of light and shade and apt touches of colour has revealed to us their beauty. Witness the Sutherland Trail, The Land of Promise, Okema, The Homestead. Krieghoff has preserved for posterity

the beauty of the homely scenes in the life of the Habitant of Eastern Quebec; Kenderdine we believe is doing the same for the pioneering homesteader of the prairies. While Kenderdine has been the most successful with the least promising of subjects, he has risen to eminence in his studies of the great trees, the majesty of the mountains, the broad river and the sheltered lake.[39]

Murray was connected in an unusual way with another famous Saskatoon artist, Ernest Lindner. Lindner, after emigrating from Austria, had spent two years on a farm at Markinch, Saskatchewan as a labourer, doing the first physical labour of his life. In the fall of 1928, he decided to spend the winter in a lumber camp and went to Saskatoon en route. Walter Murray came to the house where Lindner was staying and offered him a job at the university. First Lindner kept records of egg production in the hen house, and then he produced displays for the Better Farming Train. From this unique beginning at the university, Lindner blossomed into one of Canada's most distinguished artists. Murray assisted in this transformation as Lindner readily admits: "I must say my whole life took a different turn partly because of Dr. Murray; being encouraged by a man of such stature. He actually gave me commissions. That was very important."[40]

Lindner's assessment of the university art collection during Murray's era is perceptive. "I think it was the best which could at that time be done.... He was an older man and he was very conservative in his taste and so on, but, yes, he was the first in Saskatchewan who really promoted art. . . . It is quite a historical collection. . . . Henderson was a very good painter. . . . Kenderdine was a very capable painter. I learned a lot just sitting around in his studio watching him work."[41]

Another artist whom Murray aided personally was Nicholas de Grandmaison, a Russian aristocrat and eccentric who came to Canada in 1923. In 1926 he first saw the Plains Indians and began to do chalk pastels of them. His Indian portraits are singular and romanticized, a European portrayal of a romantic Canadian West. There are fifteen of Grandmaison's works in the University of Saskatchewan collection, and eight are labelled "source unknown." Walter Murray probably purchased most, if not all, for the university, two as a personal gift. He may well have had a hand in Grandmaison's growing reputation across the country. Murray served on a Royal Commission with Edward Beatty, the longtime head of the C.P.R., and very likely introduced Beatty to Grandmaison's work. It was an Indian pastel bought by the C.P.R.

which established Grandmaison as a leading Canadian artist. Grandmaison sent Murray a reproduction in 1936 and thanked him for being "one of my first patrons."[42]

James Henderson was another Saskatchewan artist patronized by Murray. Correspondence in Murray's papers documents a number of commissions Murray gave the artist. A few were official portraits, but most were paintings of Indians. In 1925, on Murray's initiative, the university commissioned Henderson to paint twelve portraits of Indians representing the prairie tribes of Saskatchewan and Alberta. Murray had in mind a parallel to Paul Kane's work in the nineteenth century. Because of ill health and the fact that some of the pictures were privately purchased, only nine were completed, of Indians from the Piegan, Blackfoot, Stoney, Sioux, Cree, and Blood tribes. After receiving a number of paintings in 1929, Murray voluntarily offered an increased price because "they so far surpassed our expectations."[43] Murray acknowledged that Henderson's interpretation of Indian character had given him especial pleasure.

Nineteen of Lindner's works are in the university collection, twenty-four of Kenderdine's, fifteen of Grandmaison's, and fifteen of Henderson's. Arthur Lismer, Lawren Harris, A.Y. Jackson, C.W. Jeffries, Marion Long, and Suzor-Coté are also represented. In each case their works first appeared in the collection during Murray's time, although additions were made later. Four artists patronized by Murray—Lindner, Kenderdine, Henderson and Grandmaison—are included in the National Gallery collection in Ottawa. Murray's promotion of Saskatchewan art reaped national benefits.

Lindner's comment that Murray was the first in Saskatchewan to actively promote its art is perhaps best illustrated by the exhibition in Hart House, Toronto, arranged by him in 1925. Murray suggested the idea of an exhibition to the warden of Hart House, J. Burgon Bickersteth, during a visit in the fall of 1924, and the latter took up the proposal. Murray selected the artists and collected the paintings, although he consulted Norman MacKenzie and took his advice. MacKenzie was a well-known Regina lawyer and art collector whose collection Murray obtained for the university in the 1930s. Bickersteth was enthusiastic. "I need hardly say, however, that it would arouse tremendous interest if there could be shown in this house a collection of Saskatchewan pictures."[44] His judgment was correct. The exhibition opened March 23, 1925. A catalogue was produced at Hart House from notes supplied by Murray, only the second time this had been done for a Hart House exhibition.

The exhibition was a triumphant success. Warden Bickersteth reported to Murray that "few, if any, exhibitions that have been held in Hart House have been seen by more people." On the Sunday afternoon, the Sketch Room, where the exhibition was held, "was packed all afternoon and between two and three hundred catalogues, which were supplied by us free, being taken away."[45] Bickersteth arranged an open night and invited a select audience from a list supplied by the Toronto Art Gallery to view the paintings. He assured Murray that "both the artists concerned and yourself may feel that the exhibition has been thoroughly worthwhile."[46]

Although none of the artists was a staff member of the university, through Murray the university paid all but twenty dollars of the cost of mounting the exhibition. The artists had all been Saskatchewan residents for part of their lives, and most of the works exhibited had been painted in Saskatchewan. That was sufficient in Murray's mind to justify the expense. "We believe that our artists are doing good work and that this work will be appreciated outside of the Province when it is known."[47] The exhibition was then shown in Regina, although Murray's idea of a series of provincial exhibits to show the people of Saskatchewan the quality of work being done by their own artists was rejected by Norman MacKenzie when Murray discussed it with him.

Murray thus actively encouraged art in the province by making the university a patron of art, buying pictures and commissioning them, assisting artists of talent like Kenderdine and Lindner, and publicizing the work of Saskatchewan artists through exhibitions. Art was a vital expression of a nascent Saskatchewan culture. Beginning in the 1920s Murray made sure the university nurtured both.

Agricultural Research

Murray gave strong support to the university's work in agricultural research and extension throughout the decade. In 1921 he wrote to the British Trade Commissioner in Winnipeg describing the work of the university. He stressed that "special attention has been given to research. Three problems being regarded as particularly urgent: The determination of the varieties and distribution of rust and the breeding of a rust-resistant wheat; the investigation of the effects of alkali and sub-surface waters on concrete, and the most effective method of wall insulation for house building."[48]

Research projects which were unique to the province and of practical value to its people received Murray's backing, and none more so than the soil survey undertaken by the Soils Department under Professor Hansen. Murray took a special interest in it, and according to one of the men who worked on it, the president's involvement was a mixed blessing.

> When I was working on the soil survey I found him [Murray] to be quite a dictator in administrative things. . . . Murray would not allow us to do any proper research until the survey was finished. . . . When it was completed it served as a model for all Canada. From it land value could be and was established. It was especially valuable, indeed essential, in deciding what fertilizer and what quantity was needed for the best crop. From the soil survey a manual for assessors was developed. . . . The Prairie Farm Rehabilitation Act used its results in planning at a later date as did the people involved with ecological surveys.[49]

The enormous scale of this project begun in 1921 and pushed on throughout the decade is illustrated by Murray's report to Convocation in 1924 that four million acres had been surveyed and another million and a half was underway. This was out of a total acreage of 160 million for the whole province of which perhaps 40% to 50% would be subject to survey as arable land. With the publication of revised agricultural soil ratings in 1972, the work started 50 years earlier was finished.[50]

In 1922 Murray tried to get the Royal Society of Canada to hold one of its meetings in Winnipeg and to devote a public session to wheat, especially to the problem of wheat stem rust. He believed the discussion would be of great public value.[51] Murray's interest in western agricultural problems meant not only that he was constantly on the lookout for scientific research to help overcome them but that he was also an inveterate publicist for the West and its challenges, seeking to broaden the understanding of western agriculture in the rest of Canada and trying to focus the attention of national bodies on the western prairies.

For the whole of the decade, wheat rust investigation was carried out in the university's Biology Department and in the Agricultural College. Professor J.B. Harrington commenced his plant breeding experiments in the Agricultural College in 1925; they would lead to the development of the apex strain of rust resistant wheat some ten years later.

An outbreak of swamp fever (Equine Infectious Anemia) in 1923 triggered the establishment at the University of Saskatchewan of a laboratory for the study of animal diseases. Murray informed Premier Dunning the laboratory would be housed in a building designed for the purpose. "The barn would accommodate not only horses, but cattle, sheep and pigs suffering from disease. It would contain a place for the guinea pigs used in experimental work, an office, a laboratory, a work room and a post mortem room."[52] Sixty years later a cure for swamp fever still eludes veterinarians, and it still takes a formidable toll. "It has been estimated that from 30% to 70% of affected animals die."[53]

There were other diseases to be investigated such as "Wilt" or "Take All," a fungus which attacked the roots of wheat plants. Murray wrote the Federal Minister of Agriculture in 1924 urging immediate action. "I strongly think that your Department should at once make provision for this work. If nothing is done and this disease spreads, as it seems highly probable, those responsible for this matter, both in Ottawa and in Saskatchewan, will find it difficult to justify their parsimony."[54]

Halting the ravages of plant and animal disease did not stand ahead of what might be termed general farming improvements. In his report to Convocation in 1924, Murray listed a variety of steps undertaken by the staff of the College of Agriculture. These included the introduction and popularization of sweet clover, the breeding and selling of purebred swine, a campaign to grow corn in southwestern Saskatchewan, improvement of flax culture and forage crops (the work of Dr. L.E. Kirk), experiments to develop hardy apples, and a demonstration that bee keeping was possible and profitable. He concluded this list with a statement summing up his philosophy of the value of agricultural research in Saskatchewan. "The unusual and difficult conditions of Western Agriculture can be met only by the adoption of new and improved methods discovered and tested by Science."[55]

Improving agriculture and farming went hand in hand with another project dear to Walter Murray. The Homemakers' Clubs for farm women were organized by the Extension Department to improve both the lot of these women and to organize and advance needed community work. He reluctantly reported to the university in 1924 that the money to support this work, which had come from the Dominion Grant in Aid of Agriculture, had been withdrawn "just when the clubs were rapidly extending their sphere of usefulness and becoming valuable agencies for the betterment of the rural communities. This work must not be allowed to stop."[56] As long as he was President, the university ensured that the Homemakers' Clubs continued.

A Man of Many Parts

During the 1920s Walter Murray was active in many other areas besides his two chief occupations, the university and the church. He had been elected a fellow of the Royal Society of Canada in 1918. He made a point of attending as many of its meetings as he could, and he presented three papers during the decade, each on an aspect of the history of Canadian higher education.[57] He also worked to advance the interests of Saskatchewan within the Royal Society principally by trying to arrange the nomination of some of his Saskatchewan colleagues for election. A letter he wrote in 1920 in favour of W.P. Thompson, who was later to be President of the University of Saskatchewan, is typical of Murray's efforts: "I am most anxious that some of our men should be kept in touch with other scientists in Canada and up to date the membership of this University has been overlooked by the Royal Society."[58] Thompson was elected. Murray was able to have E.H. Oliver elected in 1921, using similar tactics. In 1922, he tried without success to have John W. Dafoe nominated as "one of the most active and most interested of the men of the West, and possibly we might not limit it to the West, in the question of Canadian national development."[59]

In 1926, he was still arguing for more appointments from Saskatchewan on the grounds that his university had fewer representatives in the Royal Society than any other university in the country.[60] Murray continued his campaign for greater Saskatchewan representation in the Royal Society throughout the next decade and even after his retirement. It was primarily through his own intensive efforts that his successor at Saskatchewan, James S. Thomson, was elected a fellow of the Royal Society in 1942.

He took time out from his church-union negotiations in 1921 to attend the organizational meeting of the League of Nations Society in Toronto. Murray had written to Sir George Foster, following the latter's speech to the House of Commons on the League of Nations early in 1921, that "it is most important that the public should be given an idea of the work of the League. I think there has been a general feeling of relief and satisfaction among thinking men that the League was a success. It turned out better than many expected."[61] In 1926 Murray described himself as "an ardent supporter of the League of Nations, doing everything in my power to promote the cause of an early peace."[62]

Murray had to refuse a request from Prime Minister Mackenzie King in 1923 to act as a Royal Commissioner to inquire into industrial trouble in Cape Breton. He was too fully occupied in work on an educational commission for the Province of Manitoba.[63] One of Walter Murray's first faculty members in the College of Agriculture, John Bracken, had moved to Manitoba to become the head of the Agricultural College. He was elected to the Manitoba Legislature in the United Farmers electoral victory of 1922 and then became both party leader and provincial premier. Faced with a number of complicated educational questions, he turned to his former President and asked Murray to head a Provincial Royal Commission on Education. Murray and his Commissioners, among other things, were asked to recommend a permanent site for the university and to investigate the province's school system.

This Commission occupied a great amount of Murray's time in the latter part of 1923, but he turned to the Carnegie Foundation for assistance in looking at the connection between the University of Manitoba and the Agricultural College. The Carnegie Foundation President sent his assistant, Dr. W.S. Learned, to Winnipeg, and Learned's report, submitted along with the Commission's report, advanced two principles only too familiar to Murray, who had implemented them in Saskatchewan. One was the integration of the Agricultural College within the university, and the other was the revitalization of four denominational colleges in affiliation with the university and on a common site. Murray was delighted. He congratulated President Pritchett of the Carnegie Foundation on Learned's report. "It is an exceedingly good piece of work and I think it practically settles the University question in Manitoba. . . . The Report as an independent piece of work will have much greater influence than anything we could have done."[64]

Murray had been elected a Trustee of the Carnegie Foundation in 1919 and thus in 1923 was able to use his influence to persuade the Foundation to assist in resolving Manitoba's educational problems. This unique educational partnership of the Carnegie Foundation through its representative, Dr. Learned, and the President of the University of Saskatchewan did not dissolve in 1924; nearly ten years later it came up with a solution to the junior college issue in both Saskatchewan and Manitoba.

Murray's spare time during the 1920s was not only taken up with educational commissions. He was in demand as a Convocation speaker and occasionally as a speaker to other groups. He delivered Convocation Addresses at the University of British Columbia in 1923 and at Manitoba and Alberta in 1927, managing in each case to talk about the history of Canadian universities.

There was another theme which increasingly attracted his attention—the peaceful and harmonious blending of immigrant families on the prairies into a new Canadian unity. He took pride in recording the number and origins of immigrant students who studied at the University of Saskatchewan, and he reported to Convocation in 1929 on the contribution they made, seeking to reassure any of his listeners who might have doubts:

The most notable feature of the life of this cosmopolitan body, this miniature league of nations, has been the absence of racial consciousness. There has been cordial co-operation in every phase of student activity, generous rivalry in the pursuit of knowledge, and evidence on every hand of a pride in Canada and a devotion to the land of our birth or adoption.[65]

He dwelt on this theme in public speeches, urging Canadians to accept the background of "achievement, tradition and culture," which the New Canadians brought, "with understanding and respect."[66] The blending of races within Canada constituted the Canadian nation. Canadians had to adopt a welcoming attitude towards immigrants. "We may never expect to make Canada strong through high-handed methods. It must be by consent from a free-minded people."[67]

Murray's life, however, was not solely a constant whir of public activities. Perhaps learning a lesson from his breakdown in 1919, he began to take regular summer holidays with his wife and his three daughters at Big River. The Murray family had started holidaying at Big River during World War I. How and why this remote village on the shore of a long, narrow northern lake was chosen is a mystery. Indeed, how Murray discovered it is puzzling. It is almost 150 miles north of Saskatoon and was accessible only by poor rail service or by poorer dirt trails. It was certainly not a thriving family centre. In 1919 Mrs. Murray was in charge when accommodation of a sort was erected; her husband was in Nova Scotia vainly seeking to avoid a nervous breakdown. This first "cottage" cost $150.00 and the president's wife worried about their ability to pay this modest sum. The prospect of having a little more security than tenting, which she hated, probably made it worthwhile. The Murray's cottage was toward the end of the lake farthest from the village and was the sole cottage reached by "Murray's trail." The Murray family spent vacations at Big River through the 1920s and well into the 1930s. They often invited their close friends and colleagues, the Mortons and the Donald MacLeans. The dinner table talk was far ranging and good. It was obviously a relaxing atmosphere for Walter Murray. Donald MacLean's stepson recalls sleeping in the same tent with him. "He stretched, yawned once or twice and was asleep."[68]

On one trip to Big River, the vacationers ran into a violent thunderstorm. The Murray-MacLean convoy was halted by fallen trees blocking the road. Murray produced the necessary axe and went to work. "He was handy with an axe."[69] Such roadblocks were evidently predictable events, and an axe in the trunk a necessary precaution. No doubt Murray's skill as an axeman dated from his youth on a New Brunswick farm. Even today there are still plenty of trees on that farm available to hone the axeman's skill.

The 1920s were years of great accomplishment for Walter Murray. The university had grown rapidly in student enrollment. Faculties and departments had been added, and research had expanded into new fields with notable success in some cases and great promise in others. The physical plant had more than doubled although the Arts building remained an unfulfilled dream. The graduates provided a special pleasure and satisfaction to Murray when they donated $10,000 to build the bronze gates which stand as a memorial to the university war dead. At the dedication Murray unveiled the tablets and read the names of the sixty-seven dead. Beyond the university, Murray's evident talent was recognized and he was in demand for service on Royal Commissions, federal and provincial. In education, in the public domain, and in the church his career was at its peak.

His great contributions to Saskatchewan were recognized at a public dinner held in Regina on February 27, 1930 to commemorate both the university's 21st anniversary and Murray's 21 years of service as its President. Four hundred guests attended, half of them travelling down from Saskatoon and other provincial towns for the occasion. The Murrays received gifts of paintings and a silver tea service as well as the accolades of the university community, the public, and the government. The Lieutenant Governor termed Murray "one of the best loved men in the province,"[70] a warm tribute to his humanity which was echoed by other speakers. Premier Anderson proposed the toast to Walter and Christina Murray, and James Gardiner, then Leader of the Opposition, seconded it. Gardiner caught the spirit of the evening and of Murray. "The President of the University of Saskatchewan is a man that all learn to love. We may well afford to spare time to do him honor."[71]

Addresses were presented to Murray on behalf of the faculty and staff, the graduates, and the undergraduates. The faculty and staff praised Murray as a builder. "You, Sir, have built, with our own prairie stone, buildings beautiful, harmonious and solid. You have also built that unseen fabric of the mind and soul which is the real university, not less beautiful and harmonious than our stone buildings."

The dinner was almost too much for Murray. His wife told two of their daughters that "Dad is very surprised and upset over the dinner being such a big affair and at noon he almost went to pieces."[72] He survived the praise, but his thoughts strayed back to the crisis at the end of the war as he thanked colleagues for arranging the banquet. He praised "the steadfastness" of friends who had stood by him then and without whose help the achievements of the decade would not have been possible.[73]

It was a great occasion for Walter Murray. For the moment he could bask in the aura of his contributions and accomplishments publicly recognized and applauded. Alas, it was the pinnacle of his career. Now the Depression, which had already cancelled his cherished Arts building, would dominate his life and work to his last day as President.

■

Chapter 10

Carnegie Support

Walter Murray came to the University of Saskatchewan convinced of the importance of close ties with one of the major foundations in North America specifically dedicated to assisting higher education. Dalhousie had been admitted to the pension system for retired professors sponsored by the Carnegie Foundation for the Advancement of Teaching, and Murray was anxious that Saskatchewan professors have the same financial benefits that he and his colleagues had enjoyed in Halifax.

The Carnegie Foundation was created in 1905 with a gift of ten million dollars from Andrew Carnegie. President Henry Pritchett of M.I.T., who had helped to persuade Carnegie of the great need for pensions for university professors, gave up his university position to administer the Foundation, and the following year the Carnegie Foundation for the Advancement of Teaching was incorporated. With the income from the money donated by Carnegie, the Foundation was able to create a national system of pensions for university faculty in the United States, Canada, and Newfoundland. To be eligible, institutions had to have six full professors, raised to eight in 1921, possess an endowment of $200,000, also raised in 1921 to $500,000, and be free from debt. Institutions under sectarian control were ineligible. State universities were excluded at first but included in 1908 after Carnegie added another five million to the Foundation's capital. In 1918, the pension fund was re-organized with a provision for contributions of 5% of professional salaries.[1]

As Secretary of the Senate at Dalhousie, Murray had prepared the annual reports for the Carnegie Foundation and had been in regular correspondence with its officials. One of the first people Murray contacted after being made President at Saskatchewan was the President of the Carnegie Foundation, seeking his advice on a variety of questions ranging from the criteria for determining the university's location to whether or not the term "College" was preferable to "School" or "Faculty." He was careful to describe his vision of what the university would be and to lay the groundwork for an early application by the university for admission into the Carnegie Pension Plan. Murray told Pritchett that "we look to the Carnegie Foundation to mould University education in America and are therefore daring in the demands which we make upon your time and consideration."[2] This phrase might well be dismissed as the flattery of a new university president attempting to ingratiate himself with the Foundation, but Murray was sincere, as the future would prove.

Murray actually began what became a seventeen-year wooing of the Foundation in 1912, requesting advice from President Pritchett on the steps required for admission to the privileges of the Carnegie Foundation. The reply, after investigation by the Foundation staff, was discouraging. Murray was told not to bother applying until his university "has become quite firmly established."[3] Murray tried again in 1915 with no better result.[4] Murray readily appreciated the value of membership in the Carnegie fund as a recruiting aid to attract high-quality faculty. The security of a better pension than the university could offer on its own might make Saskatchewan more appealing to potential candidates. Affiliation, in Murray's eyes, however, meant much more than financial benefits. He summed these up in a later letter of application as "the formal recognition by the Foundation of the character of the work of the University."[5] Such recognition, of course, might bring additional financial support, but for Murray it was above all a sign of Saskatchewan's acceptance into the club of North American universities—an institutional coming of age.

After his rejection in 1915, he did not re-apply for another thirteen years, but he used the interval to develop close personal ties with the Foundation. He was elected as a member of the Board of Trustees of the Carnegie Foundation in 1919 because, as the Secretary of the Board informed him, the Board had "desired for a long time to come more in touch with the universities in the western part of the Dominion."[6] This was the beginning of a tenure of nearly twenty years on the Board. He served as Vice-Chairman of the Foundation from 1922-24 and as Chairman for the year 1934-35. The trustees received no compensation for themselves, which suited Murray's own inclinations. The compensation came instead in the form of financial assistance from the Carnegie Corporation to his university.

Manitoba actually received the first benefits from Murray's ties with the Foundation. When he was appointed to head the provincial commission on education in Manitoba in 1923, he obtained from the Foundation the services of Dr. W.S. Learned, President Pritchett's assistant, to investigate the relationship between the University of Manitoba and the provincial Agricultural College and how the four denominational colleges could fit into Manitoba's university structure. Learned was able to bring a North American perspective to his task, and his report impressed both Murray and the Manitoba officials who received it.

Five years later, in 1928, Murray decided the time had come to try again for formal admission to the associated list of universities of the Foundation. He wrote President Pritchett, enclosing a two-page summary of the university's activities since its inception. Pritchett's reply politely said that the Foundation wanted a formal inspection and report on the university before affiliation could be considered.[7] The inspection was to be carried out by Howard S. Savage, the Secretary-Treasurer of the Foundation, who elected to visit the campus during the fall, when the university was in session. Murray welcomed the inspection, confident that the University of Saskatchewan was "on par with the other Western Universities."[8]

Savage's visit to Saskatchewan in the autumn came with good omens as far as Murray was concerned. He wrote Savage a letter of thanks for bringing "the most extraordinary weather that we have had this fall. It has not been equalled in our history."[9] More important than the beautiful weather was Savage's impression of the university. His report to the Foundation examined the admission standards, the failure rate, the financial state of the university, its own pension plan as well as the provincial background. His findings are an objective and revealing analysis of the university then twenty years old.[10]

Savage discovered some weaknesses both in the number of students admitted without the prerequisite foreign language requirement and in the large number, 20-25%, who failed after the first and second years. The situation was not as bad as at certain American universities "that aspire to athletic notoriety," and Savage concluded that generally "the academic standing of the University is good, but not superlative. It would, I believe, be better if the Province were in a stronger economic and financial condition. Its deficiencies are the products of conditions which only time and prosperity can remedy." The university's pension plan, while "much more satisfactory" than those of many universities affiliated with the Carnegie Foundation, had not been examined by an actuary. "And President Murray indicates that he does not think it had better be," Savage added. In his overall assessment of the university's programs, Savage found the major omission to be a University library which reflected the priority given to the applied sciences rather than to the humanities. Savage understood, probably from talking to Murray, the reason for this emphasis in a province which was not wealthy. "The citizens of the Province must, therefore, make a living from the soil, and the agency that can assist them to get that living and teach their women-folk means of making their houses even slightly attractive, receives the farmer's trust and support. This is the basis of the relation of the University to the Province and its people."

Savage described the university's mission as follows: "so to improve conditions of life in the Province that her graduates will find happiness and a fair degree of comfort and prosperity within its borders." The university was vital to the life of the province. It had to "place modern scientific knowledge at the service of the people." University research in many instances was directed at overcoming provincial problems like wheat rust or concrete decay from the alkaline soil and water of Saskatchewan. The university had sunk deep roots within the province even though Savage noted "a suggestion of condescension" towards it from outside the borders of Saskatchewan. He went on:

> The institution is young. It does not advertize itself—indeed, its members take pride in understating its accomplishments. It is situated not in a wealthy or an impressive district, but in the midst of arid, almost treeless wheatfields, in an atmosphere heavy with dust and beside a town that can best be described as "frontier." Within the Province, nothing of this attitude of condescension is encountered. Between the farmer and the University officer or teacher there apparently exists an unusual mutual respect and co-operation. Indications are that such a relationship is not the general rule in all of the western provinces of Canada.

Savage saw an optimistic future for the university, predicting new buildings and higher standards in the next decade. He found the academic standards high already in the university's professional schools; only in Arts and Agriculture were they uneven. He attributed this in part to the qualifications of faculty, especially in the Arts where not as many possessed advanced degrees and where the Departments were not as well staffed. Even here he found improvements underway.

Savage sent a copy of his report for Murray to see. Murray could not let the comments about the qualifications of his Humanities professors go by without a rebuttal. He immediately replied detailing their academic distinctions and trying to right the balance between Humanities and Science. The reason many of the faculty in the

Humanities did not have postgraduate degrees was due to their being educated in Britain rather than Germany or the United States. "This explanation, I think, will make clear that the difference noted in the Humanities and Sciences is apparent rather than real and does not indicate lack of appreciation of the importance of the Humanities in University education."[11] Murray clearly was on the defensive about the priority given to the Humanities in his university.

The overall report was very favourable, as Savage reaffirmed in a later letter to Murray. "The University of Saskatchewan is probably doing more useful work than many people in both Canada and the United States realize. That a wide public should realize this fact is infinitely less important than that the quality of the work itself and the service that it implies should continue."[12] Savage's report opened the door for Saskatchewan's formal affiliation with the Foundation. Murray applied on behalf of his university early in April 1929 and the Carnegie Board approved the application within two weeks.[13] It had taken a long time to achieve, but the university soon began to reap the benefits.

As well as the Carnegie Foundation for the Advancement of Teaching, Andrew Carnegie had established another educational foundation. In 1911 he created the Carnegie Corporation with an initial gift of twenty-five million dollars. The following year he added another hundred million. For ten years the Corporation existed as a vehicle for Carnegie to indulge his personal philanthropic whims. Following Carnegie's death in 1919, a permanent president was appointed, and the Board of Trustees was reorganized. The Corporation's impact on higher education did not really begin until the election of Frederick Keppel as President of the Corporation in 1923.

Under Keppel various innovations were supported in American universities; these innovations included some in the fine arts, in which Keppel took a strong personal interest. The major part of the Corporation's donations went to American universities, but Canadian institutions also benefitted. Of the original endowment, the income from ten million dollars was set aside for British dominions and colonies, reflecting Carnegie's Scottish birth and continuing ties with Britain. Because of excessive spending in the early years of the Corporation, Keppel and the Trustees in 1926 decided to limit the total amount to be spent in any one year to two million dollars. From 1926 the Corporation turned to small grants either for new programs or to strengthen existing institutions. For example, beginning in 1926, the Corporation presented teaching collections of art to a number of universities.[14]

For Murray and for the University of Saskatchewan, the potential of financial aid from the Carnegie Corporation was vital if the university was to be able to undertake innovations. Saskatchewan was not a wealthy province, and it contained no magnates to provide endowments for the new university. Nor were there any comparable Canadian foundations to which the university might look for support. The University of Saskatchewan had approached the Carnegie Corporation for financial assistance, without success, prior to the formal affiliation with the Foundation in 1929. The Dean of Arts and Sciences, George Ling, had written early in 1928 vainly seeking help to build the Arts and Science Building.[15] Shortly afterward, Murray began a campaign to get funds in order to hire a Professor of Music.

The university's role in nurturing the musical life of the province had long been a personal interest of Murray's. It had not been possible to teach Music as part of the curriculum when the university opened, but Murray had recognized very early how the university could act as a catalyst to encourage musical activity in Saskatchewan. In 1909 he wrote to the Vice-President of the Provincial Music Festival:

> I think it important for the University to make some effort to stimulate the study of Music. The interest shown at the last Music Festival, and the need for something to fill up the long winter evenings is surely sufficient reason to justify the University in taking up this work.[16]

A Provincial Music Festival was first organized in 1909 and was held each year until the war forced its cancellation. Murray himself served as President of the Saskatchewan Musical Association in 1913-14. Under his auspices, the university had committed itself to appoint the adjudicators for the yearly festivals. After the war, Murray was most anxious to have the university assist in the rejuvenation of the Music Festival. He reported to Convocation in 1921:

> The public interest in Music is much keener and greater progress has been made in educating the taste and appreciation of the people. The remarkable success of the Provincial Music Festival, the excellence of the work of the various choral societies, choirs and soloists indicate an appreciation and skill that could do credit to a Province whose pioneer days had been lost in the mist of the past.[17]

By 1922 the university was releasing the assistant in the bookstore for two and a half months to act as the Secretary of the Provincial Music Festival. Two years later, the university provided a travelling secretary to assist the Provincial Musical Association to run its festivals.

Murray wanted financial assistance from the Carnegie Corporation to bring in a Professor of Music who would work closely with the provincial association and "set a standard of musical education for the people of the province."[18] The cost would be $5,000 a year for five years. Murray had to knock three times before the Corporation opened its doors, and by then the formal affiliation with the Foundation had been approved.

After Murray's second request, Keppel, the President of the Carnegie Corporation, asked the advice of Dr. W.S. Learned of the Carnegie Foundation. The reply was an unqualified endorsement of both Murray and his university. Learned testified "to the unusual quality of the institution and of its management," and went on,

> You can rely implicitly on anything that President Murray says. He is one of the few educational administrators who possesses a positive genius for understatement.
>
> Doctor Savage was at Saskatoon last year and confirms my impressions with considerable enthusiasm. I have taken the liberty of showing him this letter from President Murray and am informed that it tallies exactly with the impressions that he received during his visit. I doubt whether the Corporation could find a more secure place in which to invest a small sum of money.[19]

The vote of confidence in Murray and in the University of Saskatchewan by officers of the Carnegie Foundation ultimately was instrumental in convincing Keppel and the trustees of the Carnegie Corporation that Saskatchewan was worthy of support. Early in July 1929, Murray wrote for the third time, describing himself as an "importunate widow" requesting funds to establish a chair of music at the university.[20]

Keppel promised Murray the request would be considered by the trustees in the fall, but he was caught between conflicting advice from the Secretary of the Corporation and Dr. Savage of the Carnegie Foundation. Robert Lester, the Secretary of the Carnegie Corporation, had doubts about the value of financial aid to the Saskatchewan Musical Association. "This may be a valuable activity and worthy of encouragement, but it strikes me as diffused and amateurish, complicated by provincial and community antagonisms, and offering little field for Corporation interest. The field is shapeless, without definition, and Carncor participation would involve us in endless discrimination."[21] Savage, on the other hand, believed the Corporation could help to "bring music further into the lives of the people of Saskatchewan" and the best way to do it would be to endow a chair of music in the university. Because of "the peculiarly intimate relation of the university to the Provincial life," this would assist both the university and the provincial Musical Association, provide the necessary leadership and administration, popularize good music, and through courses in musical theory and appreciation, fill an apparent need in the province. Savage thought a grant of $10,000 for five years could accomplish "a really thorough job."[22]

To extricate himself from the dilemma posed by the advice he had received, Keppel turned to a personal friend, John Erskine, who headed the renowned Juilliard School of Music in New York. He asked Erskine to nominate a professional musician to visit Saskatchewan and report on the music situation. Erskine complied, although Saskatchewan was as mysterious a place to him as it must have been for Madame Olga Samaroff, who was chosen to visit it. Erskine wrote to Keppel that Madame Samaroff would travel during the 1929 school year "to look up that Western Canada place for you—Saskatchewan, isn't it?"[23]

Madame Samaroff and Walter Murray obviously clicked in their approach to Saskatchewan's music education. Murray shrewdly arranged for her to adjudicate the Regina Musical Festival in 1930, and she, in turn, was most impressed by him. On her return to New York, she recommended that the Corporation make a three-year grant to enable the university to hire a Professor of Music. Keppel wrote to her early in June 1930 saying, "I feel as you do about Dr. Murray, and if the grant is made, I will tell him we do not want to control the appointment in any way."[24] A few days later, the Carnegie Corporation authorized a grant of $16,500, payable over three years, to establish a Chair of Music at Saskatchewan. What is clear from the correspondence is that this money was really a personal investment in Murray himself. His reputation both at the Foundation and in the Corporation opened the way for the first of the Corporation's grants to his university.

Murray consulted closely with Madame Samaroff about the appointment itself and kept Dr. Keppel of the Carnegie Corporation informed. He and the university acted very quickly and by the beginning of 1931, they had hired Arthur Collingwood, a Scot from Aberdeen who had visited Saskatchewan in 1929, as the adjudicator for the music festivals. Murray was delighted when Collingwood accepted. Now it seemed the university could provide the leadership needed in developing the musical life of the province, something Murray had desired from the beginning of his Presidency.

Collingwood was able to achieve a great deal in a short time. He arrived when the province and the university were feeling the effects of the Depression. Everywhere he went in 1931, to his astonishment, he found that entries for the music festivals had increased, and they were breaking even financially. In a report for the Carnegie Corporation, Collingwood wrote, "It would appear, especially in the depressed areas, that they found in music a palliative or a form of recreation that helped them to endure. Can I say more? We expected considerable decrease in entries and also financial loss in every centre. Our fears were confounded, our faith in the power of music strengthened."[25]

Collingwood vividly described his experiences and sketched his vision, urging the need for better musical equipment, including pianos, a gramophone, and a library of records, which because of the Depression, the university could not afford to purchase. Apart from the intrinsic value of studying music, Collingwood stressed two other benefits for the province and the country. One was the role of music in assimilating European immigrants to a Canadian nationality, which for Collingwood was still identical with a British culture. Collingwood elaborated:

> One of Canada's big problems, with its aggregation of nationalities, is to establish not only a common language, but also a real unity in national aspiration and national consciousness. Comparatively little in respect of national unification can be done with the adult foreign population. Their roots are too deep in their native soil. But the children are the Canadian citizens of tomorrow and the day after. Through their school music, the singing of British folk songs, British poetry allied to music by British composers, they are unconsciously absorbing and establishing a British consciousness. A practical instance of the power of music as a force in the unification of diverse races. A welder of a nation.[26]

Andrew Carnegie would have agreed wholeheartedly, and Walter Murray did, too. But there was more than a little irony in the fact that it was money from an American foundation that enabled

Collingwood to apply a veneer of British culture to the children of the immigrants in Saskatchewan's farm communities.

The other value Collingwood urged was the need for the uplifting experience of musical participation to counter the economic and psychological suffering created by the Depression. "Our Festival work clearly evidences music as an uplift, a truly re-creational force during the months of depression we have already passed through. If the economic authorities' prediction proves correct, the need for music will be greater than ever during the coming winter."[27] The Corporation trustees were impressed by Collingwood's report, and in November 1931 they voted an additional grant of $2500 to the University of Saskatchewan for the musical equipment he required. By the spring of 1932, Murray was able to tell the Corporation that half of this grant had been spent on the beginning of a promising symphony orchestra and part had been used to establish a music reference library.[28]

Collingwood's success was evident as well to the members of the Saskatchewan Musical Association, who sponsored the festivals. Their president, Carl Niderost, wrote to the Carnegie Corporation in the summer of 1932 with the news that again entries to the Provincial Festival were up in spite of the worsening Depression. Much of the credit was due to Collingwood's work; his chair of music had "given a great impetus to the study, the understanding and love of music in this Province."[29]

By the summer of 1933, the Board of Governors of the university faced an extremely difficult decision. They wanted to continue the Chair of Music because, as Murray wrote to Dr. Keppel, "the results so far have exceeded the most sanguine expectations."[30] But the government grants to the university had been drastically cut, and the Board had been forced to respond by asking some faculty to take leaves of absence without pay. Murray asked the Carnegie Corporation to renew its Music grant for three more years. This "would ensure the permanence of the undertaking."[31] Keppel agreed to do this, and in the fall of 1933, the Corporation voted another $16,500, payable over three years, to keep the music program going at Saskatchewan.

Arthur Collingwood had ended his first report to the Carnegie Corporation with the words, "Is this a young man's vision, or an old man's dream? I do not know. I *do* know that visions and ideals have been transmitted into living realities, and that sometimes, dreams *do* come true." The vision both he and Walter Murray had of the university's role in stimulating the musical life of Saskatchewan did come true through the financial assistance of the Carnegie Corporation.

The Carnegie Foundation and the Corporation were also closely involved with another aspect of Saskatchewan higher education, the Regina College question. The issue dated back to the decision to locate the provincial university in Saskatoon, which had caused great disaffection in Regina. In 1910 the Methodist Church established a college in Regina. The University Act conferred a monopoly of degree granting powers, except in theology, upon the University of Saskatchewan, but the creation of Regina College and its location kept the original rivalry alive. There were repeated attempts to challenge the university's monopoly by expanding Regina College. No other matter pursued Walter Murray more relentlessly throughout a quarter century. Equally, to no other issue were his considerable talents marshalled so implacably in opposition. He was determined that one and only one state-supported university would serve Saskatchewan. Having been unable to achieve a state university in Nova Scotia, he was not about to let the monopoly concept successfully implanted in Saskatchewan be undermined by the rival claims of Regina.

His own views had been bolstered by the political support of both Premier Scott and Sir Frederick Haultain, leader of the opposition when the Province was formed and later Chancellor of the university. Successive government leaders upheld the provincial university's position until the election of the Conservative government of J.T.M. Anderson in June 1929.

In 1926, Murray forestalled any possibility of Regina College's obtaining degrees for its students through affiliation with Victoria College of the University of Toronto. Murray wrote his longtime friend, Robert Falconer, about the designs of Dr. Stapleford, President of Regina College. "Dr. Stapleford is seized with the ambition to make the College a University. . . . I told him very emphatically that I believed the policy was educationally wrong."[32] Once alerted by Murray to Stapleford's idea of affiliation with Victoria, Falconer obligingly reassured Murray that this would not be allowed to happen.[33]

The election of Anderson re-opened what for Murray was an old wound. In June 1931 Premier Anderson espoused the idea of "degree conferring powers . . . in smaller colleges of the province." Murray immediately wrote to the Premier warning of the dangers of sectarianism in higher education should church colleges be given degree granting powers. For Murray, the spectre of re-creating the educational divisions of Nova Scotia was an alarming prospect and one he would do anything to avoid.[34] The Premier replied that he had been misquoted, but to Murray it now seemed that the ambitions of Regina College and its president were being encouraged tacitly, if not openly, by the provincial government.

Stapleford had been trying for some years to curry favour with the Carnegie Corporation in the hope that Carnegie money would assist him in building up Regina College. A request for funds in 1925 was rejected, but in 1929 he tried again, seeking library support.[35] Stapleford had wanted a supporting letter from the University of Saskatchewan. The Dean of Arts, George Ling, wrote the letter, and in it he sketched the background of the Regina-Saskatoon rivalry for the officers of the Carnegie Corporation. He endorsed Stapleford's plea for library support and added he "would be very glad to see Regina College prosper in what I regard as its proper sphere of activity." However, it was not in the province's interest to create a second university and Ling added, "I feel I cannot cooperate with it or endeavour to strengthen it for this purpose."[36] Ling was obviously expressing Murray's views. The Carnegie Corporation turned down the Regina request.

With Premier Anderson's apparent encouragement, Stapleford once again approached the Carnegie Corporation in 1930. This time he asked for $10,000 a year, for five years, to add third and fourth years to the program, with the degrees to be granted by the University of Saskatchewan. Murray, sensing the danger to the university, had visited Keppel a month previously to ensure Corporation support and to alert Keppel to what was happening in Saskatchewan. Murray described it as a "political snarl" over the expansion of Regina College and asked if the Corporation might be willing to finance a study by the Foundation of the junior college problem in Saskatchewan. Murray held the upper hand. Stapleford did not get his money, and the Corporation President promised to keep in touch with Murray.[37]

More important for Murray, the Corporation agreed to finance the study Murray wanted, and Murray recruited Dr. W.S. Learned to carry it out. Learned had performed a similar task for Murray nearly ten years previously in Manitoba. Murray knew his man.

The study was carried out with remarkable speed early in 1932. Learned worked informally with Chancellor Wallace of Victoria College at the University of Toronto and President Falconer as well as Dr. George Locke, Librarian of the Toronto Public Library. Learned's study, published as the Carnegie Foundation's bulletin number 27 in 1932, was quickly accepted by both Murray and the

University of Saskatchewan.[38] Murray could have written the key recommendation himself. "The Commission holds the view that under the existing conditions, the concentration in one responsible state-controlled institution of the authority within the province to issue and evaluate educational degrees is sound and should be perpetuated."

Murray was elated with the study. It gave him all the ammunition he needed. He wrote to the President of the Carnegie Foundation, "The report is a masterpiece and was admitted by all those who agreed and those who were disappointed to be unanswerable. I believe it has disposed of the problem for at least twenty years."[39] He rejoiced even more openly after the Regina College Board accepted the university's proposals for co-operation. Murray wrote to another staff member of the Carnegie Foundation, saying that "without the assistance of the Report we would have had twenty years of demoralizing strife with political manoeuvring of the worst kind."[40]

The Learned Report effectively ended the Regina College campaign to obtain university status. Murray could now relax knowing there was no longer a real danger of the political or sectarian rivalry that he had feared might spring up in Saskatchewan higher education. What he saw as the mistakes of the Maritimes would not be repeated in Saskatchewan, certainly not while he remained the university's President.

But the Regina issue was not over yet either for Murray or for the Carnegie Corporation. Murray had never given up his idea of building a University Library, and even in the depths of the Depression he had no qualms about asking the Carnegie Corporation for $100,000 to construct "an excellent building."[41] Keppel had no intention of asking the Corporation's Trustees to fund a Library in Saskatchewan, but he wrote Murray privately that he was thinking of a $50,000 emergency grant for each of the three Canadian prairie universities. Later when the Trustees confirmed Keppel's offer, he wrote again with the official news, offering the funds for "some new and significant work . . . likely to have a stimulating effect on the morale of the institution."[42]

Murray did not have to agonize long over how to spend the money. He planned to use it to implement the recommendations of the Learned Report, and in order to do this the university had to take over Regina College. Once again the Carnegie Corporation's fortuitous grant enabled Murray to act. He met with President Stapleford and made the takeover offer. The negotiations were difficult, but by early 1934 agreement had been reached and the Board of Governors of both institutions approved the proposal.

In keeping with the Learned Report recommendations, the university offered to sustain Regina College as "a genuine community college . . . with courses far outranging the university preparatory work and touching the community in many other ways."[43] This included offering courses equivalent to the first two years of university work, expanding the work of the Music Conservatory, continuing adult education and extension classes, and when financial conditions permitted, building an Art School. For Murray this was contingent on the university buying all the land and buildings owned by Regina College, thus eliminating any possibility of the emergence of a university in Regina to rival the state university in Saskatoon. There was no intention, however, of closing Regina College.

Murray submitted his plan to the Carnegie Corporation for approval. His idea was enthusiastically endorsed by Dr. Learned in a memorandum written for Keppel and the Carnegie Corporation trustees.

> Although this use of the fund would not result in any single specific monument such as a library or endowed chair, it undoubtedly does go to the heart of the most critical situation which this institution now confronts. If through the use of the money in this manner described the University can actually bring into its possession the Regina College property, coordinate it with its own activities as a junior college, and get the City of Regina definitely committed to the ultimate solution outlined in the report made a year ago by Chancellor Wallace and myself, the result may prove little short of momentous to that community. It will clear up the existing problem forever and it will also give us a splendid example of a community service institute under university auspices . . . [44]

In the letter accompanying the formal application for approval by the Corporation, Murray was able to add that an Art Gallery would soon be created in Regina, endowed by Norman MacKenzie, a prominent Regina lawyer, which would help to create a major school of Art to accompany the Regina School of Music. Murray himself had played a prominent role in bringing this about. The Corporation Trustees were happy to approve the takeover, done after all with Carnegie money.

After overcoming the objections of the Regina College staff and administration and persuading his own university of the need to acquire Regina College, Murray faced one final obstacle. The governors of the College were appointed by the United Church, which had to approve the sale of the property. When the matter was debated in the Board of Education of the United Church in the spring of 1934, strong opposition surfaced from the Methodist wing of the church. Murray was surprised and admitted that he had not anticipated this. The Methodists did not want to surrender church control of higher education, but the plain fact was the church could no longer afford to sustain the College.

Murray may have been caught a bit off guard by the nature and strength of the opposition in the Church's Board of Education, but he used all his political expertise and connections to make sure the Executive Committee of the church gave final approval. The most important of these was the former Moderator, who just happened to be E.H. Oliver, Principal of St. Andrew's College and one of Murray's closest friends. He wrote to Oliver just before the Executive Council considered the proposal: "I know you will see that there is no misunderstanding when the matter is being considered by the Executive."[45] Oliver complied willingly and the Executive Committee agreed to the transfer.

Even Falconer was called in to help again when Murray heard there was a possibility of Regina College affiliating with Queen's. Falconer wrote the Principal of Queen's to head off any move in that direction.[46] Falconer shared Murray's triumph, as well he might since he had played an important part in it, but it was Murray himself who savoured the moment. He had been the consummate academic politician, using his ties with both the Carnegie Corporation and the Carnegie Foundation to outmanoeuvre the Regina people, as he saw them, and solidify the position of the University of Saskatchewan. When Falconer praised him for having accomplished "a great piece of work in thus unifying higher education in Saskatchewan," Murray nodded in quiet agreement.[47]

He saw the acquisition of Regina College as the last step in the realization of the original policy enunciated in the preamble to the University Act—the creation of one university for the whole province to provide "higher education in all its branches" and to enable "all persons without regard to race, creed or religion" to take full advantage of these facilities. For Walter Murray, the one was indivisible and absolute. He could step down as president having, as far as he was concerned, vanquished the Regina problem and laid to rest the rivalries which went back to the original decision to locate the university in Saskatoon.

There was one remaining item in connection with the acquisition of Regina College. On behalf of the university, Murray offered Dr. W.S. Learned of the Carnegie Foundation an honorary degree in

March 1934, three months after the offer of $50,000 from the Carnegie Corporation.[48] Learned's discretion was more acute than Walter Murray's, and he replied that he felt obliged to decline "at this time," apparently concerned about a public perception of cause and effect. Murray waited two years and repeated the offer.[49] This time Learned accepted. Both Murray and the University of Saskatchewan thus repaid the debt they owed to Dr. Learned for helping to resolve the Regina College issue.

Carnegie support and Murray's contacts with the Foundation and the Corporation were also instrumental in bringing to Saskatchewan a refugee from Hitler's anti-Jewish persecution who was to gain one of only three Nobel prizes awarded to Canadians. Gerhard Herzberg's laureate was in chemistry; he was (and is) a physicist. Herzberg's arrival at Saskatchewan in the midst of the Depression owed a great deal to Walter Murray's prompt action, his willingness again to approach the Carnegie Corporation for assistance, and his unique recruiting methods. Herzberg was the rare exception to a Canadian policy of closing the door to refugees, academics or not, who fled Hitler's Germany during the Depression. Without Murray's active intervention at every stage, he would not have been admitted.

It was the financial crisis at the University of Saskatchewan caused by the Depression which set in motion a chain of events destined to bring Herzberg to Canada. Early in 1933, Dr. J.W.T. Spinks, a young bachelor chemistry professor at the University of Saskatchewan, was called to Murray's office with other young bachelor faculty and given the choice of resigning or going on leave for a year with $500.00 salary and the hope of returning to a job. The university's financial position had forced the president to take this drastic action. Spinks and his colleagues elected to go on leave.[50] He wrote to a German physicist specializing in spectroscopy at Darmstadt, asking permission to work with him for a year. The physicist's name was Gerhard Herzberg. On reviewing Spinks' letter, Herzberg asked his wife, "Now where on earth can . . . the University of Saskatchewan in Saskatoon . . . be?"[51]

Gerhard Herzberg's academic position at Darmstadt was precarious. He himself had come under suspicion as a communist because of an invitation in 1932 to lecture at the Karpov Institute for Chemistry in Moscow, but it was the fact that his wife was Jewish which caused him to be dismissed in 1935. After Spinks returned to Saskatchewan in 1934, Herzberg wrote to him, asking whether Walter Murray, as President of the University of Saskatchewan, would write to the President of the University of Toronto on Herzberg's behalf. Murray wrote to both the President of the

University of Toronto and to Dr. Tory, the President of the National Research Council. Spinks recalled in an interview about Murray, "The letters he wrote at the time were fabulous."[52] The letter to Toronto ended, "Should neither of you feel inclined to invite him to come we would do so with joy, although we have not sufficient means to provide him with proper equipment for his work, but a man of his power and resource can make much of little."[53] Murray's commitment was made at a time when, as Spinks put it, "the bulk of the university assets in 1935 consisted of a bunch of I.O.U.'s in his safe."[54] Neither Toronto nor the NRC held out any hope of finding a place for Herzberg.

Both Herzberg and Murray had heard of a plan offered by the Carnegie Corporation to support German academics who had to flee Germany. Murray wrote to the Carnegie Corporation early in February 1935, seeking details of the plan.[55] The answer, which came within a week, was that no formal plan existed, but the Corporation was happy to receive individual proposals from universities in the British Dominions or Colonies. The conditions were that "if the University believes that there is a reasonable possibility of providing a permanent position for him, the Corporation will be glad to give consideration to a grant to cover the salary of a guest professor for a period not to exceed two years."[56]

Murray immediately applied to bring a displaced professor from Germany to serve as a guest professor at Saskatchewan for two years. Gerhard Herzberg was the first choice because of Spinks' enthusiastic support for him. Spinks, recalling the episode, still marvels at Murray's methods. "He was quite extraordinary. He went ahead and made this appointment to the Physics Department purely on my say-so."[57] The Chairman of the Department was not informed until Herzberg actually arrived on the campus. Spinks concluded: "It could only have happened under a fairly autocratic system, with a president like Dr. Murray who trusted his own judgment, and was prepared to take a bit of a gamble. The gamble paid off handsomely."[58]

The Carnegie Corporation learned that Herzberg had a very good scientific record and was therefore a candidate worth backing. The Corporation's only concern was the research facilities available at Saskatchewan, but they concluded that this was really a question for Herzberg himself.[59] Herzberg certainly had doubts about going to a university that not only lacked suitable equipment for his research and was without any funds to purchase it but which also offered only a two-year appointment and no guarantee of anything beyond; however, he really had no choice. The Carnegie Corporation allocated $2850 for each of two years to pay Professor Herzberg's salary. As soon as Murray received word from the Corporation, he offered the position to Herzberg, who promptly accepted.

Murray then had to intervene personally with A.L. Jolliffe, the Canadian Commissioner of Immigration, for Herzberg and his family to receive the necessary clearances to come to Canada. Shortly after Herzberg arrived at the university, another Physics Professor, Dr. Alty, resigned to go to Glasgow University. Dr. Herzberg related what happened next. "I had been there only three months and Dr. Murray asked me to come to his office and he told me . . . we feel we should give you a full time appointment . . . and the salary was distinctly different. . . . In three months he had collected enough evidence that I was a good scientist." Murray wrote to Dr. Alty that Herzberg "is proving to be a genuine treasure."[60]

When Herzberg's two-year visa expired in 1937, once again Murray had to battle an obstinate Immigration Commissioner on Herzberg's behalf. Commissioner Jolliffe wanted to know whether Herzberg would be displacing a Canadian. Murray responded vigorously. "Does that imply that a Canadian university cannot appoint to its staff any person, no matter how distinguished, who would in any way displace a Canadian resident? . . . Could no British, American, or European scholar then be engaged if a Canadian resident was thereby displaced?" If this was government policy, "its seriousness for higher education and research in Canada is very great—in fact, it might prove fatal."[61] Murray's forceful intervention was sufficient to pry landed-immigrant status for Herzberg and his wife out of a reluctant Immigration Branch. In 1938, after Murray's retirement as President, he assisted Herzberg again with an immigration problem, helping to get his wife's parents into Canada after the terrible pogrom against the Jews in Germany early in November. It took an Order-in-Council to admit them, and probably only Murray's intervention was sufficient to overcome the entrenched anti-Semitism of F.C. Blair, the Director of Immigration.

The collaboration of Walter Murray and the Carnegie Corporation brought Gerhard Herzberg to Canada with benefits which went far beyond the University of Saskatchewan. Not surprisingly, Herzberg dedicated the book, *Diatomic Molecules,* translated with Dr. Spinks and published in 1939, to Walter Murray.

Murray succeeded in obtaining financial assistance from the Carnegie Corporation for two other Saskatchewan academics in his last year as President. One was a Russian immigrant, T.K. Pavlychenko, who had carried out agricultural research on the root systems of weeds and cereal plants. Murray wrote to Dr. Keppel on his behalf, and the Corporation granted Pavlychenko $2,500, which aided him in doctoral research at Nebraska.[62]

One of Murray's closest friends on the faculty was the historian, A.S. Morton. For Morton, Murray was willing to break the rules. To ease the crushing financial burden of the university in 1933, the Board of Governors approved leaves of absence for a year with only three months' pay for nine professors and leaves without pay for six months for another four staff members. Morton was the exception. He had been at work on the early history of western Canada since 1920, a project Murray strongly endorsed.[63] Morton had finally gained permission to carry out research in the archives of the Hudson's Bay Company in London, England, the first such permission granted to a Canadian historian. Murray had assisted Morton in obtaining this permission. When it finally came, Murray told the historian, "You've no choice, Morton, you've got to go."[64] Morton took his first sabbatical in twenty years to go to London with his wife and two small children. He was given his full salary for the year.

Later, when the book was completed, Murray took the opportunity provided by a visit to New York to introduce his successor as President, James S. Thomson, to the Carnegie Corporation officials. He pleaded on Morton's behalf for a financial grant-in-aid of publication. The Corporation gave $2,500, without which Morton's classic study, *A History of the Canadian West to 1870-71* (Toronto, 1939), might not have been published.

Murray's requests for aid did not cease as the end of his presidency approached. In March 1937 he asked for $5,000 a year for three years to erect an Art Gallery in Regina and another $5,000 a year to begin a "badly needed" two-year program in Veterinary Medicine, as well as funds to extend two university buildings. He justified his requests to Keppel in a novel way: "There is scriptural authority for asking and even for being importunate in certain conditions. Although these conditions do not exist we persist."[65] None of these requests was granted.

Murray then joined with James S. Thomson in October 1937 to petition the Carnegie Corporation to help save the rural people of Saskatchewan "from demoralization" due to the effects of the Depression. "The churches and the schools are struggling pitifully. The social and cultural activities are at a very low ebb. A three-year programme would set the feet of our farmers upon the highway to health and prosperity and preserve a rural civilization that is worthwhile. . . . We are not appealing for help for a decaying cause but for a people who though overwhelmed by present disaster, have the possibilities of building up a fine rural civilization."[66] No record of a reply survives, but this heartfelt plea for much-needed assistance apparently did not sway the directors of the Corporation.

Other North American universities certainly received more money than Saskatchewan did from the Carnegie Corporation. Before 1928 the University of Saskatchewan had relied solely on government assistance from the province. This dependence did not change during the Depression, but as government revenue declined, the Carnegie grants for music, to help take over Regina College, and to bring Herzberg to the university were the only source of funding for innovation available to the university. The money enabled Murray to achieve two of his cherished educational goals and yielded great benefits in a province suffering desperately from the Depression and starved for resources to spend on higher education, let alone on cultural amenities like music.

The connection Murray had established with the Carnegie Foundation and the Carnegie Corporation prompted the Chairman of the Board of Governors of the university, P.E. MacKenzie, to write the Foundation seeking suggestions for Murray's successor after Murray resigned in 1937. The reply, written by Dr. Learned, highlighted the reputation Murray had made for himself in North American educational circles and gave advice which in the circumstances may have been wrong.[67] Learned wrote:

> Those of us who know Dr. Murray and have realized that his work at the University was drawing to a close have frequently felt concerned over the difficulty of replacing him. He has not only served the University of Saskatchewan with notable ability, but has been an educational leader whose exceptional power has been felt throughout the Dominion and in the United States.
>
> It is much easier to suggest the sort of man that would seem desirable than it is to name him. It would be my feeling that Dr. Murray's successor should, if possible, represent the same type of education that Dr. Murray himself exemplified in so high degree.

In effect, Learned told the Board to find another Murray, someone who had been educated in England or Scotland, and he suggested seeking names from Murray's longtime friends, Sir Robert Falconer and A. Stanley MacKenzie. The Board followed this advice and chose another Maritimer, James S. Thomson, as his successor. So strong was the stamp which he had placed on the institution that neither its Board nor even shrewd observers like Learned perceived that a different type of leadership might be required. Murray had worked so hard and so successfully to cultivate the ties with the Carnegie Foundation and its sister Corporation that when it came time to replace him, the Foundation's officers were looking for a person who resembled him. In this indirect but influential manner, the connection with the Foundation may even have affected the Board's choice to succeed Murray. Under Murray, Carnegie advice had always been accepted and acted upon. There was no reason to change after he resigned.

With Murray gone, Carnegie support also ceased. The two had come together in the late twenties, fortuitously for Saskatchewan. In many ways it was a personal connection, and that it should end after Murray left was natural. Murray's first letter as president to the Carnegie Foundation in 1908 had warned he would be "daring" in his demands. He had been, but his boldness was fully repaid.

■

Chapter 11

Depression: The Bad Years

"The long expected arts building is in sight." So reported the president in his year-end summary to Convocation in the spring of 1930. The provincial government had approved its construction and appropriated an initial $100,000 in the annual estimates. Walter Murray was jubilant. Already he could see it "immediately west of the chemistry building . . . built of local stone, the beauty of which is unsurpassed."[1] It was a lovely vision crowning years of planning, but within a few months it vanished, a victim of the Depression. Murray explained to the Chairman of the Board of Governors early in November that the provincial cabinet took almost two weeks to decide to postpone construction for a year. "While they were deliberating, if you remember, the blizzard came and the snow buried the unthreshed grains."[2] The letter concludes with a sad epitaph for the venture. "The beautiful weather would have made possible the excavation, the foundation and the collection of stone this year."[3] The cancellation of the Arts Building was the first blow of the bad years, or the seven lean years, as Murray later termed them. There would be many more.

The collapse of agriculture in Saskatchewan due to a combination of natural calamities and plummeting world grain prices undermined prairie institutions relying on agriculture for their support. Government at all levels, the university, indeed every activity in the province was affected. The cost of living was measured in what could be purchased by a bushel of wheat. One of Murray's correspondents wrote in December 1930, "In 1914, an eight-foot binder at Calgary cost 194 bushels. In November, 1930, an eight-foot binder cost 755 bushels."[4] Climatic disasters reinforced the collapse of wheat prices. Drought ruined crops in a large area of southwest Saskatchewan. The devastated area steadily widened in the years to come. Some land would not produce even enough feed for the farm animals, while the wind would whip up enormous dust storms that blackened the sky for hundreds of miles, piling the topsoil in drifts along fences where the wind-driven Russian thistle formed a barrier. The drifts reached heights of six feet and more.

Then came the exodus from the drought area to the north, where trees held the soil and there were no dust storms to uncover and blow away seed. The pathetic migrants simply deserted their farms, piled their belongings on wagons or Bennett buggies, and set out. They hoped they would find better conditions, but they knew it could not be worse. Those who managed to stay on their land, who could feed themselves and eke out a very small income would later boast they had never been on "relief." By the fall of 1933, a large fraction of the rural population could not make that boast; through government assistance they received the minimum necessities of life. Premier Anderson informed Murray in September 1933, "We are faced with a rural situation which involves providing relief to at least 40,000 farmers and their families and at an approximate cost of ten million dollars."[5] This amount translated into approximately $50 to $65 annually for perhaps 200,000 people and required a sum probably exceeding half of the province's revenue. Premier Anderson told Murray the province would have "to borrow huge sums of money to meet the situation."[6]

The Depression hung like an ugly pall over the remaining years of Murray's presidency. Murray might well have chosen to retire rather than to continue in his position as the economic situation steadily deteriorated. He gave the Board of Governors a letter of resignation dated December 11, 1930 because his 65th birthday was approaching on May 12, 1931. The University pension scheme which he had put in place made 65 the retirement age for faculty and president.[7] The letter specified that his resignation was to take effect at any time the Board thought it to be in the best interests of the university. Had the resignation been accepted, he would have been spared the onerous burdens of the depression years, but the phrase Murray used, "in the best interests of the university," suggests he submitted the letter as a matter of protocol, not expecting it to be accepted. The Board of Governors, facing the immediate task of deciding how the reductions in expenditures were to be spread among the various parts of the university and particularly how salary reductions were to be carried out, had no desire to begin a search for a new president. Murray's resignation was not accepted, but his position continued to trouble his conscience.

His letter to the Board in 1930 left the option to the university. "For the University alone is in a position to determine whether or not retirement in each case is in its best interest. This is obvious when one considers such reasons for retirement as the prevention of inefficiency due to the decline of physical or mental vigor; the introduction of new ideas and methods; and the desirability of giving younger men a chance."[8] The Board made its decision to retain him without hesitation. He then served a further six and a half years beyond the normal retirement date.

The retirement question arose in another context two years later. The Board of Governors appointed a standing committee on retirement in December 1932. Even before the committee was struck, Murray was seeking information from the Carnegie Foundation to assist the university in resolving the dilemma in which it found itself. The Province of Saskatchewan had adopted a plan making retirement at 65 mandatory for civil servants. At the university, retirement at age 65 was permissible, not mandatory. Murray's own position was one of the anomalies to be resolved, as was evident in his letter to the Carnegie Foundation.

> When the President reaches the age of retirement, should he not resign? If his resignation is not accepted should it be laid on the table to be open for acceptance whenever the Governors deem it in the best interests of the university? Or should his appointment be renewed from year to year until his retirement is desired either by himself or by the Governors?
>
> I tendered my resignation when I reached 65. It was not accepted. A professor will attain this age within a month.[9]

After the Board adopted a retirement policy, it specifically exempted Murray from the provisions of the policy.[10]

Far from experiencing a decline of mental or physical vigor which he may have feared, Murray continued to drive himself as hard as ever, shouldering tasks outside the university along with the constant struggle to maintain the university in the face of the repeated blows of the Depression. Just before the Depression struck, Murray received an invitation from Ottawa to serve as one of three members of what became the Beatty Royal Commission investigating salary rates and qualifications in the technical and professional categories of the federal civil service.[11] Murray accepted the appointment. The Commission was formally constituted on April 15, 1929. It held eight meetings and examined 67 witnesses before submitting its report in February 1930. The cost of the Commission barely exceeded $25,000, in great contrast to the millions now expended on such inquiries.

Murray took a particular interest in defending the merit system of appointment in the federal civil service. The difficulty was how to determine merit. As an academic he knew that examinations did not always discover merit, and he believed the experience of universities might prove helpful.

> If to the mechanical and impersonal examination there could be added the selection of a competent and impartial committee who could inspect the applicants, many of the howling failures of the merit system would be avoided. . . . Universities are by no means perfect models to follow but they have passed through the patronage system, the examination system, the vote of the outside body, and have found more satisfaction in the personal selection by competent judges, subject of course to the approval of a disinterested body.[12]

The Commission's work encompassed only the technical, professional, and scientific employees of the federal civil service, but the report recognized the government's growing need for specialists, especially in scientific areas. In keeping with their belief in a high-quality civil service, the Commissioners adopted an American precedent and recommended that a university degree be required for all candidates entering these special categories. The Commission, however, was more influenced by the British civil service practices in its other recommendations. Their thrust was to give deputy ministers greater control over their departments, to ensure that merit was the sole consideration for promotion, and to reduce delays in implementing promotion decisions. The Commissioners recommended the abolition of the multiplicity of categories. These would be replaced by a simplified system of seven grades within two divisions, a more rational and efficient plan. The three Commissioners also proposed changes in recruiting designed to attract the best Canadian graduates.

Walter Murray played a prominent role in the work of the Commission and basked contentedly in the praise given to it. Dr. Hincks, the Medical Director of the Canadian National Committee for Mental Hygiene, wrote to him: "Men connected with the Rockefeller Foundation told me recently that they had read your Civil Service Report. In their opinion it was the finest document of the kind they had ever seen."[13]

Two other Royal Commissions took up significant amounts of his time in the early 1930s. In 1931, he was appointed as one of the seven Commissioners on the Duff Commission on Railways and Transportation in Canada. The primary task of the Duff Commission was to advise the federal government on how to reduce the ever-growing railway debt of the country. This plunged Murray into a highly technical subject and involved him in fifty days of formal hearings, a considerable portion of the working year in which he carried full responsibility for adjusting the university's operations to large reductions in revenues. The next year, 1932, he also served on the Turgeon Commission in Manitoba investigating the impairment of the University of Manitoba trust funds and the position of the Manitoba College of Agriculture. Public service was an integral part of Murray's personal creed, and he did not use either the excuse of the Depression or his age to turn down government requests.

He did manage to lighten his workload somewhat by retiring from the National Research Council in 1931. He had been one of the Council's first appointees in 1916, and his length of service was second only to that of his great friend, A. Stanley MacKenzie of Dalhousie, who followed him into retirement a few months later. Murray's place on the NRC was filled by Dr. C.J. Mackenzie, then Dean of Engineering at Saskatchewan, who later became one of the Council's most distinguished presidents.

Murray's chief task as President of the University of Saskatchewan during the Depression years was to keep it operating. Between 1931 and 1934 the provincial grant to the university declined by over 40%, from $672,000 to $398,000. The grant was unchanged in 1935. Five years of crop failure and persistent drought had taken their toll. Murray later pointed with justifiable pride to the preservation of the institution during these, its most difficult years.

> The amazing fact remains that salaries were reduced, fees were increased, costs cut down, but no permanent employee was dismissed; no essential operation was discontinued; and no serious reduction in the number of students followed the increase of the fees.[14]

There was at least one occasion when the financial survival of the university hung in the balance. Each year the university needed bank loans in advance of the income from fees. Mr. Justice Estey recalls listening in to a conversation

> one Sunday afternoon when my father, as [Vice] Chairman of the Board of Governors, and Dr. Murray met at the President's home in the midst of a terrible dust storm. . . . The purpose of the meeting was to decide what to do in the face of the fact the Bank of Montreal could lend no further moneys to the university. The province was unable to advance any further moneys, and the payroll had to be met the following Friday at noon. I never did find out how they solved the problem but

somehow the university reeled from one such crisis to another until about 1936. Through it all, Dr. Murray carried on as though he were Chairman of the Board of General Motors without a care in the world.[15]

In fact, he had many cares and they weighed him down.

The Provincial Treasurer announced a program of wage reductions for civil servants in August 1931. The provincial plan was a deduction of 5% on the first $1,000 and 10% on any amount in excess of $1,000. The university followed with its own salary restraints which Murray devised, and he softened the impact on low wage earners and on families. On his recommendation, the Board reduced his salary by 20%.[16]

With the economic situation worse in 1932, Murray had to propose harsher salary reductions for the following year along with a policy of instituting one-year leaves of absence with three months' pay. The Board again accepted his recommendations.[17] Murray's economies, forced on him and on the university by reduced grants, bore extremely heavily on the teaching faculty. By 1935 there had been no salary increase for five years. Even worse, as Murray informed the Saskatchewan Premier early the following year, the faculty

have taken salary reductions reaching 25 p.c., much heavier than those imposed in the Dominion or other public services. Certain members have accepted leaves of absence without pay for six months, while others have undertaken greatly increased duties to permit their colleagues to go away on leave without pay. All this has been done without serious complaint or protest.[18]

The salary reductions and the compulsory leave without pay aggravated the declining morale of faculty and helped to create a depression psychology "characterized by dissatisfaction, frustration, a sense of futility and a consequent reduction in enterprise."[19] Of nine faculty members who went on compulsory leave in 1934-35, three resigned shortly after returning to take up positions elsewhere. Faculty were called on to teach larger classes with less help in the very years their salaries were cut.

The crop loss in 1930 due to wet harvest weather and a blizzard that snowed under the grain still in the fields affected eighty percent of the province. Students still wanted to come to university, but very few could afford to do so. The farm crisis brought a lineup to Walter Murray's door. Early in 1931 he wrote that "the number of students coming to me with embarrassments about money matters this year is five or six times as great as that of any other year."[20] Murray's willingness to help people in trouble was legendary, and it was never more in evidence than during the Depression years. Countless students completed their university education because of his personal assistance. His successor wrote in a tribute following Murray's death: "There was a phrase that often slipped from him, as he spoke about the practical solution to some problem. 'It's the human thing to do.' This was his philosophy of life."[21]

Murray's reputation as a soft touch was a concern to his friends. "He was always loaning people money who needed it, much of which he never got back and didn't expect to."[22] It even caused the Board of Governors to intervene. The Vice-Chairman of the Board, Mr. Estey, took the matter up with the family, to no avail according to Murray's daughter. "Mr. Estey spoke to us regarding Dad's habit of helping prodigals which impoverished him, according to Mr. Estey. Mother replied that it was his money and he could do with it what he wanted."[23] Clearly, Murray could not finance a student loan program by himself. The Board of Governors added funds to the existing Bateman Loan Fund, entrusting the President with personal responsibility for their disposition.[24]

Since the university was forced to raise fees to supplement the government grants, loans were essential for students who had no other means of obtaining funds. Soon the demand for loans exceeded the funds available, and students were allowed to sign notes for fees. From 1933 to 1936, between one-third and one-half of the student body signed notes, which piled up in the Bursar's safe.

Murray relied on "a tradition of honour" to obtain repayment, and his trust was rewarded. Eighty percent of the loans were repaid before the end of the academic year in which they were made.[25] Nevertheless, as the bad years followed one another so did the bad accounts. By the autumn of 1935, Murray decided to write off some of the arrears both for fees and room and board. The amount was not quite $2,500, a small fraction of the more than $100,000 in loans which had been given out to that date. Murray summarized his policy: "Harsh measures were never resorted to, though unremitting attention was necessary."[26]

By 1935 some debts were such that payments received double credit. One of Murray's letters illustrates his discreet approach, so at variance with the collection agency philosophy. "We are not anxious to embarrass you but if you could make some payment this year before the end of December for which you would receive double credit you would then be entitled to double credit for payments next year."[27]

Another stratagem used to help needy students was to build the Joe Griffiths Stadium with student labour. To obtain employment, arrears of fees were obligatory. Students were paid thirty cents per hour for a ten-hour day. Of the three-dollar daily wage, two went to discharge their debt, and one was retained for living expenses.[28]

Those whom Murray helped were always grateful, sometimes pathetically so. A widow whose two sons had been assisted by Murray wrote to him. One son had a job obtained through his recommendation, while the other son was allowed to continue at university although unable to cover his indebtedness. "For this help, these kindnesses, I am personally, deeply grateful, Dr. Murray. I accept them in the spirit of all good which moves in our lives, coming to our aid in just such ways as this."[29]

Walter Murray had first-hand experience of how the Depression could ruin a family. In 1932 his brother Stewart, a lawyer in Winnipeg, appealed to him for financial assistance. Stewart could no longer meet his debts. For the rest of the decade, Walter kept his brother and his family afloat with a steady series of loans and gifts. By 1940, according to Walter's own calculations, he had loaned his brother a total of nearly $7,000. He obviously knew that he would receive very little of it back.

The president, the faculty, the students, in company with the rest of the province, could not escape the terrible combination of drought and crop failure. Murray's admiration for the frugality of students scratching to make ends meet in order to complete their education shines through in his correspondence and public reports. He wrote President Wallace of the University of Alberta: "The economies practised by students are surprising. One boy is living on $15.00 a month—$6.00 being expended on room and $9.00 on food. Three others are living together and averaging less than $15 per month."[30] He echoed the same theme in his annual report for 1933. "In times of unemployment many young men and women make great efforts to attend the University rather than remain idle. This year, as never before, have they practised economies."[31] As a Victorian who believed in sacrifice for education, Murray was proud of a younger generation which was prepared to make even greater sacrifices to obtain a university degree.

Murray's personal help was not confined to the university campus. He and his wife organized and sent relief parcels to needy families far removed from Saskatoon—at Hudson's Bay Junction and south of Moose Jaw. In this he was responding to the pleas of former students. A.M. Nicholson sent Murray the names of nine of the neediest families in Hudson's Bay Junction in January 1931; within a week he had received the relief parcels.[32] When Murray heard from F.P. Grove's publishers in 1933 of the author's desperate straits, he sent him a cheque for twenty dollars. Grove wrote that the money came "like a God-send. It will enable me to get medical advice."[33]

Murray's task as President of the University of Saskatchewan was made more difficult for him during the early years of the Depression by the lack of rapport between him and the provincial Premier, J.T.M. Anderson. As President, Murray had enjoyed the friendship and support of a succession of Liberal premiers in Saskatchewan and he had worked closely with various federal members. His public status was always one of political neutrality, and he went to considerable lengths to ensure that no staff member of the university dabbled in party politics. But at heart Murray was a Liberal, and Premier Anderson was the first Conservative premier the province had known. Murray's circle of friends embraced a number of leading Conservatives including Sir Frederick Haultain, Mr. Justice MacKay and Premier John Bracken of Manitoba. Bracken had been hired by Murray as a faculty member and still regularly consulted his former mentor about western problems.[34] The differences between Murray and Anderson may, therefore, have been personal rather than political, but they were very real. Murray, of course, suspected Anderson of encouraging the hopes of President Stapleford of Regina College to obtain university status for his College, which in Murray's eyes would undermine the monopoly of the provincial university. However, he had other fears.

Just before a meeting of western premiers in December 1932 to decide on financial cutbacks, Murray wrote to Premier Anderson promising the university's co-operation to cope with the financial plight of the province, but at the same time he set out very plainly the limits to any reductions.

> We must, however, in our cutting avoid killing. If we can spread the economies to be effected over different services in such a way that life will be kept in the organism, I think we can pull through without serious sacrifices to the country. I am very much averse to panicky action but willing to make great sacrifices if they are met in a reasonable way and for a worthy purpose. Mechanical lopping off here and there without consideration of the economies is sure to do much harm. Possibly the wisest policy is for a decision to be reached as to what is necessary in the way of reduction and then distribute that reduction so that the minimum of harm will be done. It is most important that all branches of the service should feel that they are being treated justly and fairly.[35]

There are indications in this letter of more than a survival policy for the university. The references to "panicky action" and "mechanical lopping off here and there" are not symbolic of trust and understanding, and the tone of the letter is quite different from that of the correspondence between Murray and Anderson's predecessors.

Murray's specific concern was that the premiers might decide on a policy of closing professional schools to avoid duplication among prairie universities. As part of its efforts to reduce expenditures, the University of Saskatchewan investigated the possibility of closing one or more of its smaller professional schools, but it was clear such a move would run into strong opposition within the university. Instead, Saskatchewan had opted for leaves of absence with limited pay. Murray did not want to see the premiers taking such key educational decisions as a panic response to the worsening Depression. The professional schools survived and the provincial government did not impose a program of rationalization.

Underlying tension between Murray and Anderson continued until the defeat of Anderson's government in 1934 brought the Liberals back to power in Regina. Murray was delighted and admitted he was surprised by the results. The demise of Anderson's government coincided with badly needed summer rain. Both events were very welcome. Murray wrote an old crony, "The air has cleared, and with the coming of the rains and the lessening of the grasshoppers, hopes are rising. I do not think anyone has any overwhelming anxiety about the future now."[36] However, the defeat of the Anderson Government would not improve matters as much as Murray's euphoria caused him to predict, and the Depression would grind on.

The Depression years were not solely a catalogue of calamities for the University of Saskatchewan. Murray had managed, with the help of Carnegie funds, to incorporate Regina College into the university and so put to rest the divisive rivalry between the two institutions. He was also instrumental in negotiating the affiliation of the Roman Catholic St. Thomas More College as one of the federated colleges of the provincial university. This occurred in 1936, the last year of his presidency, but it was the culmination of nineteen years of patient work.

As early as 1919 the principles of such a federation had been passed by the University Council after negotiations between Murray and the Roman Catholic authorities of the province.[37] The negotiations did not then bear fruit, largely because the Archbishop of Regina, Archbishop Mathieu, still thought in terms of a separate Catholic university for the province. A start was made to establish a Catholic

College on the campus in 1926 with the appointment of the first instructor, Dr. Basil Markle. This appointment was reluctantly approved by Bishop Prud'homme under pressure from two Saskatoon laymen who played a major role in the lengthy and difficult negotiations preceding it.[38] The next year Murray vetoed the Bishop's suggestion that Markle be replaced. Relations continued to be delicate until Saskatoon itself became a Catholic diocese, and the new Bishop supported the idea of a Catholic college located on the campus and affiliated to the university. St. Thomas More College owed much to Murray's groundwork as Dr. Francis Leddy, President of the University of Windsor, recognized in a lecture on the founding of the College.

> Dr. Murray was probably the most perceptive and shrewd university president of his time, and his support of the idea of a federated Catholic College was certainly based completely on his conception that this would be good for the Province and for the University.[39]

Under Murray the University of Saskatchewan during the Depression continued to reach out to the people of the province through its varied extension programs. One of the groups which needed and received special assistance was the teachers in rural Saskatchewan. Many could only hope for such pay as the one dollar per pupil grant could provide, but when the salary came, the school district had used some of the grant for heating the school or other administrative expenses. Murray commented on the plight of these teachers in his last annual report. "The teachers of the province, particularly the rural teachers, have suffered grievously. Not only were their salaries cut 57 p.c. but their prospects for advancement were still more reduced."[40]

In a program to upgrade teacher qualifications, the provincial Department of Education instituted a rule that three university courses had to be completed in return for a permanent teaching certificate. In the Depression this was a very great hardship indeed. Murray addressed the problem with such resources as the university could muster. Aid in the form of scholarships, travel grants, and reduced rates for rooms and meals was made available. Over $20,000 was dispensed in assistance during the two years 1936 and 1937. More than 600 teachers benefitted from the scholarships alone. Walter Murray had started a program in education at Dalhousie as a professor still in his twenties; at the end of his career, nearly seventy, he was still helping teachers further their education.

He was just as committed to extension, and in spite of the biting constraints of the Depression years the university under his direction carried on its extension services. Throughout the thirties between 35,000 and 50,000 people in the province annually benefitted from one or other aspect of the university's extension programs.[41]

Murray also held strong and traditional views about these activities which he was not about to change. One of the early extension programs had been the formation of Homemakers' Clubs for farm women. They continued throughout his tenure of office. In 1932 the clubs wanted to change their name to Women's Institutes. Murray blocked the change by presenting a memorandum to the Board of Governors which then approved a resolution stating, "The Board view the proposal with disfavour and trust that the tradition associated with the origins, control and name of the Homemakers' will be continued."[42] The wave of the future broke sharply on the rocks of tradition, and the issue was not raised again while he was president. The angry reaction of the president remained vivid in the memory of Mrs. G.W. Simpson, who carried the recommendation of the Homemakers' Executive to him.

Saskatchewan had launched some very innovative extension programs in conjunction with the railways. "Better Farming Trains" had been sent through the province with displays for farm improvements. Dr. V.E. Graham, former Dean of Agriculture, recalled, "A great deal of work was done through the extension department . . . I saw farmers making cheese in tin cans with rocks on top of the cans to apply pressure to squeeze out the moisture."[43] There was plenty of scope for the university's assistance.

Early in the 1930s the Colonization Department of the Canadian National Railways instituted a Community Competition, which was based on progress in education, agriculture, citizenship, arts, and handicrafts. Robert England, the western representative of the Colonization Department, set the conditions for the competition and worked closely with the judges. Walter Murray chaired the panel of three judges for Saskatchewan and collaborated with England. The two became fast friends. The prizes for the competition were substantial—$1,000, $500, and $250. Murray and his fellow judges had to assess the relative progress attained by immigrant communities after an extensive survey of each entrant. Eighteen of the forty competitors were in Saskatchewan. Murray and his fellow judges travelled over 3,000 miles in the province on their tour of inspection.[44] Robert England remembered a day with Murray, when we had called on a Ukrainian family in northern Saskatchewan only to find that the men were out in the harvest fields and the woman of the family was going along to feed the pigs with two pails of swill. Dr. Murray went up to shake her hands and she put down one pail and shook hands and he picked the pail up and off they went together to feed the pigs. No university president in Western Canada either before or since had ever spent so much time in the homes, community halls, and churches of the Ukrainian, German, Hungarian, and Doukhobor settlements in that province as did Dr. Murray and he did it at a time when this was unique and unusual.[45]

Murray revelled in his personal inspection tour because it brought him first-hand contact with the immigrant settlers. He was able to assess not only their progress but their needs. His delight with the accomplishments of the immigrant communities was exceeded only by his praise of what the rural schools were accomplishing and his obvious pride at the attachment the immigrants felt for Canada. This was reassuring for Murray who during World War I had harboured doubts about the loyalties of some of the East European immigrants. He found no evidence of disaffection to report even though the economic conditions could not have been worse.[46]

He was particularly pleased to find "not a single child above Grade I . . . who could not understand and speak English.[47] He concluded: "The rural school in the non-English districts of Western Canada is not a failure but an effective agency in preparing the young for Canadian citizenship."[48] Here, too, he was able to reassure himself that some of his earlier misgivings had been unfounded. Education was an integral part of these immigrants' lives, and Murray had to confess that "their appreciation of the value of education surpass those of the Canadian or British."[49] He had taken a special interest in the success achieved by immigrant children at university, and now he was able to discover at first hand the desire of European settlers to have their children go to university. "The ambitions of the children and of the parents for their children to go to High School, Normal School or University was surprising. In some groups it suggested that of the famous old schools of Scotland."[50] From Murray this was indeed high praise. Everywhere he went he was the ambassador for the provincial university, and he returned to Saskatoon fully satisfied of the unqualified support for higher education by the settlers who had migrated to Saskatchewan from Central Europe.

Perhaps because of his extensive contact with immigrant communities during the early 1930s, he actively interested himself in assisting immigrants who sought his aid during the Depression.

Two doctors, Batanoff and Afanasieff, were assisted to qualify as medical practitioners in part through his efforts.[51]

Murray intervened with Prime Minister Bennett in October 1932 on behalf of the Doukhobors facing deportation to Mexico. He wrote,

> One might endure with equanimity the prospect of Peter [Veregin] himself being duped and transported to suffering in Mexico. But it is a different matter when the lives of simple men, women and children were at stake. . . . I know the Doukhobors fairly well and have respect for their simplicity, industry and childlike faith. . . . They are with rare exceptions good citizens.[52]

Bennett replied two weeks later. The answer was no. Murray could not help.

He had better luck in 1936, intervening on behalf of two Doukhobor families from Blaine Lake who had asked him to help bring their brothers from Mexico. Their story was simple. They had left Russia "like most where they could go, so we went to China as we were not far from the boundary line of China. Then in China we found it hard to live so some of us stayed there while others left where they could, like some to Mexico, some to the States and last us."[53] Through Canadian Immigration, Murray was able to arrange clearance for the brothers to come to Canada.

Murray could not remain immune from the radical political currents gusting about the Prairies during the Depression, yet he was careful not to become overtly involved in politics himself. He was personally unsympathetic to both the new socialist ideas of the Regina Manifesto and to the views of William Aberhart and his Social Credit movement, but he was acutely conscious of the suffering being caused and the difficulty of finding remedies. When he wrote in 1932 to Henri Bourassa to thank him for sending a copy of a speech on the Imperial Trade Agreements, he articulated his own personal dilemma:

> We are living in strange times. Hitherto we have been inclined to look to precedent for direction. Conditions are so fundamentally changed that many of us have very great difficulty in forming a judgment that is at all trustworthy. I fear that we have at least two or three years of floundering in front of us—perhaps more.[54]

After the Regina riot in 1935, Murray found it much harder to keep the university out of politics. The editors of *The Sheaf*, the student paper, published a series of editorials that were viewed as radical and Marxist. This aroused the local Canadian Legion in Saskatoon, the Rotary Club and some prominent citizens who urged Murray to act and who also complained to the provincial government. One of the Legionnaires wrote to Murray, "I pay for my Daughter to go to a patriotic Canadian Institution, not to mingle with a bunch of Reds."[55]

Murray tried to defuse things on two levels. He met privately with the editors to urge them to moderate the tone of their editorials. He told them that "they must refrain from doing things that are objectionable to the great body of people in the university,"[56] a message which probably did not endear him to the editors. At the same time he wrote to those who were complaining, playing down the importance of the editorials and trying to moderate the demand for punishment. To the president of the local Legion branch, Murray pointed out that "repressive measures only provoke, but consultation and friendly discussion of things usually lead to a better understanding and to the disappearance of the matters that are offensive."[57]

In a lengthy explanation to the university Chancellor, Murray revealed a shrewd understanding of the mentality of the students, even if he did not share their opinions.

> Things are difficult this year because of the trouble at Regina. The boys got very much worked up over the young lads who were like themselves. They had made preparations and had reasonable expectations of employment, but were unfortunate. Many of the young students felt very keenly the lack of employment and the somber outlook for the future. I think we older folk do not realize how intensely they feel on this matter.
>
> When we finished our studies we felt sure of good employment and a reasonable prospect of success if we were willing to make the effort. During the last three years many of our graduates have been able to get nothing. They have used up their resources; they have worried and fretted about the lack of opportunity and have, in some cases, given up in despair. If we could be responsible for things and keep alive hope, be patient with them and where opposition arises give them a little assistance, we would tide them over a very difficult time and save this country from serious disorder.[58]

This was the philosophy that governed his actions. When the Minister of Education, J.W. Estey, attacked the students in a public speech, Murray responded equally vigorously, telling Estey he should know better. "These boys are not Communists neither are they allied with them . . . simply young men who are much exercised by an unfortunate state of affairs. I am less surprised at their outbreaks than I am at sober sensible people being disturbed by the outpourings of excited boys."[59] The tempest passed, but the political passions stirred up by the Depression could not bypass the university completely. One of the surprising aspects of these years is how little the university was involved in the new political movements emerging on the prairies.

It was not only the movements on the prairies that Murray observed with concern in his last years as president. Along with other observers of Europe, he became increasingly alarmed by the tendency of Europeans to gravitate towards the political extremes of right and left. He feared the coming of another war and what it might do. He articulated these fears in a radio broadcast for Education Week in February 1936, sponsored by the Wheat Pools. In it he stressed society's vulnerability to war and how education promoted the interest of peace. He was both eloquent and prophetic:

> It is not merely that War will destroy the youth of nations, but War will destroy the very fabric of civilization when it obliterates great masses of people, destroys ancient institutions and crushes into dust all those agencies that minister to the health, the comfort and the happiness of mankind. Never before were the instruments of war more destructive; never more uncontrollable than they are today; never more accessible to the basest of mankind.[60]

As a Victorian liberal, he lamented the fact that concern for the rights of the individual were being swept aside not just in repugnant ideologies like Hitler's Nazism, but even in the popular socialist thinking of some of the students in North America. He sympathized with youth seeking a better social order, but as he looked around in the middle 1930s there was not a lot to make him optimistic. His pessimism was in part attributable to his age and the strain of his unbroken years as president, especially the burden he had carried during the Depression. Quite simply, he had overworked himself and it began to show.

In 1934 he saw the resignation of Dr. James MacLean, President of the University of Manitoba, announced in the paper. His letter to

MacLean reveals his own troubled state of mind as he contemplated the fact that most of his friends were now retired. "I often wonder if it would not have been wiser to have left here when the retiring age made it possible. The years since have been full of trouble and a minimum of satisfaction. . . ."[61] The underlying melancholy persisted. At the end of August, he wrote to another old friend, "Things in Saskatoon have changed considerably since your day. Many of those who were here in those days have gone and only a few relics are left. The spirit today is nothing to the spirit of the years when you were here."[62]

That summer, as they had for so many years, Murray and his family went to Big River. There he and his wife, Christina, were in a light plane which overturned on the lake, but fortunately neither was injured. The plane overturned in shallow water—luckily for both of them since neither could swim.[63] The mishap was naturally a further cause for serious concern at this time.

By 1935 he was thinking seriously of retirement as he realized that economic recovery for the province would require a number of years. He had seen the university through the worst period of the Depression. Soon it would be time for someone else to take over. He wrote another retirement letter when Dr. Buller left Manitoba. Buller, with Murray's help, had led in the battle against wheat stem rust. Murray wrote: "You suffered the inconveniences and hardships of pioneering. Intellectual pioneering is more difficult than physical."[64] Murray's pioneering days were almost at an end.

Others, too, realized this. The *Winnipeg Free Press* sent Mrs. Kenneth Haig, one of its ablest reporters, to write a reflective assessment of Murray's career which appeared in February 1935.[65] She caught the man and his accomplishments very accurately. She described Murray as having "a definite core, a definite policy, a definite hope and faith." He held firmly to the principle of one university for the province, a university which kept itself out of politics, but one which accepted the province's dependence on agriculture, placing it first in priority. Both research and extension were directed towards serving the interests of the province. It was a warm and humane tribute to a man "who found a prairie wilderness and built thereon a university at once an heir of the rich ages and a product of the long trail and unhampered horizons."

Murray naturally was also in a reflective mood as he completed his work as president. He addressed the university's twenty-fifth Convocation in 1936, listing the accomplishments of his presidency: the buildings, the students, the faculties, the graduates, and the impact of the extension program. The following year he addressed his last graduating class, sounding much like an Old Testament prophet as he chronicled the university's history. He saw his thirty years neatly divided into periods with strong Biblical overtones. "The first seven years were *golden* years filled with high hopes and plans for the university . . . the next seven years were black with the storm clouds of War and the miseries of readjustment. . . ." Then came "the fat years when prosperity flourished as never before. . . . The last seven years were *lean* years when drought, depression and disease conspired to withhold food for man and beast and the necessaries for a modest living." He told his audience that in his lifetime the West had survived two "great tribulations"—war and depression. Both had been nearly overwhelming, but he emphasized in closing that "as never before the public has accepted responsibility for the unfortunate and placed the rights of humanity before all else."[66] This was certainly his credo.

■

Chapter 12

The Years Far On

Walter Murray retired on August 31, 1937. It had been twenty-nine years since he stepped off the train in Regina to build the University of Saskatchewan. The rolltop desk he had bought with his own money when he first became president and which he had used ever since was trundled from the president's office to a small room behind the stage of the then convocation hall. There he was to share the space with James Clinkskill, whose job was to countersign the university's cheques. The room was not easy of access, it was certainly not spacious, and it was not private. Murray made little use of it.

In the months before he left the office that looked out on the bowl toward the chemistry building and the river, he pored over the files he had accumulated, stripping from the official university papers anything he regarded as sensitive or personal. These he transported to the president's house and sorted again. Much was kept and has now been returned to the university after the death of his last surviving daughter, Jean. But a large amount of material was handed to her at the time. She was required to throw it into the fireplace without examining the contents.

Murray and his family had lived in the president's house as its sole occupants for a quarter of a century. They had moved in before the stairs were installed, using a ladder to reach the second floor. Now they had to vacate what they had all regarded as their home. The move was a hard one to make, even if they did not go far. The Murrays moved to 1233 Elliot Street which was nearby. There the kitchen table became his desk, where he busied himself writing portions of A.S. Morton's manuscript history of the University of Saskatchewan.[1]

The authority, power, and prestige of office had now passed to a new president, J.S. Thomson. Murray worked hard to help Dr. Thomson get off to a good start, as Thomson acknowledged later in his own memoirs.

On his part, Dr. Murray was most cordial in his welcome and he did all within his power to ease my way into the chair which he had vacated. For the first few months he was assiduous in giving me the benefit of his experience and he undertook to introduce me personally to members of the Faculty, and also to the Premier with the ministers of the Government. Afterwards he accompanied me to the heads of different Foundations where I discovered the respect with which he was universally regarded.[2]

Thomson was not noted, however, for his tact and empathy. Scarcely more than two months after taking office, he omitted to invite his predecessor to the annual memorial service held at the university on November 11. Murray was deeply hurt at being left out.

A second wound occurred from the complete rupture of his long and intimate friendship with George Ling, the longtime Dean of Arts whom Murray had appointed as Dean in 1911. Another of Murray's successors as President, W.P. Thompson, recalled later:

> Everyone expected that Ling would be Murray's successor. In fact for many years he was called the crown prince even by Murray himself. When he was passed over . . . he became bitter and blamed Murray. . . . When I tried to patch up their differences Ling told me firmly to go to hell.[3]

There is no evidence that Murray attempted to manipulate the selection of his successor, but he certainly knew what was happening and who the leading candidates were. In this sense he flouted the convention that a retiring president of a university should avoid involvement in the selection process. Ling blamed him for the outcome.

Murray wrote to his old friend, A. Stanley MacKenzie, in May 1937 with a knowledgeable assessment of the candidates to succeed him. Both MacKenzie and Sir Robert Falconer had suggested James S. Thomson, another Maritimer, and Murray told MacKenzie, "Your suggestion of Thomson as a suitable person and Falconer's reference to him made the committee of the Board of Governors anxious to learn more about him, and others." Murray added, "Their choice will narrow down to one within the Faculty and one from outside."[4]

Murray's letter does not imply he thought the Board should automatically choose Thomson over Ling.

Thomson, according to your report and Falconer's, seems to be the most acceptable in personality of those on the outside. There are, however, certain things which should be carefully considered. Conditions here are so different to anything that he has been acquainted with. The life of the people in the province, economic and political issues and the relation of a state university to political matters and also to the people would be quite new and strange to him.[5]

MacKenzie hastened to qualify his original recommendation. "I would not urge Thompson [*sic*] as I do not know him well enough. But he has grown on me, and I feel he has some of the important qualifications for the post." He then stated Thomson's great drawback, "his entire lack of acquaintance with the spirit and issues of the prairies."[6]

The Board of Governors chose Thomson and the Chairman of the Board, Mr. Justice P.E. MacKenzie, announced the choice as unanimous. George Ling, Murray's old friend and loyal supporter throughout his term as president, believed Murray had double-crossed him. There was nothing Murray could do to repair the broken friendship.[7] When Dean Ling retired in 1939, a banquet was held in his honor. He made it a condition of his attendance that "that old SOB will not be there."[8]

Murray's sensitivity to the war and to Remembrance Day ceremonies at the university involved him in another incident in 1938. The student paper, *The Sheaf*, in its Remembrance Day issue published an editorial about World War I alleging that a Canadian officer had lined Germans up against a wall and machine-gunned them to save food. Murray was outraged by this apparent violation of the sanctity of Remembrance Day and blasted the student editor in a letter.

Remembrance Day is to many of us a sacred day, a day of sorrow and tender memories. On this day of all days your ill-timed efforts have stirred up strife, provoked anger and filled our hearts with bitterness.[9]

Murray made it clear he believed the university should repudiate all responsibility for the opinions published in the paper. He certainly left no doubt he would have done so had he remained president. He ended his letter by pointing out that since he was no longer responsible for the management of the university, he spoke only for himself. He did not want his letter published. He wrote it to let the editor "know how it appears to an onlooker who is deeply interested in both the students and the university."[10] What was so galling to him was the fear that students did not appreciate the sacrifices made by an earlier generation.

The Alumni decided to present his portrait to the university and set about raising money for it. Immediately, Murray commissioned Ernest G. Fosberry without consulting the Alumni executive, whose members were a bit miffed. They were even more upset that he arranged with the artist to provide a rather expensive frame. As a result the total cost slightly exceeded the amount raised; the Murrays paid the excess, although the Alumni could easily have raised it.[11] The portrait was painted in Ottawa, and from there Murray wrote to his daughter describing the process from the sitter's viewpoint: "It has been a very long and shall I say serious business. The actual sitting is tiresome—an hour at a stretch without movement and an alert expression are not the lazy thing they suggest."[12] Murray's own interest in art won out as he went on to describe how the artist worked:

He first made a study for form and expression. Then he made two studies for position and colour and when he had satisfied himself as to these he began to paint the head. He began to build for shape and proportion. It was interesting to Mother how he picked out the MacKenzie features with the Murray suggestions. I should say four-fifths MacKenzie and very little Murray. During this he was under painting as distinguished from the premier coup method which seeks to give the final colour at the first attack—a method liable to great mistakes, as the mood, light, line, fatigue etc., change. . . .

The final painting is a matter of an infinite number of touches following rapid inspections of the figure and movements to the canvas. With this there is observation from all angles so that the eyes will see colour with little suggestion of form. . . .

You understand why it is taking so long. When it is done it will not be a thing of daubs and patches—the corrections or the marrings which spoil the work of the inexpert.[13]

At the Spring Convocation in 1938, the university awarded honorary degrees to both Walter and Christina Murray. The honor was even greater for Christina who became the first woman to receive an honorary degree from Saskatchewan. She was recognized as his co-partner and for her many volunteer activities as President of the Local and Provincial Councils of Women, the first President of the League of Arts and Crafts, and her support of the Y.W.C.A. and the Homemakers' Clubs.

During the winter following his retirement, the Murrays vacationed with the Robert Falconers in Florida. The holiday was largely paid for by their daughters. No doubt the complete change, the rest, the sunshine, and the company of old friends all helped Walter to adapt to retirement. He was not content to be inactive for long. Both his friends, A. Stanley MacKenzie and Robert Falconer, advised him "to cut loose absolutely from the University for a time."[14] He was, in MacKenzie's words, "a free rigger," but that was not a synonym for idleness.

He returned to Saskatoon to find there were many tasks waiting for him. He had always been involved in a wide range of areas outside the university. No doubt he was happy to discover he was still sought after. When Sir Frederick Haultain gave up the chairmanship of the Rhodes Selection Committee, Murray took it over until 1940. He continued to be a patron of civic groups such as the Philharmonic Society of Saskatoon and the Choral Society as well as the St. John's Ambulance Society and the Poppy Day Committee. He served as Chairman of the Board of Governors of the Saskatoon City Hospital from 1939 to 1945. These were local undertakings, but his services were also sought by national groups and in one case by an imperial body.

A British parliamentary body calling itself the Imperial Policy Group wanted to include him in the list of its correspondents.[15] Nearer home The Canadian Association for Adult Education sought and obtained his services for the Advisory Board of a series of publications entitled *The New Dominion Books*. Murray was asked to pass judgment on the first two titles in the series and to make suggestions for additional volumes.[16]

The Canadian Society for the Protection of Science and Learning, a group of academics formed to help bring refugee scientists and scholars to Canada, asked his consent to be nominated as a vice-president. When Murray did not reply immediately because he was spending part of the winter in the south, the Society went ahead and placed him on the Council. Murray believed J.S. Thomson, his successor as president, would be better able to assist, but the organizers would have none of it. W.C. Wallace, the Librarian of the University of Toronto, wrote to him saying, "If you don't mind, I should prefer to have your name . . . since it is so much better known than that of President Thomson."[17]

Murray took a leading role in what for him was a completely new field, film, beginning in 1939. He interested himself in the work of the Canadian Film Committee whose library of British and Dominion films was distributed under the aegis of the National Film

Society. Murray became a Director of the Society headed by Sidney Smith, President of the University of Manitoba and Chairman of the Canadian Film Committee. Murray and Smith journeyed to Ottawa in March 1939 to take part in a meeting designed to increase the scope and importance of Canada's work in films. They met with five of Prime Minister Mackenzie King's Cabinet. From this meeting, directly or indirectly, came the National Film Board, which was to serve as a liaison between the government, documentary film production units, national educational bodies, and the National Film Society of Canada.[18]

The Act creating the National Film Board was passed in 1939. The Board was to be composed of eight members, two from the government, three from the civil service and three "other citizens." Murray was asked by W.D. Euler, the Minister of Trade and Commerce, who chaired the National Film Board, to serve a one-year term as one of the "other citizens."[19] He happily accepted. The Board's first task was to find someone to fill the position of Film Commissioner. After the first person selected had declined, Murray suggested that the post be offered to a Scot named John Grierson, who had visited Canada and worked closely with the National Film Society. Murray wanted Grierson to launch the work even if he stayed only for six months or a year.[20]

John Grierson took up the task of Film Commissioner, but within the year he became embroiled in a row with the Deputy Minister and the Minister of Trade and Commerce, under whose Department the Film Board was to operate. Murray was one of Grierson's strongest supporters. Prior to one of the Board meetings called to discuss the crisis which seemed likely to precipitate Grierson's resignation, Murray, who was unable to attend, wrote to a fellow Board member: "We are in agreement about the great value of Grierson's services to Canada as Film Commissioner. His departure would be a national calamity."[21] When Grierson's opponents dug in their heels, Murray and C.G. Cowan, another of Grierson's allies, approached both the Prime Minister and the Minister, trying to head off Grierson's resignation. On behalf of Grierson, Murray wrote an eloquent testimonial to the Prime Minister early in 1941, indicating his own perceptive judgment both of Grierson and of the importance of film for Canada.

Mr. Grierson in the short time he has been Film Commissioner has demonstrated beyond the shadow of a doubt his great capacity as a director of film production. He is without doubt a genius and has displayed a rare talent of imagination in the production of films and an unusual power in awakening the interest of the public in the making, the distribution and use of films of a very high quality. . . .

No words of mine are needed to support the claims that the Film may become an agency rivalling in power that of the Radio and the Public Press in the moulding of public opinion and the directing of human action. . . .

Mr. Grierson has not only unrivalled insights into the possibility and powers of the Film but he has an unsurpassed skill in the selection of subjects, their imaginative treatment and in giving to his pictures a rare human and lifelike quality. If we lose his services the production of National Films in Canada may degenerate into a dull, uninspired lifeless affair. . . .

In a few months Mr. Grierson has accomplished in quantity what many thought would require two or three years and of a quality that not a few thought impossible.[22]

The Prime Minister's reply was encouraging, and the Minister of Trade and Commerce also wrote Murray to reassure him that every effort would be made to keep Grierson, even though he opposed Grierson's demand to remove the Moving Picture Bureau Branch from the Department.[23]

Murray's intervention helped the Film Commissioner who in the end did not resign, but there was a sequel. Murray was serving a one-year term, and two months after his personal pleas on behalf of Grierson, he received a polite letter from the Minister informing him he would not be reappointed. The reason given was that "the members of the Board should be changed from one locality to another, in order that others might become better acquainted with what we are endeavouring to do."[24] Murray drew the obvious conclusion; he was convinced that his support of Grierson was responsible for the Minister's dropping him from the Film Board.[25]

His health had been one of the reasons prompting his retirement in 1937. Robert Falconer wrote to him saying he was sorry to hear that Murray had suffered from heart trouble and dizziness, but "this shows you were very wise in insisting on your resignation."[26] A holiday in Florida during the winter following his resignation was beneficial, but the next winter he was seriously stricken. It happened when he was in Ottawa for a meeting of the Film Committee, which he combined with sittings for his portrait. His leg began to bother him, and he was eventually admitted to hospital—the diagnosis was phlebitis. He was able to return to Saskatoon, but there he had a much more severe attack. Treatment for an embolism resulted in a long stay in hospital and a lengthy recuperation lasting into the spring. His wife was also sick and after Walter's release from hospital both were bed patients at home.[27] Recuperation was slow. He went to his summer cottage in July 1939, but he was unable to attend a dinner to honour the Hon. W.R. Motherwell, the longtime Minister of Agriculture first in the Saskatchewan provincial government and then in Mackenzie King's federal government.

The attack on his health had been severe; at age seventy-three he could not expect a rapid recovery, but his health did return eventually. With the outbreak of war there were renewed requests for his services to which he responded. By the late summer of 1940 he had agreed to serve on the Y.M.C.A.'s National War Services Committee. The next year his work for the War Services Fund was acknowledged by R.S. McLaughlin, its patron.[28]

During 1940 he played a part in the arrangements for the National Registration for which he was thanked by Saskatoon's mayor, Carl Niderost.[29] Earlier in the year he had been in Ottawa where he judged there was some lack of the proper spirit. He reported to his daughter Christina, "The war is more remote in Ottawa than in Saskatoon."[30] Such being the case in his eyes, he proceeded to urge further action in a letter to the Hon. James G. Gardiner. That careful politician made a careful reply: "I note your references to the support which we would receive from Canada in case there was a desire to go further than the Government has gone up to the present. I can quite understand that that would be the position at present, but there is always the possibility that there might be some serious reactions later on."[31] The view of the Government about Canada's war effort was indeed somewhat less vigorous than the seventy-four year old patriot deemed appropriate.

He did what he could in Saskatoon to help. In 1942 he was elected General Chairman of the "Vote Yes" campaign in the conscription referendum. No provision was made for expenses, and Murray paid part of the remaining accounts himself. His friends made efforts to see he was reimbursed.[32] Throughout the war he provided "smokes" for the boys overseas who appreciated his kindness in much the same way Saskatchewan soldiers in World War I welcomed the Christmas packages he and others from the university had arranged to send.

He also served as Chairman of the Board of Saskatoon's City Hospital. Among his other duties, he delivered addresses to the graduating class of nurses in 1940 and 1941. He assured the citizens of Saskatoon they were getting good value for the money spent and argued for better dormitories for the nurses in training. In 1941 he dealt with the challenge of war, still in a spirit of optimism. "War always called for the best, in physical fitness, in youthful vigour and in public spirit."[33] The war had other effects on the hospital. Murray reported it had suffered a "devastating attack of matrimony." Twenty-three nurses had resigned to be married. He continued to be active as Chairman of the Hospital Board through much of the war years. Some of the medical staff thought he was perhaps a little too active. One recalled "he took an interest in everything at the hospital. Doctors don't like interference in affairs that affect them. They just like the board to be there but not to do anything that touches them or their work."[34]

During this period Murray was able to complete one last piece of scholarship with the help of his friend, the historian A.S. Morton. This lengthy paper on the history of the University of Saskatchewan, for presentation to the Royal Society, was a labour of love for both of them. Whether it was lingering health problems or some other cause, he was not able to present it in person. Morton summarized it on his behalf to the 1941 meetings and reported on the occasion to Murray.

> The only reaction I got was from a professor at Guelph, (anonymous) who sighed that Guelph and the University of Toronto were not on the same campus, and grew eloquent about the constitution of the University of Saskatchewan precluding all political interference. He as good as said "Would to God it were so at Guelph."[35]

As the decade of the forties approached its midpoint, Murray's health and vigour both declined. When he was asked in 1944 to write an obituary for a longtime friend, the distinguished journalist J.W. Dafoe, he had to decline because of illness. One of his last ventures was to lend his support to the nomination of a former Saskatchewan politician, J.W. Estey, to the Supreme Court of Canada. Estey had lectured in law at the university and had served on its Board of Governors for eight years, including a period as Vice-Chairman, before going into the provincial Cabinet. Murray was one of his unwavering admirers and approached both Gardiner and Mackenzie King to urge Estey's appointment to the Court. The Prime Minister made a point of acknowledging Murray's efforts. "I have noted your representations on behalf of Mr. Estey, and shall not fail to see that they are brought to the attention of my colleagues in the Cabinet for consideration when judicial appointments are being considered."[36] Gardiner also thanked Murray as he took great satisfaction in seeing a fellow Saskatchewan liberal appointed to the Supreme Court.[37]

Assisting in Estey's nomination was, indeed, Walter Murray's last accomplishment. By 1944 all his old friends were dead. These included Principal Oliver and his two great friends who had also been university presidents, Falconer and MacKenzie. The careers of Murray, Falconer, and MacKenzie had many parallels: All three were maritimers; Murray and Falconer had studied together at Edinburgh; each of the three had been a professor in Halifax—Murray and MacKenzie at Dalhousie, and Falconer at the Pine Hill theological college. Within a few years of each other, all were appointed university presidents, and together they placed a dominant maritime stamp on Canadian higher education for a generation. Murray served the longest tenure of the three as President, but both Falconer and MacKenzie continued in office until the Depression. What especially marked the close relationship that Murray retained with his two closest maritime colleagues was the warmth of mutual affection. He consulted both of them regularly on all aspects of university administration. Even in retirement they kept in regular touch with suggestions of books to read, accounts of old friends, comments on the world scene, and, as time went on, tales of illness and the deaths of friends. Murray's last piece of public writing was his obituary of Sir Robert Falconer. It ended with a line that applied equally to his own life. "Nothing is here for tears; nothing to wail."[38]

Death was approaching Walter Murray. He lingered in a coma for a long period in the hospital where he had served as Board Chairman. He died on March 23, 1945. Three days later his funeral was held in Knox United Church. The hymns were those he had selected each year for the university memorial service. In his honour the university suspended all classes for the day. It was a simple service without sermon or eulogy, as he had wished.

■

Chapter 13

Murray: Some Measure of the Man

More than any other Canadian university, the University of Saskatchewan was the product of one man's vision. Borne upon and contributing to a strong current of progressive innovation in maritime academic life, Walter Murray came to the raw Saskatchewan prairie, newly formed into a province, with firm ideas on the nature of the university he had been chosen to build. He had been unable to persuade colleagues in the maritimes of the virtue of one state university; now in Saskatchewan he had a unique opportunity to construct his own. His colleague and longtime friend, Dr. A.S. Morton, wrote that Murray "had the imagination to see in small beginnings the great ultimate ends."[1]

When he arrived in Saskatchewan he came not just with an idea of what his state university should encompass but what it should do. In his first annual report, he defined the purpose of the university:

> What is the sphere of the university? Its watchword is service— service of the state in the things that make for happiness and virtue as well as in the things that make for wealth. No form of that service is too mean or too exalted for the university.[2]

The concept of service was both a personal and an institutional philosophy. Walter Murray was a Victorian Canadian who believed in serving whenever he was asked, and his record of service to education, to his church, and to the state—provincial and federal— speaks for itself.

Murray's belief in the service which the university owed the state did not spring up suddenly after he moved west. It evolved out of his maritime experience. He devoted a Founder's Day address at the University of New Brunswick in 1905 to an elaboration of the theme, arguing that the University rivalled the church in its power to influence the life of the society. It must be "ready to serve all sects and classes with equal favour."[3]

For a new university in a developing province, service took on a special importance. Its role was not confined to teaching students who were able to attend the university. Walter Murray believed the university had an obligation to reach out to the people of the province wherever they were to be found and wherever there was a need. His commitment to service, manifested in the university's extension programs, was accepted by his colleagues and contributed greatly to the success of Saskatchewan. The people of the province were willing to support their university because so many benefitted from it.

Murray, although not a prolific scholar, did find time especially during the 1920s to write a number of papers on various aspects of state universities.[4] Most were presented to the Royal Society of Canada. In one of the first, written in 1922, he expanded the definition of a state university. His eloquence and idealism reach across sixty years with a message that is as relevant today as it was when he first delivered it.

> The State University does not ignore the necessity of training, or the desirability of residence, yet it is open to all sects and occupations, and it makes the advancement of learning and the application of science to the service of man a fundamental aim. Moreover, since it receives its support from the people it must be subject to their control and carry to them what they need but cannot receive within its walls. Such a university, instituted, supported and controlled by the State, is in duty bound to the State to train its young men and women for good and useful citizenship, to engage in research and the application of science to the needs of man, and to extend the sphere of its usefulness far beyond the narrow limits of its campus. Teaching, Research and Extension are the three forms of its service. Its purpose is not to combat the religious or other interests of the people, but to co-operate with them. As it cares for the different phases of public well-being it increases in usefulness and merits the support which the people generously give.[5]

Two essential elements comprised the foundation of the state university he came west to build. One was that wherever it was located, the university was not to be divided, and in a small province like Saskatchewan there were to be no rivals. He had feared the potential of Regina College and succeeded in eliminating the rivalry, at least during his lifetime. The other pillar was the priority to be given to agriculture. Replying in 1908 to the official letter asking if he would be a candidate for the presidency of the university, he had advanced the claims of agriculture in a typically forthright way: "The College of Agriculture must be regarded as the sheet anchor of the university."[6] He made sure that it became the central part of the university. In his first annual report he advocated the primary role of agriculture: "In a province, destined for many years to be predominantly agricultural, the Provincial University should place the interests of agriculture in the forefront, or renounce its title to provincial service."[7]

Saskatchewan had the distinction of being the first Canadian university to include agriculture on the same campus with other subjects, governed by the same academic policies. It was a popular move, as Murray knew. Assessing it four years after he retired, he wrote: "The decision to include the College of Agriculture within the fold of the university, situated on the same site, and directed by the same Board of Governors, met with the warmest approval of the government, the legislature and the people of the province."[8]

Because of the importance of agriculture to the people of Saskatchewan, the university, with agriculture as its centrepiece, could identify itself with the people's needs far more effectively and readily than was then possible in any of the eastern universities. Murray's philosophy of service imbued the whole outlook of the university and explained why he associated extension activities with teaching and research as the three pillars of service in his definition of the state university. As early as 1914 he wrote of the University of Saskatchewan that "through its extension department in agriculture the university reaches every part of the province and not only makes the people realize the university is touching their daily life, but prevents the agricultural interests from becoming separated from the other interests of the province."[9]

The university, as Murray conceived it, belonged to the people of the province; it was open to all and it was there to serve the whole community. It could not remain aloof from the society in which it existed. He wrote in 1928 that "the large university is the state in miniature. All the interests of the larger world without are reflected within the university."[10] The university had to respond to these interests, and its response took the form of service through teaching, research and extension.

Murray's success in making his vision a reality was obvious to anyone surveying the buildings and the faculties of the University of Saskatchewan. He had largely accomplished what he had set out to do, but his success was marred in his own mind, if not in the minds of others, by two gnawing failures. He had not succeeded in having either a Library or an Arts building constructed, and he as a humanist himself, had been forced into the unhappy position of defending the Humanities in his university against the implied criticism contained in the Carnegie Foundation report of 1928. Measured by buildings, the Arts had greater trouble seeding themselves in Saskatchewan soil during Murray's presidency than the flourishing professional faculties.

Murray's vision of the University of Saskatchewan was shared by those he recruited as colleagues. He had a nose for able people. He sought them out and brought them to Saskatchewan where he then encouraged their development as teachers and researchers. Many later remembered with gratitude what he had done for them and wrote him letters after his retirement to thank him once again. Professor Allen, who had been injured in the First World War, wrote, "To you, more than to any other person am I indebted for the salvage of my life after my disablement."[11] Another who took the time to write personally was Frank Underhill. "Having been one of the infants whom you assisted through the early years of his professional life, I think I should write . . . and say how much I owed to your sympathetic and kindly guidance."[12] More than twenty years had passed, but the memory of Walter Murray's kindliness was still vivid and warm for this distinguished Canadian historian.

Murray was not revered by every one of his colleagues. During the 1930s some younger faculty members resented the one-man control he exercised over the university, as well as his Victorian attitudes. One was Carlyle King, then a faculty member in the English Department. When King later came to edit Dr. A.S. Morton's manuscript history of the university, he deliberately left out any mention of the 1919 crisis; he did not agree with Morton's account and did not want to hurt the feelings of Murray's daughters, one of whom was a faculty member in the History Department. King's own investigation of what had happened led him to conclude "that Dr. Murray was no Knight in Shining Armour maligned by a group of envious or disgruntled professors. I may add that my own personal experience of Dr. Murray in the 1930s did not lead me to dismiss as improbable the complaints that Professors Hogg, MacKay and McLaurin made fifteen or twenty years earlier."[13] Neither Walter Murray nor any member of his family could forget the searing experience they and the university had gone through in 1919. The interpretation of those events has been debated ever since, affecting individuals' assessment of Walter Murray and colouring the early history of the University of Saskatchewan.

Building the university was the central mission of Walter Murray's life after he moved to Saskatchewan. As his contemporaries recognized, it was a monumental work and one for which he deservedly received the accolades of his peers. On top of this, he performed many other roles in the church, in the National Research Council, on the Carnegie Foundation, and in numerous committees and commissions. The sheer volume of what he accomplished would have taxed, even overtaxed, the energy and capability of very strong and talented individuals; not so with Walter Murray. For many who knew him, it was not what he had achieved in higher education and the other areas that marked him as outstanding; it was the personal qualities he displayed.

Professor R.A. Wilson, formerly the head of the English Department at Saskatchewan, a distinguished scholar and a colleague of Murray's for more than twenty-five years in university and the church, told him in 1941, "To help people has been your real life work."[14] Wilson's shrewd judgment was correct; it was the way Murray operated that endeared him to so many. Not only did he exude an intense love of life, he had a genuine interest in people.

J.S. Woodsworth was one who experienced Murray's generosity.

> When you slipped into my hand a bill to get something for the kiddies I thought of a box of chocolates or something of that nature—When later, I saw the denomination of the bill I hardly knew what to think, "A mistake?"—but you don't make mistakes—I hope it is no lack of independence—I have decided to accept gratefully and to use freely, your very generous gift.[15]

Nor was his assistance confined to western Canada. From the other end of the country a minister in North Sydney wrote,

> I duly received yours of June 24th with its contents. I don't know how to begin to say my thanks to you for your time to time kindnesses—I have surmised that you had largely to do with the unpaid for interest which Dr. McDougall took in my case. All I could get from him was that I owed him nothing.[16]

During the Depression the cries for help were almost overwhelming, but he responded.

> Dear Dr. Murray, President
>
> I am a mother of six children and have nothing at all to dress them, and I will soon be a mother again in April and have nothing at all for the poor little one when it come.... I am not asking for new things, I am asking for old close I can make over for the children. We are farmer but it is 3 years we did not get a

bushel of wheat not a strew. . . . I have no shose for myself and no shose for the 2 year old baby. . . . Please do answered and let me no what you can do for me.[17]

Just four days after the date of this letter a box of clothing was on its way.[18]

Then there were the students on whom his mark was more deeply impressed. "Little did I think I would be an engineer when you first found us on our homestead. . . . I know that the only way to repay you is to perform a similar act to some less fortunate person."[19] Another and even more revealing testament comes from Dr. Georgina Hogg who recalls the experience of her family during the Depression.

> In the fall of 1931, my sister, two brothers and I all registered for the first time in the University of Saskatchewan—Isobel in Household Science, Peter in Agriculture and Allen in Engineering. I was in Arts and ultimately Medicine . . . our parents were farming at Landis, 100 miles or so west of Saskatoon . . . the drought was severe and crops and income both pitifully small.[20]

Murray must have been told of this family coming to university without any means of reasonable support. Within a few days of their arrival he had called in Isobel, the eldest, and arranged for her to assist the woman who headed extramural studies. "For stuffing, addressing and stamping envelopes Isobel earned the then very acceptable sum of $30.00 a month. I believe she paid the rent for our light housekeeping rooms with about $5.00 left over each month. . . . I have never known a university President so loved and respected by the students and I believe by the faculty. I'm sure part of it was his willingness to invest in people."[21]

During both World Wars Murray devoted time and personal attention to sending parcels overseas. His "smokes" for the boys were greatly appreciated, and the soldiers loved hearing from him since it renewed contact with their university. He continued helping until ill health made it no longer possible. A letter to him in 1944 underlines the impact that this contact had.

> This is just a short note. It's getting late, and the last patrol has just reported in and things are squared away for the night, so I should turn in. I meant to write you in time for Xmas but we were kept pretty busy about that time. I often think how grand it would be to arrive at one of your grand old Christmas parties. I do want to thank you for your cigarettes. I've had two cartons since I last wrote. They certainly come in handy.[22]

In 1931 the university yearbook contained a color photograph of the president who had just been honored for twenty-one years' service. The photographer wanted to remove the wart on his chin, feeling it would detract from the photograph of which he was justly proud. The editor thought otherwise. Finally the matter was referred to Murray himself who settled the issue. "Show me with all my warts."[23] What were they?

As even his closest admirers admitted, in university administration Murray did not delegate very much, and he insisted on making a great many minor decisions. Marian Evans Younger, the assistant registrar from 1929 to 1941, was more direct. She said, "He made all the decisions."[24] Mary Murray, no relation to the president, whose whole working life was spent as a secretary at the university and whose father worked closely with Murray for many years in Knox Church, recounted, "Dr. Murray was a dictator . . . all decisions had to be referred to him."[25] Gerhard Herzberg recalled that his appointment was made "over the head of the physics department. Murray just went ahead without getting his agreement."[26] Yet Murray's fussiness over small details and his unwillingness to delegate were not seen as serious flaws. Dr. C.J. Mackenzie judged him to be "an excellent administrator."[27]

Several people interviewed for this book, all of whom knew him well, accused him of collecting gossip. Perhaps this undue concern with being privy to everything that went on in the university was one of the effects on him of the events of 1919. It may also have been an extension of the all-consuming interest, which he undoubtedly had, in every aspect of university life. No one, however, accused him of using information gleaned from gossip to the detriment of anyone.

Walter Murray was the product of a strict religious, Victorian background, and throughout his life, whether in church or in university, he was determined to set a high moral standard. As president, he would not serve liquor in his house or permit it to be served on the campus. He supported prohibition in Saskatchewan when it was a political issue. As he grew older, he became more tolerant, recognizing the desires of others, especially younger faculty, to drink. Not until he retired would he accept a glass of sherry.

His views on co-education, while more complex, were shaped by the same background. In 1930, he wrote, "For the young folk between 12 and 21 it is possible it may not be ideal. . . . I think co-education in secondary schools is open to more objection than co-education in universities."[28] The principal reason he gave for these views was economy, but his bias was obvious. "Without it I do not believe women would have equal chances with men."[29] This was the judgment of a prominent Canadian educator, then 64, whose university teaching had started almost forty years before.

Did women have equal chances with men in the University of Saskatchewan? Dr. Margaret Cameron, professor of French and later head of the Department, became a faculty member in 1924. "Dr. Murray told me at the time they would naturally have expected to appoint a man."[30] Certainly, this was a curious statement because Dr. Cameron succeeded a woman who resigned to marry. Dr. Cameron added, however, "I remember someone did say to me that Dr. Murray had no bias in favour of men . . . he was not inclined to discriminate against women."[31]

The women living in the university residences might have amended that somewhat. They were subject not only to the general discipline rules of the university but to a set of rules, established by the president, specifically applicable to the women's residence. Infractions were dealt with summarily, sometimes by expulsion from the residence. Some relaxation occurred after a House Committee of the residence petitioned for reform in 1934, but the women chafed under what they saw as restrictive and discriminatory regulations. Murray evidently was a firm advocate of strict rules and restrictions for young women, fearing that if given their independence they were not to be trusted to act as mature individuals. In part, this was attributable to his own Victorian upbringing, but his wife, Christina, was even more rigid in her views than her husband and undoubtedly influenced him.

Christina Cameron Murray was completely devoted to her husband and his career. She subordinated her life and those of her children to the demands of her husband's job. One of her daughters said flatly, "Mother ruled the roost."[32] Walter returned the affection and trust in full. Christina knew everything that went on. She was his confidante and adviser, as is evident from her letters to him, especially during the crisis of 1919. But not everyone regarded Christina in the same way as her husband did.

Dr. C.J. Mackenzie was a close observer of the family. "He [Murray] played little part in the upbringing of the family. That was left to Mrs. Murray and she ruined those three girls. No she didn't ruin Christine who got away. . . . Mrs. Murray was forever stopping the children from doing things because they were daughters of the University President, or because it wasn't ladylike."[33] Christina Murray looked upon cheek-to-cheek dancing as "almost obscene. . . . She hated teas and would not let the girls attend that waste of time."[34] Her ideas, too, were rooted in a rigid, Victorian family background, and she was a woman of strong principles.

Her daughter Jean described another side of her mother, a commitment to service in volunteer agencies that echoed Walter Murray's philosophy of public service. Christina organized the local and Provincial Councils of women in Saskatchewan; she was an active member of the Business and Professional Women's Club and a member of the YWCA. During the First World War she took the initiative to provide social amenities such as dances with coffee and food for the soldiers. Her daughter Lucy was banned from helping in this as she was judged by her mother to be too friendly to the troops.[35]

Murray's commitment to the university, to service in the church, and to other public responsibilities carried a price in terms of his own family relations. On two occasions at least, in 1926 and again in 1939, he felt he had to justify, on paper, his own financial position and the estate he was leaving for his daughters. The fact that he wrote what amounted to two confessions, apparently meant for his children, suggests he was unable to talk to them in person and that his conscience nagged him about money. The latter was understandable. He had very little because he was constantly giving it away. He admitted to his eldest daughter, Christina, in 1926 that "nearly all my life I have been forced to ask for overdrafts or loans and had not my position been good I would have been refused more than the twice or thrice which I remember with not a little chagrin." After detailing the family's assets, he added, "I wished to give each of you the best education you desired so that you could always make the most of your life."[36]

This was what his own father had tried to do, but had not succeeded in giving the younger children. Murray had taken over after his father's money ran low and old age overcame him. Murray assisted two of his brothers to complete their schooling and provided a home for one of his sisters who attended Dalhousie. Now he was passing on the same philosophy to his own children. "We have never had any question or dispute about what each should have received, and each has made the most of his or her opportunities."[37]

Murray reiterated the same theme in a "Personal Statement" he prepared in 1939—about the same time as he drafted a will—going into lengthy detail on the education that each of his three daughters had received. Still, he could not convince himself he had treated them equally because in this document, he committed himself to set aside $2,000 in his will for Christina, the eldest, "to make the opportunities to each of the three girls less unequal." Lucy and Jean each went on to postgraduate education, and Christina went into nursing. In the actual will he changed this and left each of the girls $2,000, the remainder of his small estate being allocated as a reserve fund to help any of the daughters in case of financial difficulties. In his "Personal Statement" he seemed to be trying to expiate some inner feeling of guilt about how he had treated his daughters, confessing that "it was impossible to make things equal" among them.[38]

He had hired his daughter Jean to teach History at the university in 1931. Later he hired another, Lucy, to teach at Regina College. In each case he paid the salaries out of his own pocket, and he felt obliged to explain Jean's salary arrangement to the Premier.[39] (When leaves without pay became necessary, Jean was included in those asked to take a year's leave.) Her appointment was bound to stir controversy, and when Hilda Neatby was unable to obtain the promise of a faculty position at Saskatchewan, her resentment was directed at Walter Murray. In fact, he later hired her to teach at Regina College.[40]

His "Personal Statement" contains his own justification for the appointments of his daughters and hints at his emotional turmoil over his relationship to them.

> When the younger ones were ready and eager to work, there were few or no opportunities. They would have been self-supporting had there been positions available, had they been given a fair chance. The device of turning back my salary to give Jean and Lucy (particularly Jean) a chance to engage in self-respecting work may have seemed partial but no one should ever question the motive or result. It gave me and my wife great pleasure to help each to the uttermost. Our great reward will be the unselfish devotion and loyalty of the sisters to one another at all times and in all conditions.[41]

Walter Murray certainly had his warts, but on the whole they were minor defects on a large canvas. Beside the man's contributions to his profession, to his community, to his church, to Saskatchewan, and to Canada, they were small indeed.

"I don't hesitate to say that I think in the first thirty years or so of this century in Canada he was by all odds the most effective university president in Canada."[42] That is the opinion of another university president, Dr. J. Francis Leddy, who was a student at Saskatchewan during Murray's presidency, was appointed to the faculty by Murray, and who knew him as a neighbour after Murray's retirement. Dr. C.J. Mackenzie, a colleague of Murray's for many years, Dean of Engineering at Saskatchewan before he became President of the National Research Council and subsequently President of Atomic Energy of Canada, concluded, "There was none better than Murray."[43]

Murray's contemporaries also recognized what he had achieved. His lifelong friend, Sir Robert Falconer, wrote to him in 1936, as Murray's career at Saskatchewan was coming to an end.

> What I did in Toronto has been neither so enduring nor so important as your work in Saskatchewan. You have built up a great university from the bottom on lines that will never change. With great self-sacrifice you have created a standard of liberal education for a new province. Those things I could never have done. . . .[44]

The two old comrades were much given to mutual back-slapping in their later years, but Falconer's judgment about Murray's contribution to higher education in Saskatchewan was widely shared. Murray was seen to be at the top of his profession as a university president; his unusual combination of traits of mind and heart no doubt contributed to his success in his position, but they contributed much more to his success as a human being.

People of all walks of life were attracted to him: immigrant farmers and their families; faculty members; students; staff, including the farm foreman and "Barney," the janitor of the men's residences; university presidents; heads of corporations; cabinet ministers; premiers and a prime minister. All sought or enjoyed his help or advice and valued his friendship. His warm, deep, personal interest was obvious to everyone as was his kindliness. "This man with a twinkling eye" was a happy man and it was infectious.[45]

Two anecdotes from many capture the kindliness which was the essence of the man. Mr. Justice Willard Estey remembered

> the practice Dr. Murray followed of driving one of the few cars mobile in Saskatoon during the winter, and on stormy mornings driving over the 25th Street Bridge and picking up students such as myself and delivering them to City Park Collegiate a mile down the river. I believe he had several such routes that he plied in the stormy days of winter, and all about 8.15 in the morning.[46]

Grant MacEwan, in a tribute to Murray given on the CBC a year after his death, recounted the following episode:

> I was riding with him in his car one day when we encountered an old sheep herder on the trail, fifteen miles south of Saskatoon. We chatted with the old-timer as he munched his evening meal on the roadside. We learned that he was out of tea

and out of tobacco. That could be serious. Well, we returned to Saskatoon in sufficient time for our evening meal, but Dr. Murray couldn't stop; he phoned home to say he wouldn't be there. Instead of going home for supper he got a bottle of tea at one restaurant and a supply of tobacco at another and started back on a thirty-mile drive, to bring a bit of cheer to the old shepherd whom he had never seen before.[47]

As a maritimer, Walter Murray was immediately at home in Saskatchewan. The spaciousness of the prairies evoked the sea vistas of Nova Scotia. Like the maritimes, the prairies were not an industrial society, and both regions shared common beliefs on the value of higher education. Walter Murray was one of the prairie pioneers and Saskatchewan quickly adopted him. When he died the *Winnipeg Free Press* referred to him simply as "Murray of Saskatchewan."[48] At his funeral no eulogy was spoken. Across the river stood his monument, the greystone buildings of the university he had built.

■

Abbreviations used in notes

WCM — Walter Charles Murray
 USA — University of Saskatchewan
        Archives
 SAB — Saskatchewan Archives Board
 PAC — Public Archives of Canada
  US — University of Saskatchewan
TRSC — Transactions of the
        Royal Society of Canada

Notes

Chapter 1

1 Mss. Murray Family History, n.d., compiled by WCM, USA, Jean E. Murray Collection.

2 *Ibid.*

3 Lucy Murray to Jean and Lucy Murray, June 28, 1957, USA, Jean E. Murray Collection.

4 As cited in Terry Gordon Cook, "Apostle of Empire: Sir George Parkin and Imperial Federation" (Ph.D. thesis, Queen's University, 1977), p. 104. See also George Parkin, "Uppingham, an Ancient School Worked on Modern Ideas," *The Century Magazine* 36 (Sept. 1888), pp. 643-57.

5 As cited in Cook, p. 118.

6 University of New Brunswick Senate Minutes, October 28 & 29, 1884, USA, Jean E. Murray Collection.

7 *The Bunswickan*, February 12, 1942, USA, Jean E. Murray Collection.

8 WCM, Mss. notes for Convocation Address, University of New Brunswick, 1905, USA, Jean E. Murray Collection.

9 Sir Robert Falconer, "The Gilchrist Scholarships: An Episode in the Higher Education of Canada," *Proceedings and Transactions of the Royal Society of Canada*, 3rd series, XXVII (1933), Sect. 11, pp. 5-13.

10 I am indebted to Walter Murray's niece, Mrs. Elizabeth Thompson, for this anecdote.

11 *The Weekly Record*, Sussex, N.B., October 7, 1887.

12 Sir Robert Falconer, "In Edinburgh Fifty Years Ago," *Queen's Quarterly* 44 (Winter, 1937-38), p. 454.

13 WCM, "The Function of Philosophy in a Liberal Education," *The University Monthly* XI, no. 2 (Fredericton, November 1891), pp. 17-24.

14 As reprinted in *The Educational Review*, St. John, N.B., September 1892.

15 For accounts of the transformation of Dalhousie, see D.C. Harvey, *An Introduction to the History of Dalhousie University* (Halifax, 1938), pp. 101-2, and Robin Harris, *The History of Higher Education in Canada 1663-1960* (Toronto: University of Toronto Press, 1976), p. 105.

16 WCM, "Educational Ideals," *The Dalhousie Gazette*, October 16, 1893, pp. 4-21.

17 WCM, "Public Schools and Ethical Culture," *The Educational Review*, August 1896, pp. 50-7.

18 Murray wrote an account of this meeting for *The Dalhousie Gazette*, February 13, 1903.

19 Dalhousie Senate Minutes, November 7, 1908.

20 *The Dalhousie Gazette*, January 12, 1903, p. 109.

21 WCM, "History of St. Matthew's Church, Halifax, N.S.," *Collections of the Nova Scotia Historical Society* 16 (Halifax, 1912), pp. 137-70.

22 WCM, *Local Government in the Maritime Provinces,* University of Toronto Studies in History and Economics, vol. II, no. 4 (Toronto: University of Toronto Press, 1907), p. 57.

23 *Daily Echo,* March 25, 1905.

24 *Ibid.,* April 27, 1905.

25 Peter Macdonald, George Sedgewick and Kenneth Mackenzie to WCM, May 8, 1905, USA, Jean E. Murray Collection.

26 WCM, "Civic Pension Fund," *The Canadian Municipal Journal,* vol. III, no. 12 (December, 1907), pp. 570-1.

27 *The Halifax Herald,* May 1, 1909.

28 *Local Government in the Maritime Provinces,* p. 61.

29 F.H. Bell, *Tax Reform in Halifax* (Halifax, 1896), p. 22.

30 *The Morning Chronicle,* May 18, 1908.

31 WCM to J.A. Johnson, November 19, 1910, USA, Jean E. Murray Collection.

32 Lemieux to WCM, July 21, 1907, *ibid.*

33 Grant MacEwan, *The Sodbusters,* p. 228.

34 WCM to Parkin, October 2, 1908, USA, Jean E. Murray Collection.

35 The Rev. John Kerr, *Curling in Canada and the United States, a record of the tour of the Scottish team, 1902-3, and of the game in the Dominion and the Republic* (Edinburgh, 1904), pp. 112-13.

36 *The Dalhousie Gazette,* October 20, 1908, p. 4.

Chapter 2

1 Haultain to Sifton, Jan. 14, 1899, PAC, *Journals of the Legislative Assembly of the North-West Territories,* 1899.

2 *Saskatoon Star-Phoenix,* Jan.- 1907.

3 Thorvaldur Johnson, "Rust Research in Canada," Agriculture Canada publication #1098.

4 PAC, Council of the North-West Territories, 1885.

5 1883-46 Victoria Chapter 47. See also Jean E. Murray, "The Early History of Emmanuel College," *Saskatchewan History,* 9 (1956), pp. 81-101.

6 Resolution of North-West Territories Legislative Assembly, Nov. 20, 1889. See also A.S. Morton, *Saskatchewan: The Making of a University,* revised and edited by Carlyle King (University of Toronto Press, 1959), p. 7.

7 Morton, *Saskatchewan,* p. 10.

8 W.C. Sutherland to Scott, March 5, 1907, SAB, Scott Papers, fol. 36216.

9 Caucus members to Scott, March 16, 1907, *ibid.,* fol. 36217.

Chapter 3

1 Morton, *Saskatchewan,* p. 21.

2 *Regina Morning Leader,* Sept. 11, 1907.

3 W. Stewart Wallace, *A History of the University of Toronto, 1827-1927* (University of Toronto Press, 1927), pp. 173-4.

4 J.A. Macdonald to Sir Edmund Walker, Jan. 23, 1907, University of Toronto, Board of Governors Papers, A-73-015/51.

5 Clinkskill to McColl, Apr. 21, 1908, USA, Controller and Treasurer's Papers, III, Miscellaneous Records, File 1.

6 Falconer to McColl, May 4, 1908, *ibid.*

7 The letter dated May 23, 1908 is in USA, Controller and Treasurer's Papers, III, Miscellaneous Records. See also Morton, *Saskatchewan,* pp. 34-5.

8 WCM to McColl, June 6, 1908, *ibid.*

9 Calder to Levi Thomson, June 15, 1908, SAB, Calder Papers, fol. 3864; R.G. MacPherson to Scott, June 12, and reply, June 17, 1908, SAB, Scott Papers, fols. 36232, 32234.

10 A.K. Maclean to WCM, July 13, 1908, USA, Jean E. Murray Collection.

11 MacKenzie to WCM, April 1, 1910, *ibid.*

12 Forrest to WCM, June 22, 1908, *ibid.*

13 MacKenzie to WCM, July 23, 1908, *ibid.*

14 MacMechan to WCM, August 12, 1908, *ibid.*

15 WCM, "Recollections," *The Rotunda*, vol. 12, no. 1 (Easter, 1938), pp. 5-7.

16 *Ibid.*

17 *Ibid.*

18 Dixon to Scott, Sept. 7, 1908, SAB, Scott Papers, fol. 36242.

Chapter 4

1 WCM to MacMechan, August 15, 1908, Dalhousie University Archives, MS 2/82/L598, MacMechan Papers.

2 WCM to McColl, June 6, 1908, USA, Controller and Treasurer's Papers, III, Miscellaneous Records.

3 Jean Murray, "The Contest for the University of Saskatchewan," *Saskatchewan History* 12 (1959), pp. 1-22.

4 WCM to Christina Murray, August 20, 1908, USA, Jean E. Murray Collection.

5 WCM, "The University of Saskatchewan," *Transactions of the Royal Society of Canada*, Third Series, vol. 35 (1941) Sect. 2, p. 107.

6 WCM to Christina Murray, Sept. 5, 1908, USA, Jean E. Murray Collection.

7 WCM to Scott, private and confidential, Oct. 8, 1908, SAB, Scott Papers, fols. 36244-53. Drafts of the letter can be found in the USA, Jean E. Murray Collection.

8 WCM to Christina Murray, October 18, 1908, USA, Jean E. Murray Collection.

9 Christina Murray to WCM, November 8, 1908, *ibid.*

10 WCM to Christina Murray, October 13, 16 & 23, 1908, *ibid.*

11 WCM to Christina Murray, October 23, 1908, *ibid.*

12 WCM to Christina Murray, November 4, 1908, *ibid.*

13 WCM to Christina Murray, November 13, 1908, USA, Jean E. Murray Collection.

14 Christina Murray to WCM, Nov. 18, 1908, *ibid.*

15 WCM, "Notes on trip," October 1908, *ibid.* He incorporated these in his submission to the Premier. See WCM to Scott, December 7, 1908, SAB, Scott Papers, fols. 36260-63. See also Jean Murray "The Contest," p. 16.

16 WCM, "Notes on trip," October, 1908, *ibid.*

17 Scott to McNab, December 15, 1908, cited in Jean Murray, "The Contest," p. 17.

18 WCM to H. Tory, March 19, 1909, University of Alberta Archives, 902-3 (d), Tory Papers.

19 WCM to Christina Murray, March 21, 1909, USA, Jean E. Murray Collection.

20 Jean Murray, "The Contest," p. 20-1.

21 WCM to editor, *Daily Phoenix*, telegram, April 7, 1909, USA, Jean E. Murray Collection.

22 Tory to WCM, April 13, 1909, University of Alberta Archives, 902-3 (d), Tory Papers.

23 McLeod to Scott, April 17, 1909, SAB, Scott Papers, General Correspondence "M," 1908-9.

24 *Ibid.*

25 WCM to Christina Murray, April 11, 1909, USA, Jean E. Murray Collection.

26 WCM to Christina Murray, June 6, 1909, *ibid.*

Chapter 5

1 Scott to W.W. Andrews, August 31, 1908, USA, Jean E. Murray Collection.

2 Alan R. Turner, "W.R. Motherwell and Agricultural Education, 1905-1918," *Saskatchewan History* XII (1959), pp. 92-3.

3 WCM to Christina Murray, Sept. 25, 1908, USA, Jean E. Murray Collection.

4 WCM to Tory, Nov. 4, 1908, USA, Presidential Papers, RG1, Sl.

5 Recommendation of Committee of Board of Governors, Regina, Nov. 15, 1908, SAB, Saskatchewan, Department of Education, File 14B. See also USA, Jean E. Murray Collection.

6 Report of the President re relation of the Agricultural College to the University, April 5, 1909, USA, Jean E. Murray Collection.

7 WCM to Christina Murray, Nov. 22, 1908, USA, Jean E. Murray Collection.

8 WCM, "History of Education in Saskatchewan," in Shortt and Doughty (eds.), *Canada and its Provinces*, vol. 20, pp. 469-70.

9 Young to WCM, March 19, 1910 and reply April 5, 1910, USA, Jean E. Murray Collection.

10 Report of commission, June 28, 1910, *ibid.*

11 WCM to Wesbrook, May 11, 1914, USA, Jean E. Murray Collection.

12 Wesbrook to WCM, May 19 & 30, 1914, *ibid.*

13 WCM to Christina Murray, October 16, 1908, USA, Jean E. Murray Collection.

14 Vallance to WCM, April 8, 1911, USA, Presidential Papers, RG1, Sl.

15 Don Kerr, "Building the University of Saskatchewan, 1907-1930," *Prairie Forum*, vol. 5, no. 2 (1980), p. 168.

16 WCM to Scott, May 19, 1912, USA, Presidential Papers, RG1, Sl.

17 Kerr, "Building the University of Saskatchewan," p. 170.

18 Kerr, "Building the University of Saskatchewan," p. 171.

19 W.P. Thompson, *The University of Saskatchewan, a Personal History* (University of Toronto Press, 1970), p. 37.

20 Edmund Oliver Diary, Sept. 19, 1909, USA, Jean E. Murray Collection.

21 Oliver Diary, Sept. 18, 1909, *ibid.*

22 Oliver Diary, Jan. 25, 1912, *ibid.*

23 WCM to Falconer, Dec. 18, 1909, *ibid.*

24 Morton Manuscript History, p. 121, USA, Jean E. Murray Collection.

25 *The Morning Leader*, July 30, 1910.

26 Tory to WCM, Aug. 23, 1909, USA, Jean E. Murray Collection.

27 WCM to Mackay, Dec. 28, 1909; reply Jan. 1, 1910, USA, Presidential Papers, RG1, Sl.

28 WCM to Hon. E.L. Wetmore, Oct. 17, 1912, *ibid.*

29 Wetmore to WCM, Oct. 22, 1912, *ibid.*

30 C.H. Bell to WCM, Dec. 29, 1913, *ibid.*

31 WCM to Haultain, Jan. 18, 1913, *ibid.*

32 Falconer to WCM, January 27, 1913, University of Toronto Archives, Falconer Papers.

33 WCM to Calder, October 29, 1909, SAB, Calder Papers.

34 A.S. MacKenzie to WCM, Jan. 16, 1910, USA, Jean E. Murray Collection.

35 WCM to E.B. Roach, Dec. 22, 1910, USA, Presidential Papers, RG1, Sl.

36 WCM to Falconer, Nov. 1, 1910, USA, Jean E. Murray Collection.

37 Calder to WCM, confidential, Nov. 22, 1910, USA, Presidential Papers, RG1, Sl.

38 WCM to Calder, Feb. 7, 1911, *ibid.*

39 Scott to WCM, May 6, 1913, SAB, Scott Papers, fol. 36353.

40 Scott to WCM, May 13, 1913, *ibid.*, fol. 36361.

41 *Regina Leader Post*, May 2, 1913.

Chapter 6

1 Don Kerr and Stan Hanson, *Saskatoon: The First Half Century 1882-1932* (NeWest 1982), p. 46.

2 Scott to Lord Strathcona, May 6, 1913, SAB, Scott Papers, fol. 36355.

3 WCM to C.H. Mitchell, April 5, 1910, USA, Jean E. Murray Collection.

4 Scott to WCM, Jan. 2, 1913, USA, Presidential Papers, RG1, S1.

5 WCM to Tory, February 1, 1912, *ibid.*

6 WCM to Falconer, February 7, 1913, *ibid.*

7 WCM to Gordon, January 12, 1911, *ibid.*

8 WCM to Falconer, May 23, 1914, USA, Jean E. Murray Collection.

9 Report of the Commission appointed to consider the granting of degree-conferring powers to Calgary College, Edmonton, December 29, 1914, *ibid.*

10 WCM to Glazebrook, November 29, 1911, USA, Jean E. Murray Collection.

11 WCM to E.J. Wylie, January 31, 1912, *ibid.*

12 James Eayrs, "The Round Table Movement in Canada, 1909-1920," *Canadian Historical Review*, vol. 38, no. 1 (March 1957), p. 11.

13 The article was published as "Canada and the Navy," Part 3, *Round Table*, no. 8 (September 1912), pp. 650-6.

14 John E. Kendle, *The Round Table Movement and Imperial Union* (University of Toronto Press, 1975), pp. 116-29.

15 *Ibid.*

16 WCM to Hill, October 21, 1914, USA, Presidential Papers, RG1, S1.

17 *Ibid.*

18 Major McKergow to WCM, December 8, 1915, *ibid.*

19 WCM to Lieutenant-Colonel W.E. Thompson, August 2, 1915, *ibid.*

20 Lieutenant-Colonel Thompson to WCM, August 9, 1915, *ibid.*

21 WCM to Oliver, April 7, 1916, *ibid.*

22 Press handout, March 20, 1916, *ibid.*

23 WCM to Tory, March 16, 1916, Univ. of Alberta Archives, Tory Papers, File 902-3d (b).

24 WCM to Miss H.N. Bircholdt, April 30, 1917, USA, Presidential Papers, RG1, S1.

25 Major McKergow to WCM, January 26, 1916, *ibid.*

26 "A farm boy's mother" to WCM, n.d., 1916, *ibid.*

27 George Taylor to WCM, March 6, 1916, USA, Jean E. Murray Collection.

28 WCM to Taylor, March 8, 1916, *ibid.*

29 WCM to Tory, February 29, 1916, USA, Presidential Papers, RG1, S1.

30 WCM to Halpenny, March 3, 1916, *ibid.*

31 A.I. Oliver to Mrs. Oliver, July 24, Aug. 1 & 13, Oct. 2 & 4, USA, Oliver Papers.

32 Oct. 2, 1916, *ibid.*

33 Oliver to Mrs. Oliver, Feb. 6, 1917, *ibid.*

34 *Ibid.*

35 Morton Manuscript History, p. 173, USA, Jean E. Murray Collection.

36 Chief of the General Staff to WCM, March 26, 1917 and replies, April 4 & 10, 1918, USA, Presidential Papers, RG1, S1.

37 WCM to Burrell, May 28, 1912, *ibid.*

38 WCM to Burrell, November 28, 1912, *ibid.*

39 Brief to the Royal Commission on Technical Education and Industrial Training, December 20, 1910, *ibid.*

40 WCM to Editor, *The Canadian Courier*, November 14, 1910, *ibid.*

41 WCM to Macallum, Aug. 30, 1918, *ibid.* For the story of the early work on rust research, see Thorvaldur Johnson, "Rust Research in Canada," Department of Agriculture, no. 1098.

42 Foster to J.C. McLennan, May 26, 1916, as cited in M. Thistle, *The Inner Ring: The Early History of the National Research Council* (University of Toronto Press, 1966), p. 7.

43 Foster to WCM, November 9, 1916, USA, Presidential Papers, RG1, S1.

44 Tory to WCM, Feb. 6, 1917, *ibid.*

45 WCM to Wesbrook, Feb. 26, 1917, *ibid.*

46 *Ibid.*

47 USA, Board of Governors' Minutes, March 22, 1917.

48 *Greystone* [1934], Message of the President.

49 Cameron to WCM, Aug. 7, 1915, USA, Jean E. Murray Collection.

50 Glower to WCM, Nov. 23, 1917, *ibid.*

51 WCM to Falconer, October 21, 1916, *ibid.*

52 WCM to MacKenzie, Oct. 28, 1916, *ibid.*

53 Oliver to wife, May 29, 1917, USA, Oliver Papers.

54 WCM to Duval, Oct. 9, 1917, USA, Jean E. Murray Collection.

55 *Saskatoon Phoenix*, Dec. 5, 1917.

56 WCM to Wallace, Nov. 5, 1934, USA, Presidential Papers, RG1, S1.

57 *Regina Leader*, 1910?, USA, Jean E. Murray Collection.

58 WCM, "Address to the Ruthenians," 1917? *ibid.*

59 Dominions Royal Commission, Appendix III, "Western Immigration," USA, Jean E. Murray Collection.

60 WCM to Calder, Dec. 22, 1917, *ibid.*

61 Tory to WCM, April 3, 1917, *ibid.*

62 WCM to Tory, Nov. 26, 1918, *ibid.*

63 WCM to Armstrong, May 5, 1917, *ibid.*

64 WCM to Falconer, Nov. 25, 1918, *ibid.*

65 WCM to Oliver, April 12, 1918, *ibid.*

Chapter 7

1 WCM to Greenway, March 26, 1919, USA, Presidential Papers, RG1, S1.

2 WCM to Falconer, March 19, 1918, *ibid.*

3 Interview, C.J. Mackenzie, September 8, 1977.

4 WCM to Martin, Dec. 31, 1918, USA, Jean E. Murray Collection.

5 Martin to WCM, Jan. 4 & 16, 1919, *ibid.*

6 *Saskatoon Phoenix*, Jan. 28, 1919, *ibid.*

7 Martin to WCM, Jan. 28 and reply Jan. 29, 1919, *ibid.*

8 WCM to J.H. Holmes, Feb. 27, 1919, USA, Presidential Papers, RG1, S1.

9 Interview, Dr. Jean Murray, Oct. 4, 1980.

10 WCM to MacKenzie, pvt. & confid., April 11, 1919, USA, Jean E. Murray Collection.

11 WCM to Falconer, pvt. & confid., April 11, 1919, and WCM to MacKenzie, pvt. & confid., April 11, 1919, *ibid.*

12 *Ibid.*

13 *Ibid.*

14 Falconer to WCM, April 16, 1919, *ibid.*

15 MacKenzie to WCM, May 3, 1919, *ibid.*

16 McColl to J.L. Hogg, April 22, 1919, *ibid.*

17 WCM to Falconer, April 22, 1919, *ibid.*

18 W.P. Thompson, "A University in Trouble," *Saskatchewan History*, vol. XVII, no. 3 (1964), pp. 86-87.

19 Pp. 87-8, *ibid.*

20 WCM to Falconer, May 5, 1919, USA, Jean E. Murray Collection.

21 Board of Governors' Minutes, May 2, 1919, *ibid.*

22 WCM to McColl, June 16, 1919, *ibid.*

23 WCM to Board to Governors, July 10, 1919, *ibid.*

24 WCM to Board of Governors, "Memo re Tenure of Office," July 10, 1919, *ibid.*

25 Christina Murray to WCM, July 30, 1919, *ibid.*

26 *Ibid.*

27 WCM to Board of Governors, July 25, 1919, *ibid.*

28 WCM to Christina Murray, Aug. 9, 1919, *ibid.*

29 McColl to WCM, Aug. 12, 1919, *ibid.*

30 WCM to Rutherford, Aug. 16, 1919, *ibid.*

31 *Ibid.*

32 WCM to Christina Murray, Aug. 17, 1919, USA, Jean E. Murray Collection.

33 WCM to Clinkskill, Aug. 20 & 23, 1919, *ibid.*

34 Clinkskill to L.R. Murray, Aug. 21 & 23, 1919, *ibid.*

35 Clinkskill to WCM, Aug. 23, 1919, *ibid.*

36 Mundie to Hedley Murray, Sept. 1, 1919, *ibid.*

37 WCM to Christina Murray, Aug. 31, 1919, *ibid.*

38 Falconer to WCM, Sept. 22, 1919, *ibid.*

39 Taylor to WCM, Sept. 30, 1919, *ibid.*

40 Clinkskill to WCM, Sept. 29, 1919,*ibid.*

41 Christina Murray to WCM, Oct. 6, 1919, *ibid.*

42 Christina Murray to Martin, Dec. 21, 1919, *ibid.*

43 WCM to Tory, Feb. 16, 1920, University of Alberta Archives, Tory Papers, 902 3d (c).

44 *Saskatoon Star*, Aug. 12, 1919.

45 John G. Diefenbaker, *One Canada: Memoirs of the Right Honourable John G. Diefenbaker*, vol. 1 (Macmillan, 1975), p. 79.

46 Interview, Mr. Justice Emmett Hall, Sept. 27, 1979.

47 Martin to McCraney, Aug. 27, 1919, USA, Jean E. Murray Collection.

48 Martin to WCM, Aug. 28, 1919, *ibid.*

49 Auld to WCM, Aug. 30, 1919; Macallum to WCM, Sept. 5, 1919, *ibid.*

50 Dunning to WCM, confid. Aug. 28, 1919, *ibid.*

51 WCM to Christina Murray, Oct. 9, 1919, *ibid.*

52 MacKenzie to WCM, Sept. 26, 1919, *ibid.*

53 *Saskatoon Star*, Sept. 29, 1919.

54 WCM to Ling, Nov. 8, 1919, USA, Jean E. Murray Collection.

55 Moxon to WCM, Dec. 5, 1919, *ibid.*

56 Interview, Mr. Justice Emmett Hall, Sept. 27, 1979.

57 Thompson, "A University in Trouble," p. 95.

58 Jean Bayer to Christina Murray, Nov. 22, 1919, USA, Jean E. Murray Collection.

59 Moxon to WCM, Dec. 5, 1919, *ibid.*

60 Weir to Martin, Dec. 13, 1919, *ibid.*

61 "The University Trouble, Summary of Events and Discussion of Principles Involved," Citizens' Committee of Saskatoon, 1919, *ibid.*

62 Martin to Endicott, Dec. 24, 1919, USA, Jean E. Murray Collection.

63 WCM to Adam Shortt, Feb. 13, 1920, *ibid.*

64 WCM to Tory, Feb. 16, 1920, University of Alberta Archives, Tory Papers, file 902 3d (c).

65 Transcript of evidence of C.A. Dunning, March 26, 1920, USA, Jean E. Murray Collection.

66 *Saskatoon Star-Phoenix*, April 7, 1920.

67 WCM to Sidney Smith, June 17, 1935, USA, Jean E. Murray Collection.

68 University of Saskatchewan, Judgement of Visitor, April 30, 1920, *ibid.* For a modern legal summary see Bora Laskin, "Some Cases at Law," Appendix A of George Whalley, ed., *A Place of Liberty: Essays on the Government of Canadian Universities* (Toronto: Clarke, Irwin & Co., 1964), pp. 182-4.

69 *Canadian Chemical Journal*, January, 1920.

70 WCM to MacKenzie, May 13, 1920, USA, Jean E. Murray Collection.

71 WCM to Frank Adams, May 11, 1920, *ibid.*

72 G.S. Mundie to WCM, Aug. 11, 1920, *ibid.*

Chapter 8

1 *Dalhousie Gazette*, October 10, 1893.

2 *Dalhousie Gazette*, March 20, 1895.

3 *Presbyterian Witness*, Sept. 7, 1901 and Jan. 18, 1902.

4 WCM, "History of St. Matthew's Church, Halifax, Nova Scotia," *Collections of the Nova Scotia Historical Society*, vol. 16 (Halifax, 1912).

5 *Ibid.*, p. 147.

6 *Dalhousie Gazette*, March 20, 1906.

7 It was published that same year as *The Way to Union . . .* , (Toronto: William Briggs, 1912). See also WCM to Morton, August 28, 1912, USA, Jean E. Murray Collection.

8 WCM, undated paper (1906?) entitled "For the Maritime Local Committee of the Joint Union Committees," US, St. Andrew's College, Murray Papers, File 1.

9 Falconer to WCM, July 22, 1906, *ibid.*, File 3.

10 T.C. James to WCM, Dec. 1, 1906, *ibid.*, File 3.

11 Falconer to WCM, July 9, 1906, *ibid.*, File 3.

12 WCM to Oliver, Aug. 4, 1911, US, St. Andrew's College, Oliver Papers.

13 WCM to Oliver, Aug. 26, 1911, *ibid.*

14 WCM, "A Theological College in Saskatchewan," *The Presbyterian*, March 28, 1912.

15 WCM, "The University and the Theological Universities," March 21, 1921, USA, Jean E. Murray Collection.

16 WCM, "Church Union," *ibid.* Analysis of voting in the Presbyterian Church, 1911?

17 See letters to Munro, Fullerton, Glover, Feb. 22, 1911 and Haddow to WCM, March 8, 1911, *ibid.*

18 WCM, "Church Union Vote and Comparisons," Sept. 1911?, *ibid.*

19 WCM to D.M. Ramsey, R.M. Haddow, Dr. MacKay, Aug. 25, 1911, *ibid.*

20 WCM to Rev. J.W.A. Nicholson, March 13, 1912, *ibid.*

21 WCM, "Benefits for Saskatoon," *ibid.* Draft article for the *Presbyterian Witness*, 1911?.

22 WCM to Chancellor Burwash, June 19, 1912, *ibid.*

23 *Toronto Daily Star*, June 11, 1912.

24 WCM to the editor of the *Presbyterian Witness*, Feb. 13, 1914, USA, Jean E. Murray Collection.

25 WCM to Dr. W.J. Clark, June 27, 1914, *ibid.*

26 *Ibid.*

27 Falconer to WCM, Jan. 4, 1916, *ibid.*

28 WCM to the editor of *The Presbyterian*, Jan. 21, 1916, *ibid.*

29 "An Appeal to the General Assembly of the Presbyterian Church meeting in Winnipeg, June 9, 1916," *ibid.*

30 WCM to Fraser, Nov. 8, 1916, enclosing "Has the Assembly broken faith?" and "Was the Winnipeg Assembly Insane?" *ibid.*

31 WCM to Taylor, Nov. 25, 1916, enclosing "Why did the Winnipeg Assembly feel obliged to reach a decision about Church Union?" *ibid.*

32 WCM, "Early Plans and Negotiations Looking Toward Union," *The New Outlook*, June 10, 1925.

33 *Manitoba Free Press*, May 28, 1921.

34 F.M. Morter to WCM, May 3, 1921 and reply May 11, 1921, US, St. Andrew's College, Murray Papers.

35 *Ibid.*

36 *Saskatoon Star Phoenix*, June 6, 1921.

37 WCM to Pidgeon, Oct. 4, 1921, US, St. Andrew's College, Murray Papers, File 6.

38 WCM to Pidgeon, Nov. 2, 1921, *ibid.*

39 Pidgeon to WCM, July 28, 1922, *ibid.*, File 7.

40 WCM to Edmison, Oct. 11, 1922, *ibid.*

41 Falconer to WCM, Dec. 2, 1922, *ibid.*

42 WCM to Pidgeon, Dec. 8, 1922, *ibid.*

43 WCM, "The Cry for Another Vote: Reasons Why There Can Not and Ought Not to be Another Vote on Church Union," 1923, *ibid.*

44 *Ibid.*

45 *Ibid.*

46 File 8, Newton Powell to WCM, March 28, 1923; George Pidgeon to WCM, Jan. 26; WCM to Edmison, April 6, 1923; Pidgeon and Edmison to WCM, Apr. 13; Wilson to WCM, Apr. 17, 1923, *ibid.*

47 R.S. Wilson to WCM, March 21, 1924, *ibid.*, File 9.

48 WCM to G.B. Johnston, M.L.A., Jan. 7, 1924, *ibid.*

49 WCM to Calder, Jan. 7, 1924, and reply March 26, 1924. See also WCM to Motherwell, Jan. 7 and reply Jan. 26, 1924, *ibid.*

50 WCM to Falconer, Feb. 29, 1925, USA, Jean E. Murray Collection.

51 MacKinnon to WCM, April 2, 1926, *ibid.*

52 Minutes of Knox Church Session, May 6, 1945.

Chapter 9

1 *Winnipeg Tribune*, March 30, 1925.

2 Don Kerr, "Building the University of Saskatchewan," p. 174.

3 President's Report, 1930, USA.

4 President's Report, 1920-21, USA.

5 President's Report, 1924-5, USA.

6 WCM to Brown, Sept. 24, 1924, USA, Presidential Papers, RG1, S1. See also Don Kerr, "Building the University of Saskatchewan 1907-1930," *Prairie Forum*, vol. 5, no. 2 (1980), p. 129.

7 Archibald MacMechan, "Impressions of a Train-Flight Across Canada," *Halifax Herald*, [1927], USA, Jean E. Murray Collection.

8 WCM to Rand McNalley, Feb. 24, 1923, USA, Presidential Papers, RG1, S1.

9 WCM to R.M. MacGregor, Dec. 20, 1921, *ibid.*

10 WCM to Tory, Feb. 15, 1922, USA, Jean E. Murray Collection.

11 Dunning to WCM, Jan. 30, 1923, USA, Presidential Papers, RG1, S1.

12 Interview, H.C. Rees, stepson of Donald MacLean, April 23, 1978.

13 WCM to Heisler, April 7 & 10, 1926, USA, Presidential Papers, RG1, S1.

14 Riches to WCM, Dec. 14, 1928, *ibid.*

15 Riches to WCM, March 20, 1927, USA, Presidential Papers, RG1, S1.

16 Interview, F.F. MacDermid, April 13, 1978.

17 *Saskatoon Phoenix*, May 27, 1921.

18 Interview, F.F. MacDermid, April 13, 1978.

19 WCM, "Professional Education in a Western University," Convocation Address to the University of Manitoba, 1913, USA, Jean E. Murray Collection.

20 *Ibid.*

21 WCM to A.S. MacKenzie, Jan. 17, 1913, USA, Jean E. Murray Collection.

22 *Ibid.*

23 President's Report, 1922-23, USA.

24 Memorandum for the Rockefeller Foundation, [1919], USA, Jean E. Murray Collection.

25 *Ibid.*

26 President's Report, 1926-27, USA.

27 *Ibid.*

28 WCM to Tory, May 29, 1924, USA, Presidential Papers, RG1, S1.

29 WCM to Tory, Jan. 23, 1929, *ibid.*

30 WCM to Tory, January 12, 1929, *ibid.*

31 Cited in W.P. Thompson, *The University of Saskatchewan*, p. 45.

32 Interview, Dr. Jean Murray, April, 1978.

33 President's Report, 1926-27, USA.

34 President's Report, 1921, *ibid.*

35 *Ibid.*

36 University of Saskatchewan, Catalogue of Permanent Art Collection, 1980.

37 *Ibid.*

38 Interview, Mrs. A.S. Morton, Sept. 9, 1977.

39 WCM, "Tribute to Gus Kenderdine," April 17, 1936, USA, Jean E. Murray Collection.

40 Interview, Ernest Lindner, April 20, 1978.

41 *Ibid.*

42 Grandmaison to WCM, Aug. 14, 1936, USA, Presidential Papers, RG1, S1.

43 WCM to Henderson, May 3, 1929, *ibid.* See also Paul C. Hamilton, *Grandmaison, Henderson and Kenderdine: Painters of the Prairies,* (University of Saskatchewan, 1979).

44 Bickersteth to WCM, Feb. 7, 1925, *ibid.*

45 Bickersteth to WCM, April 3, 1925, *ibid.*

46 *Ibid.*

47 WCM to Bickersteth, Feb. 10, 1925, USA, Presidential Papers, RG1, S1.

48 WCM to L.B. Beale, March 15, 1921, *ibid.*

49 Interview, Harold Moss, April 22, 1978.

50 H.C. Moss, "The University of Saskatchewan, 1917-1924," unpublished manuscript.

51 WCM to Charles Camsell, Oct. 31, 1922, USA, Jean E. Murray Collection.

52 WCM to Dunning, Oct. 15, 1923, USA, Presidential Papers, RG1, S1.

53 "Control of Equine Infectious Anemia," Agriculture Canada Publication, 1973.

54 WCM to the Hon. W.R. Motherwell, April 5, 1924, USA, Presidential Papers, RG1, S1.

55 President's Report, 1923-24, USA.

56 President's Report, 1923-24, USA.

57 "University Development in Canada" *TRSC,* Third Series, vol. 16 (1922), Sect. 2, pp. 77-105; "State Support and Control of Universities in Canada," *TRSC,* Third Series, vol. 19 (1925), Sect. 2, pp. 19-32; "Manitoba's Place in University History," *TRSC,* Third Series, vol. 22 (1928), Sect. 2, pp. 57-84.

58 WCM to R.B. Thompson, December 17, 1920, USA, Jean E. Murray Collection.

59 WCM to Pelham Elgar, Jan. 23, 1922, *ibid.*

60 WCM to MacMechan, Feb. 3, 1926, *ibid.*

61 WCM to Sir George Foster, April 2, 1921, *ibid.*

62 WCM to John Fredstrom, July 5, 1926, USA, Jean E. Murray Collection.

63 Mackenzie King to WCM, telegram, Sept. 12, 1923 and reply Sept. 24, 1923, *ibid.*

64 WCM to Pritchett, December 29, 1923, Carnegie Corporation Files, General 444. See also W.L. Morton, *One University, A History of the University of Manitoba, 1877-1952,* (McClelland and Stewart, 1957), pp. 132-136.

65 President's Report, 1929, USA.

66 *Manitoba Free Press,* April 9, 1929.

67 *Ibid.*

68 Interview, H. Rees, April 23, 1978.

69 *Ibid.*

70 *Regina Leader,* Feb. 28, 1930.

71 *Ibid.*

72 Christina to Lucy and Tina Murray, Feb. 26, 1930, USA, Jean E. Murray Collection.

73 WCM to Ling, March 4, 1930, *ibid.*

Chapter 10

1 On the Carnegie Foundation, see Robert S. Lester, *Forty Years of Carnegie Giving* (New York, 1941); Howard J. Savage, *Fruit of an Impulse: Forty-five Years of the Carnegie Foundation* (New York, 1953); Abraham Flexner, *Funds and*

Foundations: Their Policies Past and Present, (New York, 1976); Merle Curti and Roderick Nash, *Philanthropy in the Shaping of American Higher Education*, (Rutgers University Press, 1965).

2 WCM to Pritchett, August 25, 1908, Carnegie Foundation, File 665.

3 Pritchett to WCM, May 26, 1913, Carnegie Foundation, File 689.

4 WCM to Pritchett, Sept. 10, 1915, *ibid.*

5 WCM to Pritchett, Feb. 15, 1928, Carnegie Foundation, File 689.

6 Secretary to WCM, Nov. 19, 1919, Carnegie Foundation, File 99.

7 WCM to Pritchett, Feb. 15 and April 12, 1928, reply May 10, 1928, Carnegie Foundation, File 689.

8 WCM to Pritchett, May 15, 1928, *ibid.*

9 WCM to Savage, November 26, 1928, *ibid.*

10 Savage to Pritchett, Oct. 15, 1928, *ibid.*

11 Savage to WCM, Dec. 1, 1928 and reply Dec. 6, 1928, *ibid.*

12 Savage to WCM, Dec. 11, 1928, *ibid.*

13 WCM to Pritchett, April 3, 1929, and reply April 13, 1929, *ibid.*

14 For the Carnegie Corporation, see Flexner, *Funds and Foundations*, pp. 113-24; Lester, *Forty Years of Carnegie Giving*, pp. 57-64; Curti & Nash, *Philanthropy in the Shaping of American Higher Education*, pp. 212-237.

15 Ling to Keppel, Jan. 4 & 18, 1928 and reply Jan. 11, 1928, Carnegie Corporation, Saskatchewan University, 1928-33.

16 WCM to F.W. Chisholm, Sept. 16, 1909, USA, Jean E. Murray Collection.

17 President's Report 1920-21, USA.

18 WCM to Keppel, March 26, 1928, Carnegie Corporation, Saskatchewan University, 1928-33.

19 W.S. Learned to F.P. Keppel, March 11, 1929; WCM to Keppel, Feb. 23, 1929, *ibid.*

20 WCM to Keppel, July 5, 1929, *ibid.*

21 Lester to Keppel, July 17, 1929, Carnegie Corporation, Saskatchewan University, 1928-33.

22 Savage to Keppel, July 19, 1929, *ibid.*

23 Erskine to Keppel, Sept. 5, 1929, *ibid.*

24 Keppel to Samaroff, June 2, 1930, *ibid.*

25 Collingwood to Lester, August 5, 1931, *ibid.*

26 *Ibid.*

27 *Ibid.*

28 WCM to Lester, May 31, 1932, *ibid.*

29 Niderost to Lester, June 10, 1932, *ibid.*

30 WCM to Keppel, July 24, 1933, *ibid.*

31 *Ibid.*

32 WCM to Falconer, October 8, 1926, USA, Presidential Papers, RG1, S1.

33 Falconer to WCM, October 15, 1926, *ibid.*

34 WCM to Anderson, June 16, 1931, and reply June 18, 1931, USA, Presidential Papers, RG1, S1.

35 Keppel to Stapleford, Oct. 6, 1925; memorandum of interview, April 24, 1929; Stapleford to Keppel, Oct. 12, 1929, Carnegie Corporation, Regina College.

36 Ling to Keppel, Confidential, Oct. 24, 1929, *ibid.*

37 Memorandum of a conversation between F.P. Keppel and WCM, Nov. 17, 1931, Carnegie Corporation, University of Saskatchewan. Memorandum of a conversation between F.P. Keppel and Stapleford, Dec. 10, 1931, Carnegie Corporation, Regina College.

38 W.S. Learned, "Local Provision for Higher Education in Saskatchewan," Carnegie Foundation Bulletin #27, 1932.

39 WCM to Suzzalo, June 14, 1932, Carnegie Corporation, Univ. of Sask.

40 WCM to Savage, June 25, 1932, *ibid.*

41 WCM to Keppel, July 24, 1933, *ibid.*

42 Keppel to WCM, August 7, and Nov. 30, 1933, *ibid.*

43 University of Saskatchewan to the Governors of Regina College, January 19, 1934, encl. in WCM to Keppel, Jan. 22, 1934, *ibid.*

44 Learned to Keppel, Feb. 9, 1934, *ibid.*

45 WCM to Oliver, April 20, 1934, USA, Jean E. Murray Collection.

46 Falconer to WCM, Jan. 15, 1934. *ibid.*

47 Falconer to WCM, Jan. 26, 1934, *ibid.*

48 WCM to Learned, March 12, 1934, USA, Presidential Papers, RG1, S1.

49 Learned to WCM, March 20, 1934, *ibid.*

50 J.W.T. Spinks, "Memories of the '30's," *The Green and White*, (May 1977), p. 4.

51 B.P. Stoicheff, "G. H.," *Physics in Canada . . .* , vol. XXVIII, Special Issue (April 1972), cited in Lawrence D. Stokes, "Canada and an Academic Refugee from Nazi Germany: The Case of Gerhard Herzberg," *Canadian Historical Review*, LVII (1976), p. 157.

52 Interview, Dr. J.W.T. Spinks, Sept. 24, 1978.

53 WCM to Cody and Burton, Jan. 31, 1935; WCM to Tory, Feb. 7, 1935, USA, Presidential Papers, RG1, S1.

54 Spinks, "Memories of the '30's," p. 5.

55 WCM to Lester, Feb. 8, 1935, Carnegie Corporation, University of Saskatchewan.

56 J.M. Russell to WCM, Feb. 18, 1935, *ibid.*

57 Interview, Dr. J.W.T. Spinks, Sept. 24, 1978.

58 Spinks, "Memories of the '30's," p. 6.

59 Memorandum, March 5, 1935, Carnegie Corporation, University of Saskatchewan.

60 WCM to Alty, Oct. 29, 1935, USA, Jean E. Murray Collection.

61 WCM to Jolliffe, Jan. 30, 1937, USA, Presidential Papers, RG1, S1. Cited in Stokes, "Gerhard Herzberg," pp. 163-4.

62 WCM to Keppel, June 23, 1937; Pavlychenko to Keppel, August 16, 1937, Carnegie Corporation, University of Saskatchewan.

63 Interview, Mrs. A.S. Morton, Sept. 9, 1977.

64 *Ibid.*

65 WCM to Keppel, March 1, 1937, USA, Presidential Papers, RG1, S1.

66 WCM to Keppel, Oct. 19, 1937, USA, Jean E. Murray Collection.

67 MacKenzie to Learned, Personal, April 14, 1937 and reply, April 27, 1937, Carnegie Corporation, University of Saskatchewan.

Chapter 11

1 President's Report, 1930, USA.

2 WCM to Mr. Justice MacKenzie, Nov. 7, 1930, USA, Presidential Papers, RG1, S1.

3 *Ibid.*

4 Sterling to WCM, Dec. 19, 1930, *ibid.*

5 Anderson to WCM, Sept. 20, 1933, *ibid.*

6 *Ibid.*

7 WCM to Board of Governors, Dec. 11, 1930, USA, Jean E. Murray Collection.

8 *Ibid.*

9 WCM to Savage, Sept. 26, 1932, Carnegie Corporation, University of Saskatchewan.

10 Board of Governors' minutes, April 17, 1933, USA.

11 Hon. J.A. Robb to WCM, March 6, 1929, USA, Jean E. Murray Collection.

12 WCM, undated memorandum, 1929?, *ibid.*

13 Hincks to WCM, August 16, 1930, *ibid.*

14 Morton Manuscript History p. 361, *ibid.* Murray wrote the section on the Depression years.

15 Mr. Justice Willard Z. Estey to R.A. Murray, March 28, 1980.

16 Board of Governors' Minutes, Sept. 16, 1931, USA.

17 Board of Governors' Minutes, December 30, 1932, USA.

18 WCM to Premier Patterson, Feb. 10, 1936, USA, Jean E. Murray Collection.

19 W.P. Thompson, *The University of Saskatchewan—A Personal History* (University of Toronto Press, 1970), p. 127.

20 WCM to Ellis, Jan. 12, 1931, USA, Presidential Papers, RG1, S1.

21 James S. Thomson, *Proceedings and Transaction of the Royal Society of Canada*, 3rd Series, vol. XXXIX (May 1945), Appendix B, p. 108.

22 Interview, C.J. Mackenzie, September 8, 1977.

23 Interview, Jean Murray, April 1978.

24 USA, Morton Manuscript History, p. 369.

25 *Ibid.*

26 *Ibid.*

27 WCM to D.H. MacPherson, Nov. 31, 1935, USA, Presidential Papers, RG1, S1.

28 WCM to D. Heim, May 17, 1935, *ibid.*

29 Mrs. Tallman to WCM, Oct. 24, 1934, *ibid.*

30 WCM to Wallace, March 2, 1933, USA, Presidential Papers, RG1, S1.

31 President's Report, 1933, USA.

32 A.M. Nicholson to WCM, Jan. 27 & Feb. 5, 1931; WCM to Rev. L.S. Cust, Jan. 3, 1931, USA, Jean E. Murray Collection.

33 Grove to WCM, Apr. 12, 1933, *ibid.*

34 Bracken to WCM, Oct. 5, 1934, *ibid.*

35 WCM to Anderson, Dec. 10, 1932, *ibid.*

36 WCM to McColl, July 9, 1934, *ibid.*

37 Dr. J. Francis Leddy, "An Address at St. Thomas More College, Saskatoon, May 22, 1976," p. 12.

38 *Ibid.*, p. 16.

39 *Ibid.*, p. 25.

40 President's Report 1937, USA.

41 The figures are given in the President's annual reports.

42 Board of Governors' Minutes, Oct. 10, 1932, USA.

43 Interview, Dr. V.E. Graham, Apr. 23, 1978.

44 WCM, "Continental Europeans in Western Canada," *Queen's Quarterly* XXXVIII (Winter, 1931), pp. 63-75.

45 Robert England, *Living, Learning, Remembering* (Centre for Continuing Education, University of British Columbia, 1980), p. 165.

46 WCM, "Continental Europeans in Western Canada," pp. 63-75.

47 *Ibid.*, p. 67.

48 *Ibid.*, p. 67.

49 *Ibid.*, p. 68.

50 *Ibid.*, p. 68.

51 WCM to Young, Apr. 7, 1931, USA, Jean E. Murray Collection.

52 WCM to Bennett, Oct. 7, 1932, *ibid.*

53 Sherstobitoff to WCM, Jan. 27 and Feb. 28, 1936, *ibid.*

54 WCM to Bourassa, Nov. 4, 1932, *ibid.*

55 Tee to WCM, Oct. 26, 1935, USA, Presidential Papers, RG1, S1.

56 WCM to Haultain, Nov. 18, 1935, *ibid.*

57 WCM to Philpott, Nov. 1, 1935, *ibid.*

58 WCM to Haultain, Nov. 18, 1935, *ibid.*

59 WCM to Estey, Nov. 18, 1935, *ibid.*

60 WCM, "Training for an International Outlook," Radio broadcast, February 1936, USA, Jean E. Murray Collection.

61 WCM to Maclean, March 12, 1934, *ibid.*

62 WCM to Aikin, Aug. 1, 1934, USA, Jean E. Murray Collection.

63 Interview, Jean Murray, Sept. 1977.

64 WCM to Buller, May 16, 1936, USA, Jean E. Murray Collection.

65 "Murray of Saskatchewan," *Winnipeg Free Press*, February 23, 1935.

66 WCM, "To the Class of 1937," USA, Jean E. Murray Collection.

Chapter 12

1 It was published in 1959 as *Saskatchewan, The Making of a University* after being revised and edited by Carlyle King.

2 J.S. Thomson, *Yesteryears at the University of Saskatchewan, 1937-1949* (University of Saskatchewan, 1969), p. 6.

3 W.P. Thompson, *The University of Saskatchewan, A Personal History*, p. 152.

4 WCM to MacKenzie, confidential, May 19, 1937, USA, Jean E. Murray Collection.

5 *Ibid.*

6 MacKenzie to WCM, May 27, 1937, *ibid.*

7 Interview, Dr. Jean Murray, Oct. 3, 1980.

8 Interview, H.C. Rees, April, 1978.

9 WCM to Mowes, Nov. 11, 1938, USA, Jean E. Murray Collection.

10 *Ibid.*

11 Interview, Marian Evans Younger, Sept. 29, 1977.

12 WCM to Jean Murray, April 10, 1938, USA, Jean E. Murray Collection.

13 *Ibid.*

14 MacKenzie to WCM, Sept. 28, 1937, USA, Jean E. Murray Collection.

15 Kenneth de Courcy to WCM, Feb. 2, 1939, *ibid.*

16 C.M. Dickinson to WCM, March 7, 1938, *ibid.*

17 W.S. Wallace to WCM, Apr. 24, 1939, *ibid.*

18 PAC, Mackenzie King Papers, M G 26, J4, C 138042, file 1832, meeting of March 30, 1939.

19 Euler to WCM, July 27, 1939, USA, Jean E. Murray Collection.

20 Minutes of National Film Board, Oct. 5, 1939, *ibid.*

21 WCM to C.G. Cowan, n.d., 1940, *ibid.*

22 WCM to Mackenzie King, Jan. 18, 1941, *ibid.*

23 Mackenzie King to WCM, Jan. 20, 1941; J.A. Mackinnon to WCM, Jan. 27, 1941, *ibid.*

24 Mackinnon to WCM, Apr. 5, 1941, *ibid.*

25 Interview, Dr. Jean Murray, Oct. 3, 1980.

26 Falconer to WCM, June 25, 1937, USA, Jean E. Murray Collection.

27 Interview, Marion Evans Younger, Sept. 24, 1977.

28 R.S. McLaughlin to WCM, Apr. 14, 1941, USA, Jean E. Murray Collection.

29 Niderost to WCM, Aug. 31, 1940, *ibid.*

30 WCM to Christina Murray, Jan. 22, 1940, USA, Jean E. Murray Collection.

31 WCM to Gardiner, May 14, and reply, May 25, 1940, *ibid.*

32 S.W. Johns to R.M. Pinder, Aug. 22, 1942, *ibid.*

33 WCM, Graduation addresses, Saskatoon City Hospital, Sept. 2, 1940 & Aug. 29, 1941, *ibid.*

34 Interview, Dr. James H. Campbell, April 18, 1978.

35 Morton to WCM, n.d., 1941, USA, Jean E. Murray Collection.

36 Mackenzie King to WCM, Aug. 24, 1944, *ibid.*

37 Gardiner to WCM, Oct. 26, 1944, *ibid.*

38 *Winnipeg Free Press*, Nov. 6, 1943.

Chapter 13

1 Morton Mss. History of the University of Saskatchewan, p. 438, USA, Jean E. Murray Collection.

2 President's Report, 1908-09, p. 11, USA.

3 WCM, Notes for Address at the University of New Brunswick, Founder's Day, 1905, USA, Jean E. Murray Collection.

4 "University Development in Canada," *TRSC*, Third Series, vol. 16 (1922), Sect. 2, pp. 77-105; "College Union in the Maritime Provinces," *Dalhousie Review* 2 (1923), pp. 410-24; "State Support and Control of Universities in

Canada," *TRSC*, Third Series, vol. 19 (1925), Sect. 2, pp. 19-32; "University Development in Canada since Confederation," *Dalhousie Review* 7 (1928), pp. 479-86; "Manitoba's Place in University History," *TRSC.*, Third Series, vol. 22 (1928), Sect. 2, pp. 57-84; "The University of Saskatchewan," *TRSC.*, Third Series, vol. 35 (1941), Sect. 2, pp. 95-117.

5 WCM, "University Development in Canada," *TRSC.*, Third Series, 16 (1922), pp. 80-1.

6 WCM to McColl, June 8, 1908, USA, Controller and Treasurer's Papers, III, Miscellaneous Records.

7 President's Report, 1908-09, p. 2, USA.

8 WCM, "The University of Saskatchewan," *TRSC.*, Third Series, vol. 35 (1941), Sect. 2, p. 111.

9 WCM, "History of Education in Saskatchewan" in Shortt and Doughty, eds., *Canada and its Provinces*, vol. 29, pp. 469-70.

10 WCM, "University Development in Canada since Confederation," *Dalhousie Review* 7 (1928), p. 482.

11 Wm. Allen to WCM, May 4, 1938, USA, Jean E. Murray Collection.

12 Frank Underhill to WCM, June 12, 1937, *ibid.*

13 Carlyle King report to Board of Governors on W.P. Thompson manuscript, June 19, 1968, USA.

14 R.A. Wilson to WCM, Oct. 17, 1941, USA, Jean E. Murray Collection.

15 J.S. Woodsworth to WCM, undated, *ibid.*

16 L. Jock to WCM, July 2, 1918, *ibid.*

17 Mrs. B. Corcoran to WCM, Feb. 17, 1930, *ibid.*

18 WCM to Mrs. Corcoran, Feb. 21, 1930, *ibid.*

19 George to WCM, Dec. 19, 1942, *ibid.*

20 Dr. Georgina R. Hogg to R.A. Murray, Apr. 11, 1979.

21 *Ibid.*

22 Capt. R.W. Potts to WCM, Jan. 24, 1944, USA, Jean E. Murray Collection.

23 R.A. Murray, personal recollection.

24 Interview, Mary Evans Younger, Sept. 24, 1977.

25 Interview, Mary Murray, Apr. 18, 1978.

26 Interview, Dr. Gerhard Herzberg, Sept. 15, 1977.

27 Interview, Dr. C.J. Mackenzie, Sept. 8, 1977.

28 WCM to Principal MacKenzie of Victoria, Oct. 29, 1930, USA, Presidential Papers, RG1, S1.

29 *Ibid.*

30 Interview, Dr. Margaret Cameron, March 20, 1978.

31 *Ibid.*

32 Interview, Dr. Jean Murray, Oct. 4, 1980.

33 Interview, Dr. C.J. Mackenzie, Sept. 8, 1977.

34 Interview, Dr. Jean Murray, Oct. 4, 1980.

35 *Ibid.*

36 WCM to Christina Murray, Sept. 18, 1926, USA, Jean E. Murray Collection.

37 *Ibid.*

38 WCM, "Personal Statement," [1939?]; WCM Will, July 31, 1939, USA, Jean E. Murray Collection.

39 Murray to Anderson, Dec. 28, 1931, USA, Presidential Papers, Ser. 1, B6.

40 M. Hayden, ed., *So Much to Do, So Little Time*, pp. 16-17.

41 WCM, "Personal Statement," [1939?], USA, Jean E. Murray Collection.

42 Interview, Dr. J. Francis Leddy, Aug. 20, 1977.

43 Interview, Dr. C.J. Mackenzie, Sept. 8, 1977.

44 Falconer to WCM, March 9, 1936, USA, Jean E. Murray Collection.

45 Interview, Marian Evans Younger, Sept. 24, 1977.

46 Mr. Justice Willard Z. Estey to R.A. Murray, March 28, 1980.

47 Grant MacEwan to Mrs. W.C. Murray,
   Aug. 23, 1946, enclosing the text of
   "The Man Murray," a radio talk given
   on the CBC, Aug. 22, 1946, USA, Jean
   E. Murray Collection. MacEwan
   included the talk as a chapter in his
   book, *The Sodbusters* (Toronto, 1948)
   pp. 226-31.

48 *Winnipeg Free Press*, March 28, 1945.

Index

About the authors

Robert Murray was born in Saskatchewan in 1910, graduated from the University of Saskatchewan in 1934 and now lives in Ottawa. He is a veteran of the Second World War having served in Canada, Alaska, Britain and Northwest Europe. Since retirement from the public service he has engaged in research and writing. He is married to Margaret Stone, also a graduate of the University of Saskatchewan, and is the father of David Murray.

Dr. David R. Murray is a graduate of Bishop's University, the University of Edinburgh, and the University of Cambridge. He is currently Professor of History and Dean of the College of Arts at the University of Guelph, where he has taught since 1967.

Dr. Murray served as Resident Historian in the Department of External Affairs in the early 1970s and edited two volumes of the series, *Documents on Canadian External Relations*. He is the author of *Odious Commerce*, a study of the abolition of the Cuban slave trade, and various articles on Latin American history and Canadian-Latin American relations. For the past five years he has lectured on Canadian-Latin American relations at the Canadian National Defence College. He is married to Ann Stockwell and they have three children, Heather, Robert and Deborah.

■